Development Issues in South Africa

Also by Ibrahim A. Elbadawi

REGIONAL INTEGRATION AND TRADE LIBERALIZATION IN SUBSAHARAN AFRICA
Volume 1: Framework, Issues and Methodological Perspectives
(*editor with Ademola Oyejide and Paul Collier*)

Development Issues in South Africa

Edited by

Ibrahim A. Elbadawi
Research Coordinator
African Economic Research Consortium
Nairobi
Kenya

and

Trudi Hartzenberg
SAPES Trust
Harare
Zimbabwe

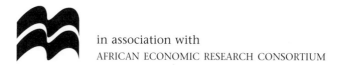

in association with
AFRICAN ECONOMIC RESEARCH CONSORTIUM

First published in Great Britain 2000 by
MACMILLAN PRESS LTD
Houndmills, Basingstoke, Hampshire RG21 6XS and London
Companies and representatives throughout the world

A catalogue record for this book is available from the British Library.

ISBN 0–333–77716–6

First published in the United States of America 2000 by
ST. MARTIN'S PRESS, INC.,
Scholarly and Reference Division,
175 Fifth Avenue, New York, N.Y. 10010

ISBN 0–312–22948–8

Library of Congress Cataloging-in-Publication Data
Development issues in South Africa / edited by Ibrahim A. Elbadawi and Trudi
Hartzenberg.
p. cm.
"This volume is a product of an AERC conference on Transnational and
Long-term Development Issues in South Africa, held in November/December
1995 in Johannesburg." — Foreword.
Includes bibliographical references and index.
ISBN 0–312–22948–8 (cloth)
1. South Africa—Economic policy. I. Elbadawi, Ibrahim A. II. Hartzenberg, Trudi.
HC905 .D484   2000
338.968 — dc21

99–052521

This book is printed on paper suitable for recycling and made from fully managed and sustained
forest sources.

10   9   8   7   6   5   4   3   2   1
09   08   07   06   05   04   03   02   01   00

Printed and bound in Great Britain by
Antony Rowe Ltd, Chippenham, Wiltshire

Contents

List of Tables

List of Figures

Foreword

This volume explores some of South Africa's development options. The volume is a product of an AERC conference on 'Transitional and Long-term Development Issues in South Africa', held in November/December 1995 in Johannesburg, in collaboration with the South African Parliamentary Committee on the Reconstruction and Development Programme (RDP), the National Institute for Economic Policy (NIEP), University of Cape Town, and several other universities and research and policy institutions in South Africa. In addition to the papers presented at the workshop, and published in this volume, several contributions were made by representatives from the South African government, the labour movement and business community, as well as distinguished personalities from the international development community. Through the rigorous policy-oriented economic research facilitated by this initiative, AERC hopes to contribute to a process of enhancing dialogue between various stakeholders concerned with economic and social development in South Africa.

The South African economy presents a rather infrequent blend of characteristics, challenges and prospects. Given its very developed manufacturing sector and sophisticated financial sector, it has immense capacity to produce growth and prosperity for all the people of South Africa in the future. On the other hand, the extremely unequal income and asset distribution currently prevailing in South Africa – which is a direct result of the deliberate policy of deprivation engineered by the apartheid regime – are unparalleled anywhere in the world. Therefore, moral imperatives and good economic sense suggest that strategic redistribution measures and investment in basic needs, health and education should be at the top of the national development agenda. As such, this volume is a small but important contribution to the debate in South Africa on how best the South African society could develop a social covenant that ensures sufficient equity and social development for the disenfranchised majority, without endangering sustained future economic growth.

Ibrahim A. Elbadawi
Trudi Hartzenberg

Notes on the Contributors

Janine Aron, Centre for the Study of African Economies, Institute of Economics and Statistics, University of Oxford, UK, and Centre for Research into Economics and Finance in South Africa, LSE, London.

Haroon Bhorat, Development Policy Research Unit, University of Cape Town, South Africa.

Rashad Cassim, Trade and Industrial Policy Secretariat, Johannesburg, South Africa.

Ibrahim A. Elbadawi, African Economic Research Consortium, Nairobi, Kenya, and the World Bank.

Ben Fine, School for Oriental and African Studies, University of London, UK.

Lungisa Fusile, Central Statistical Services, Pretoria, South Africa.

Bill Gibson, Department of Economics, University of Vermont, United States.

Abdallah Hamdok, African Development Bank, Abidjan, Côte d'Ivoire.

Trudi Hartzenberg, SAPES Trust, Harare, Zimbabwe.

Brian Kahn, School of Economics, University of Cape Town, South Africa.

Newman Kusi, Department of Economics, University of Natal, Pietermaritzburg, South Africa.

Murray Leibbrandt, School of Economics, University of Cape Town, South Africa.

Kupikile Mlambo, African Development Bank, Abidjan, Côte d'Ivoire.

Kevin Nell, Department of Economics, University of Fort Hare, South Africa.

Lala Steyn, Department of Land Affairs, Pretoria, South Africa.

Dirk Ernst van Seventer, Development Bank of Southern Africa, Johannesburg, South Africa.

Ingrid Woolard, Data Research Africa, Pretoria, South Africa.

Harry Zarenda, Department of Economics, University of the Witwatersrand, Johannesburg, South Africa.

1
Introduction and Overview

Ibrahim A. Elbadawi and Trudi Hartzenberg

Following the remarkable democratic transformation in the country the South African government made explicit commitment to a long-term development strategy for generating rapid and widely shared growth, while firmly stressing basic macroeconomic stability in the short to medium term. This strategy was based on at least two highly publicised programmes: South African Reconstruction and Development Prog- ramme – RDP – and especially its successor programme for Growth, Employment and Redistribution – GEAR. These almost ideal initial conditions led many observers to predict that South Africa was poised for a sustained econ-omic takeoff, where the strength and sophistication of its financial market, its strong civil society, and transparent and democratic governance were seen as its clear comparative advantage. However, while we still marvel at the successful democratic transition in South Africa, economic performance during the first half of the 1990s reveals that the task of managing the economic transition and laying the structural foundations for a coherent long-term development strategy remains both challenging and elusive.

An appraisal of the performance of the South African economy since mid-1994 focuses on the policies that have succeeded in turning around the dismal performance of the previous decade. Progress in a number of areas has led to cautious optimism as the process of transition and longer- term development planning gathers momentum. The reduction in the fiscal deficit, reform of the tax system and setting new priorities for public expenditure, and the checking of inflationary tendencies are noteworthy achievements. The process of transforming public sector institutions has been enthusiastically embarked upon and the economy is opening to international competition and gaining access to new markets. The growth performance of the economy, however, suggests that although a marked improvement on the previous decade, the development goals the government has identified may not be within grasp. This is so despite the fact that the longer-term trend exceeds the population growth.

For example, GDP growth was projected to have slowed to only 2.1% in 1997 compared with 3.1% in 1996. Based on past and projected GDP trends, 'the country seems to be facing the supposed impossible: slower economic growth during the 1990s than in the apartheid- and sanctions-dominated 1980s' (EIU. 1997b: 1). The slumps in the gold price, the lingering political uncertainty at the start of the political transformation and a protracted drought were cited as the main factors behind the economic setbacks of the 1990s. Other contributing factors relate to economic policy uncertainty arising from 'perceived' differences within the government and between the government and other key stake-holders (e.g. COSATU). The inherently conflictive policy targets and instruments between the short and longer runs, and between the real and financial sectors of the economy, were made all the more challenging by the peculiar nature of the South African economy. These are also the main factors that compromised the ability of South Africa to attract steady and stable flows of private capital finance, while avoiding financial crises.

Therefore, the unemployment crisis makes the spectre of jobless growth loom large and the demand for civil services ever more significant. The persistent account deficits and unstable private capital flows still present a structural barrier to economic growth, given the import–export profile of the country. The exchange rate depreciation and instability of 1996 tested the resilience of the economy and highlighted the complex interplay of internal and external, economic, social, and political forces.

It is within the context of the search for an integrated economic strategy leading to sustainable economic growth, increasing job creation, and unequivocal improvement in the distribution of income and wealth, that the chapters in this volume are being made available. They were presented at the 'Conference on Transitional and Long-term Development Issues in South Africa', which was held in November/December 1995. The active participation by South Africa and international policy-makers and academics has contributed to carefully considered revisions and/or elaboration of the issues probed in the conference presentations. The chapters boldly explore the cutting-edge policy concerns and debates, ferreting out the questions that need to be grappled with in the process of policy-making for South Africa's transitional and long-term development strategies.

1. An overview of the chapters

Chapter 2, 'Understanding South Africa's Inequality', highlights two of what are perhaps the most significant defining characteristics of South Africa's economic history: inequality and exclusion. In the final analysis, the outcome of economic policy may be measured in terms of its impact on inequality and economic participation or exclusion. This contribution probes the markers of South African's inequality profile, tracing the changes in between-group and within-group inequality. To gain insight into the economic and social forces producing such stark inequality in the distribution of income, the paper hones in on the specific labour market and social features implicated in what may be the most unequal distribution of income in the world. A particular contribution of this chapter is to mark those areas that, through select policy interventions, would affect the most disadvantaged groups in the South African society.

In Chapter 3, 'Fiscal Policy in Post-Apartheid South Africa', the focus falls on the challenge of balancing the objectives of reducing the budget deficit while addressing the need for delivery of social and economic services. Keeping in mind the objective of expanding productive capacity, medium-term expenditure planning has to reflect the growth of government revenue. Within the framework of the broadly defined objectives of the government's Reconstruction and Development Programme (RDP), the paper examines the implications of budget priority setting for macroeconomic management.

The fourth chapter, 'Public Policy and Private Investment: An Empirical Investigation', examines private investment as an essential ingredient in a successful growth strategy. This postulate hinges on the contribution of private investment as a substantive participant in the research and development process and as an attractor of foreign direct investment. Local private investor confidence is perceived as a spark to foreign investor interest and confidence. The chapter stresses the role of government in the creation of a stable macroeconomic environment; in particular, monetary and fiscal policies are singled out as especially important in inducing private investment and supporting sustainable economic growth. An environment characterised by low and stable rates of inflation, manageable foreign debt, a credibly-valued exchange rate, and controlled fiscal deficits will nurture confidence and inspire private investment.

'Industrial and Energy Policy: A Partial Review', the fifth chapter, critically reviews South African industrial policy through the lenses of the three different approaches that have been most influential in South

Africa: those of the World Bank, the Industrial Strategy Project and the Monitor Group. Each of these approaches has had a marked impact on the development of industrial policy in South Africa despite not having been developed specifically for South Africa. This chapter concludes that none of these approaches will motivate policies that make more than a limited impression on the unemployment crisis in the labour market and on basic needs requirements. From the perspective of the South African economy as a minerals–energy complex, the paper stresses importance of continuity in industrial policy framed within the context of the RDP. The strategic alternatives presented for industrial policy in particular underscore the challenges facing policy-makers in the search for a coherent blend of macroeconomic policy ingredients.

Chapter 6, 'Land Reform as a Strategy for Development: The Relevance of the Zimbabwe Experience for South Africa', cogently compares the experience of Zimbabwe and South Africa's more recent endeavours in land reform as a component of an overall development strategy. The peculiarities of the colonial legacy and the economic history have led in both countries to land grievances and the disarticulation of rural society, the rural economy and institutions. The chapter uses the Zimbabwe experience to test the proposed programmes and policies in South Africa and highlights the error traps to be avoided.

In Chapter 7, the focus shifts to South Africa within the Southern African region. 'Regional Economic Integration: Reflections on South Africa and the Southern African Region', asks some fundamental questions about South Africa's economic future in the region. It explores the question of how regional economic integration features in South Africa's development strategy. It does not take as a *sine qua non* that South Africa's economic prospects are inextricably linked with those of the region. The importance of addressing national economic development issues and not substituting regional integration for domestic economic policy development is emphasised. This sober approach to South Africa's role in the regional context hones in on different regional integration configurations. It asks, for example, if the hub-and-spoke is feasible and desirable in Southern Africa – can South Africa be the driving wheel for the smaller economies? The questions raised in the paper bring clarity to the debate on South Africa in the Southern African region – regionalism alongside multi-lateral liberalisation.

Chapter 8, 'Real and Monetary Determinants of the Real Exchange Rate in South Africa', focuses on a key policy variable in the South African economy – the real exchange rate. Within a cointegration framework, single-equation equilibrium error correction models are used to investigate the short-run and long-run determinants of the quarterly real exchange rate for the period 1970 to 1995. The chapter examines the policy implications of trade liberalisation and the potential for increased long-term capital inflows, and cautions against too much hesitancy in the removal of exchange controls. A key conclusion is that too stringent an adherence to nominal and real exchange rules imposes a straitjacket on the management of the exchange rate.

Finally, Chapter 9 tracks 'The Macroeconomic Effects of Restructuring Public Expenditure by Function in South Africa'. The paper uses a model that takes account of demand and supply-side effects. The first variant of the dynamic multi-sectoral computable general equilibrium model examines the impact of a strategy that focuses on current spending and transfers. The second gives prominence to fiscal discipline and the third emphasises economic services and infrastructure investment. The third produces the most impressive growth performance but is not the most egalitarian. A key conclusion from the chapter is that higher growth is associated with lower wages; however, following a simple strategy to force real wages down could cause the growth process to reverse, in a downward spiral of contraction and unemployment. The model simulations confirm the virtues of coordinated economic policies, stimulating simultaneously demand and supply sides in a careful functional balance of government expenditure.

2.   The challenges ahead: growth, employment and redistribution in South Africa

The most recent South African government macroeconomic strategy for Growth, Employment, and Redistribution (GEAR) (Ministry of Finance, 1996), identifies four objectives:

- A competitive fast growing economy that creates enough jobs for all work-seekers.
- A redistribution of income and opportunities in favour of the poor.
- A society in which sound health, education and other services are available to all.
- An environment in which homes are secure and places of work are productive.

The macroeconomic strategy outlined in GEAR sounds a clear echo of the fundamental vision of the Reconstruction and Development Programme. It is an attempt to map a more coherent plan for meaningful social transformation and a strategy to effect a structural economic reform programme. It aims to launch the South African economy on a job-creating, income and wealth redistributing growth path toward the next century. Perhaps it was intended as a rescue mission for the RDP, which was to have been South Africa's New Deal. It remains to be seen whether GEAR is based on a sound perception of the intricate tradeoffs and delicate balances of the costs of economic reform and the measures that need to be put in place to provide some cushion to those who will bear those costs.

Indeed, in a country with such high rates of unemployment (more than 30%), programmes that commit to avoid short-run macroeconomic populism (such as the GEAR) are likely to be met with some scepticism, no matter how well articulated or thoroughly negotiated by most of the stakeholders in the society. For example, fiscal laxity in 1997 was characterised as having posed a serious threat to the GEAR strategy, 'which is already under-performing – to the unconcealed delights of the bizarre left-right alliance that so dislikes it. Not only is GEAR missing its growth and employment targets, but interest rates have had to be kept much higher than intended, and it now looks as if the budget too will overshoot its target' (EIU, 1997a: 4). This analysis clearly exposes the conflict between short-run and longer-run objectives and the political economy that underlies the conflict. Moreover, even within the longer-term strategy, there are some 'perceived' conflicts between the export-oriented growth path promised by the GEAR and the currently considered labour bill. It is argued that some terms of the labour bill (overtime provisions and the extension of the rights of permanent workers to 'non-standard employees') may endanger the job-creating potential of small and medium-sized enterprises (SMEs) by dramatically increasing corporate costs. The argument further holds that 'recent experience in OECD economies – and in particular the marked contrast between strong job creation and falling unemployment in the USA and UK, and high joblessness in continental Europe – suggests that legislation such as the Basic Condition of Employment Act benefits the "insiders" lucky enough to have jobs at the expense of unemployed outsiders' (EIU, 1997b: 12).

Relative to its recent history, however, it cannot be denied that much progress has been recorded in South Africa since the successful and peaceful democratic transition. The budget deficit has been reduced, inflation has been kept in check, a programme of trade liberalisation is opening the economy to international competition and access to new markets is being sought. Nevertheless, it is clear that despite these laudable achievements, the fundamental challenges of sustained and job-creating growth, income and wealth redistribution, and the provision of social services have yet to record significant steps.

This brief review surveys the South African economy since April 1994 and highlights the key challenges that will test the mettle of policy-makers and the resilience and flexibility of the economy as the policy reforms are implemented.

Growth and employment

In 1995 the economy grew by 3.5%, but total (non-agricultural) employment by only 0.6%. Effectively (given the rate of growth of the labour force), this means that the number of unemployed people in South Africa increased by 280,000. The first three-quarters of 1996 recorded a decline in private sector employment of 5.8%, 3.6% and 2.8%, respectively, while public sector employment dropped 0.2% in the first quarter and rose by 4% and 1.1% in each of the subsequent quarters (SARB, 1996).

The costs of economic reform are most keenly felt by those who do not have the skills and the opportunities to get aboard the roller coaster of adjusting markets – inferior education for blacks during the apartheid years has left a legacy of unskilled labour that is, by domestic market standards, relatively cheap but not very productive, and a premium on skills, which are scarce. The shackles on the labour market are clearly not only a result of strong unions and labour protection. The challenge is therefore to balance hard-won worker rights, productivity-enhancing measures and flexible adjustment in a process of industrial restructuring and competitiveness building, mindful of the fact that production requires cooperation among all factors of production. Labour productivity is undeniably tied to that of other factors of production. A focus on all factor markets and factors of production, and reform of organisation structures and the development of a dynamic entrepreneurial culture, are all key inputs to improving the labour absorptive capacity of the economy.

Trade liberalisation, globalisation and competition policies

Having inherited one of the most unequal distributions of income and wealth anywhere in the world, the government needs to be aware that despite an improvement in the country's per capita income, income and wealth inequality combined with lack of sustainable employment opportunities will prove to be a shaky foundation for longer-term development. In the final analysis an improvement in the income and wealth distributions and real access to economic opportunities may be regarded as a litmus test of performance.

It is true that many years of shelter from the influence and the pressures of international competition harboured many organisational dinosaurs, unprepared to adapt to more flexible and demanding domestic markets and the rapid process of globalisation. Policy-makers are faced with finding a mix of labour market, trade, industrial and competition policies that will enable the shaping of a competitive private sector, a productive, streamlined public sector, and efficient, flexible markets for all factors of production, products and services. The process of trade liberalisation that has been started – but which until 1995 was not bold enough to include import liberalisation – has to be complemented by these other policies, in order to develop the capabilities and competencies of labour, capital and entrepreneurship in the context of markets that are contestable and organisations whose behaviour will enhance competitive market processes.

Significant developments in competition policy are awaited, a key area for an economy still characterised by extreme levels of market concentration. It appears that after much pre-election discussion on the dangers of high levels of market concentration and anti-competitive behaviour, cold feet have kept policy-makers out of what have come to be seen as the depths of big business waters. Competition policy can and should play a key role in defining the rules for the market game, and in clarifying for organisations what constitutes acceptable and unacceptable behaviour – what is and what is not in the public interest.

National saving, private capital finance and growth

To emphasise the importance of strong national saving – even in this era of investible foreign savings in the form of private capital flows – Williamson (1997) makes the following argument: according to robust international evidence drawn from a vast set of developing countries, a 6% real growth rate would require an investment rate of about 28%, while more than 5% external private debt usually violates the principle of current account sustainability (see also Edwards, 1997). Both considerations would therefore suggest a minimum 23% national saving rate for the achievement of desired long-term growth without the risk of destabilised currency and financial crisis – which could substantially undermine the growth objective. Therefore, long-term policies and institutions to enhance domestic saving are now considered to be the emerging key prerequisite for avoiding financial crises and ensuring that – in an era of integrated capital markets and private capital flows – the real exchange rate remains competitive in the long run (Williamson, 1997).

In such a framework, the main impediments to an accelerated rate of economic expansion – in support of the much needed employment creation and income and wealth redistribution in South Africa – are low national saving rates and inadequate and unstable foreign private capital finance. From a peak of 25% in the early 1980s, a level of 16.5% was recorded for 1996, the long-term decline being particularly attributed to the rising levels of gross government dissaving, without any compensating increase in savings by the private sector, exacerbated by capital flight and a decline in the availability of foreign savings.

The generation of domestic savings is needed to finance domestic investment that will enhance the economy's growth potential and send positive signals to foreign investors to attract stable capital flows. This critical structural feature also has important implications for the sustainability of the government's budget deficit. Careful checks on the government's consumption expenditure need to be made so as to enhance domestic saving and investment behaviour.

Private consumption expenditure has, despite relatively high interest rates, increased strongly since 1994 and the net savings ratio for the total private sector declined from 7.5% of GDP in 1995 to 7% in 1996. For 1997, though, a slowdown in domestic private consumption expenditure is expected.

The importance of foreign capital inflows, to supplement domestic savings, cannot be underestimated. Those amounted to approximately 4% of GDP in 1995, but shrank to 0.7% in 1996. Events in 1996 showed quite unambiguously that capital inflows are unpredictable and reversals can occur quite unexpectedly. Such events adversely affect business confidence and also caused a ripple effect in the exchange rate and domestic interest rates.

Fiscal reforms, employment and social services

On the fiscal front, policy-makers were faced with an unsustainable situation, including an overall fiscal deficit of 7.9% of GDP that was recorded in 1992/93. Fiscal policy since 1994 has been guided by a number of key considerations: reduction of the budget deficit and level of government dissaving, not increasing the overall tax burden, reduction of government consumption expenditure, and increasing government's contribution to gross domestic fixed investment (MoF, 1996).

The reduction of government dissaving still remains to be worked on and the budget deficit is moving towards 3% of GDP by the year 2000 target. In pursuit of the fiscal target, the 1997/98 budget has pledged a thorough audit of government expenditure including RDP allocations. In order to support the objectives of monetary policy, it is important that the deficit and dissaving be reduced so that financial stability can be attained and the way for lower interest rates can be paved.

The process of budget reform has been strengthened by the introduction of a multi-year fiscal model to be updated annually to track performance in terms of public expenditure priorities. Similar tracking of expenditure in the inter-governmental fiscal arena requires the development of institutional capacity. Managing the synergies among national, regional and local government priorities and checking expenditure-performance quotients is crucial.

Public spending, especially on social services that are not effectively provided by the private sector, can prove a major tool for redistribution. Yet caution needs to be exercised in terms of cost effectiveness and good management of expenditure programmes. Engineering a balance between market-oriented reform and providing social security and assistance is a difficult and costly task.

Recognising that the private sector needs to take a lead in the creation of productive employment, government expenditure can and should play a dual role: employment creation and provision of social infrastructure. Herein lies a key ingredient in the concerns of the labour movement about GEAR. Government has a responsibility, given the historical legacy, to create a policy environment that will enable employment creation by the private sector, yet it has to accept that it too has to contribute to this process while meeting its responsibility to provide a more comprehensive safety net for the very poor. If not, the government risks the overspill of labour's cauldron of discontent at the perceived neglect of its 1994 manifesto and a key government constituency: stayaways, strikes, violence and consequently an even more uncertain and insecure economic environment.

The formulation and implementation of a strategy for the development of an economy in which the private sector eagerly creates employment opportunities, government efficiently provides basic services for all and support for the very poor, and labour contributes productively – and where the economic process produces a more equitable distribution of income, wealth and economic opportunity – is still the policy-makers' dream.

Policy-makers are indeed aware that grappling with domestic economic reform within a more focused Southern African configuration where South Africa's role is key to the development of the region, and within a vigorous international economic environment, presents unique opportunities – but also carries enormous risks.

Macroeconomic stability and foreign exchange markets

Avoiding high inflation crises is a prerequisite for sustained growth, while achieving low and stable inflation is important for the smooth operation of currency and financial markets in an era of private capital flows. Both considerations are important for South Africa. In the last three years, the rate of inflation has been below 10% – a notable achievement after almost two decades of double-digit levels. These lower levels contribute to a more stable decision-making environment via stable price expectations and a reduction in the distorting effects of inflation on resource allocation. The objective of reducing inflation to levels more in line with those of South Africa's trading partners is certainly key. Expectations of lower inflation would support the trade liberalisation process and feed through to lower interest rates, which would affect investors' costs and ease government's expenditure constraint. With low savings and high consumption propensities comes the risk of high inflation and therefore this remains a chief concern for the South African Reserve Bank (SARB).

The market for foreign exchange was remarkably stable during 1994 and 1995, and the economic recovery and concomitant increase in imports caused the balance of payments to swing from a surplus of R5.8 billion in 1993 to a deficit of R12.7 billion in 1995 (SARB, 1996). An impressive turnaround on the capital account from an outflow of R15 billion in 1993 to an inflow of R22 billion in 1995, however, provided cover for the current account deficit, for all outstanding short-term loans to be repaid and for total foreign reserves to reach a level of R19 billion by the end of January 1996 (SARB, 1996).

The relative stability of the real exchange rate was rudely shaken in February 1996. The initial depreciation of the weighted real exchange rate of the rand can, however, be explained in terms of economic fundamentals such as inflation differentials, purchasing power parity and the growing deficit in the current account of the balance of payments. A further depreciation (from end March to end July 1996) – the impact of speculative activity and negative news about South Africa's socio-political situation – pushed the rand down to levels that were not consistent with the country's true economic potential.

After many years of exchange controls, a process of relaxing these constraints was started with a number of measures introduced in July 1997. Given the distorting effects of these controls in the capital foreign exchange markets and the impediments posed to monetary policy, this was arguably overdue. The authorities are committed to a process of phased liberalisation – at this stage, though, unlimited outward transfer of capital is not permitted. In an interesting check on the liberalisation process, individuals and companies whose tax affairs are not in order are not allowed to take advantage of the new opportunities to expatriate funds.

A stable macroeconomic environment and a more liberalised capital account regime, as well as interventions by the South African Reserve Bank (SARB) for 'smoothing' adjustments in the foreign exchange market, are all necessary ingredients for attracting foreign investors. Except for the last one, SARB has in the past deployed these policies with some measure of success. The problem here, however, is that the Bank might have gone too far in its attempt to support the market when prices (the exchange rate) are declining. This is not only very costly but it is also 'inversely related to the underlying level of liquidity in the foreign exchange market' (CREFSA, 1996).

The same leading policy research periodical argues that liquidity could be more effectively increased through more longer-term and institutional approaches for developing the market:

> As foreign investment into South Africa broadens into new sectors and as exchange controls on domestic institutions and individuals are further liberalised, the diversity of the population of investors participating in the foreign exchange market will increase. Greater diversity among market participants enhances the two-sided depth of the foreign exchange market, thereby increasing its liquidity. This, in turn, will decrease the need for intervention to smooth exchange rate adjustment.

This analysis obviates the need for anchoring short-run adjustment policy in currency and financial markets to an explicit export-oriented development strategy aimed at enhancing the current account position of the economy and hence providing the basis for a stable capital account regime in South Africa.

Exchange rate policy and export orientation

There is very little disagreement that the South African economy is not likely to benefit from any further import substitution (IS) beyond the fairly substantial industrial capacity created during the apartheid regime. If anything, the real challenge facing the South African economy is to successfully turn this capacity into a strong base for export-led growth. However, there may be some differences as to the appropriate approach for supporting the export-orientation drive. A focus on the relatively sophisticated formal manufacturing and financial sectors would suggest that priority be accorded to macroeconomic stability, especially stable exchange rates and orderly foreign exchange and financial markets, and microeconomic efficiency. This is because this enclave of the South

African economy might have passed the phase of real exchange rate-led export promotion (EP), and is poised to reap the returns of sustained growth in productivity, which in turn will lead to secular real currency appreciation (Balassa, 1964). Obviously, this enclave could not be looked at in isolation from the rest of the economy. For example, the labour market link suggests that dynamic growth in these sectors will be substantially limited by the formidable skills and education gaps that characterise the majority of the population in South Africa. A more fundamental, and related, point is that the kind of export-led growth that the country is looking for – as envisaged by official government development strategies (e.g. RDP and its successor GEAR) – requires that growth should not only be adequate and sustained but it should also be job-creating and widely shared.

Therefore, taking into account the fundamental objectives of economic development in South Africa, the South African economy is still in the real exchange rate phase of its EP strategy, where export competitiveness requires strategic real currency depreciations. However, in an era of global capital market integration, the temptation to abandon (or the inability to maintain) an orderly process of depreciation before the economy is sufficiently developed to sustain secular equilibrium real exchange rate appreciation has proved to be quite formidable in many developing countries, including of course South Africa. The recent Asian financial crisis makes clear that even the most successful developing countries may fall prey to this problem.

References

Balassa, B. 1964. 'The purchasing power parity doctrine: a reappraisal'. *Journal of Political Economy*, 72.

CREFSA. 1966. *CREFSA*. Centre for Research into Economies and Finance in Southern Africa. April.

Economist Intelligence Unit (EIU). 1997a. 'South Africa'. October.

Economist Intelligence Unit (EIU). 1997b. 'South Africa'. November.

Edwards, S. 1997. 'Exchange rate issues in developing and transition economies'. In Elbadawi and Soto, eds, *Foreign Exchange Markets and Exchange Rate Policies in Sub-Saharan Africa, Journal of African Economies*, Supplement to vol. 6, no. 3: 37–73.

Ministry of Finance. 1996. *Growth, Employment and Redistribution: A Macroeconomic Strategy*. June. Pretoria.

SARB (South African Reserve Bank). 1996. *Quarterly Bulletin*. Various editions. Pretoria: SARB.

Williamson, J. 1997. 'The Washington consensus revisited'. In Louis Emmerij, ed., *Economic and Social Development in the XXI Century*. Washington, DC: The Inter-American Development Bank/Johns Hopkins University Press.

2
Understanding South Africa's Inequality

Haroon Bhorat, Murray Leibbrandt and Ingrid Woolard

1. Introduction

The dominant themes of South Africa's economic history are inequality and exclusion. Given this history, a key benchmark against which all contemporary economic planning must be assessed is the role of such plans in narrowing inequality and breaking down the barriers that exclude participation in the economy on the grounds of race, gender or location.

Such planning requires an information base detailing the dimensions of inequality and poverty in South Africa in the mid–1990s. This base should be nuanced enough to allow for assessment of programmes that are narrowly targeted at different segments of the South African population. An accurate information base is also a *sine qua non* for any more ambitious social development modelling that sets out to inform the policy selection process.

Some aspects of South Africa's lamentable inequality record are well documented. The most careful of the recent research (McGrath and Whiteford, 1994; Whiteford *et al.*, 1995) shows that a Gini coefficient of 0.68, using 1991 census data, or 0.65, using 1993 survey data, is among the highest to be found internationally. What is particularly notable is how high this coefficient is relative to countries with equivalent, dollar-denominated, gross domestic products.

South Africa's Gini coefficient has always served as the starkest indicator of the country's distorted 'development path'. Between 1975 and 1991, the Gini coefficient remained stubbornly fixed at 0.68. However, in a particularly useful piece of analysis, McGrath and Whiteford (1994) show that this static aggregate fails to reflect significant movements within the distribution of income. The period from the mid–1970s to the early 1990s has been characterised by stagnant and even negative economic growth performance. The burden of this macroeconomic stagnancy has been unevenly borne. The income share of the lowest 40% of income earners fell by 25% over this period while the income share of the top 10% of earners rose by 4.1%. This same picture was reflected within each race group with the income share of the poorest 40% falling 48% for African earners and 30.5% for whites and the top 10% share rising 43% for Africans and 24.7% for whites. Even in absolute terms, the top 20% of African incomes rose 38.2% on average and the bottom 40% of white incomes fell 39.8% on average; indicating the beginnings of a blurring of the previously rigid racial breakdowns within the overall distribution. (See also Appendix I.)

This chapter intends to contribute to the development of this information base. A range of inequality decomposition techniques will be used to build a few bridges between the description of South Africa's inequality and the analysis of the processes undergirding that inequality. There are *four* major sections to this chapter. Section 2, 'Sources of income and national inequality', uses a decomposition analysis of income inequality by income components to focus attention on the key labour market, asset ownership and state welfare processes driving South Africa's inequality. Section 3, 'The importance of race in national inequality', then overlays the racial fault line onto this picture of national inequality through the use of various categorical decomposition techniques. Once the aggregate importance of 'between racial groups' versus 'within racial groups' inequality has been examined, Sections 4 and 5 of the chapter disaggregate, respectively, the between-race group and the within the African group pictures. As Section 2 of the chapter highlights the importance of wage income, Sections 4 and 5 focus on the labour market.

In South African policy debates there is generally insufficient scrutiny of empirical results. For example, there is scant recognition that different measurement techniques are going to generate different results. In contrast to this, the international theoretical literature on inequality has paid a great deal of attention to the fact that different measures of inequality do not define inequality in exactly the same way and therefore do come up with different magnitudes of inequality.[1]

The importance of this literature lies in its questioning of the extent to which the inequality results of any context are technique driven rather than neutral representations of the circumstances prevailing in that society. Wherever possible, control for this possibility is exercised, using a variety of techniques. Conflicting results will then serve as an indication that the situation really is not as clear cut as any of the techniques individually indicate.

Of course, in a chapter that is already dominated by the presentation and discussion of statistics, there is a danger that this cross-checking could squeeze out the last small remnants of entertainment value. This is simply what needs to be done in a chapter that sets out to derive a set of baseline information that is as reliable as possible. However, it seems sensible to situate as much of the technical discussion as possible in Appendixes I and II.

There are two recent data sources available for analysis of national inequality: the 1994 *October Household Survey* (OHS) conducted by the South African Central Statistical Service and the survey undertaken as part of the Project for Statistics on Living Standards and Development (PSLSD) by the Southern African Labour and Development Research Unit at the University of Cape Town in late 1993. The OHS required households to specify their income from *employment* and *self-employment* sources only, whereas the PSLSD survey offers full coverage of cash and in-kind sources of income. The PSLSD data are preferred for the current study, since the study's broad income coverage is more useful for analysing welfare – especially as the focus is on the contribution of different income sources to inequality. The analysis of the labour market in Sections 4 and 5 of the chapter draws on references from a broader set of empirical sources.

2.   Sources of income and national inequality

Over the last decade, a busy international literature has developed around the derivation and refinement of techniques for decomposing the Gini coefficient by income sources.[2] Such decompositions highlight those income sources that dominate the distribution of income and, as such, offer a bridge between description of inequality and the key economic processes generating inequality in a society.

The application of such work to South Africa provides an immediate addition to the knowledge of South African inequality. The PSLSD data set contains detailed information on all sources of income and, therefore, is an ideal data set to apply such analysis. Clearly, the level of aggregation that is chosen is determined by the context under consideration and the questions that the analysis is addressing. For the purposes of this chapter, it is useful to distinguish between the relative importance of the major focuses of policy attention. Total income for each household is therefore divided into six sources:

- *Remittances*: remittances from absent family members and marital maintenance.
- *Wage income*: regular and casual employment and value of benefits such as subsidised housing, transport and food.
- *Agriculture*: profit from commercial farming as well as small-scale/subsistence farming for both sale and own consumption.
- *Capital income*: dividends, interest, rent income, imputed rent from residing in own dwelling and private and civil (contributory) pensions.
- *State transfers*: social pensions, disability grants, poor relief, unemployment insurance and child maintenance grants.
- *Self-employment*: informal and formal business activities.

Such a breakdown is still at a fairly aggregate level and any number of more disaggregated breakdowns is possible to answer more specific questions. The detailed derivation of this decomposition technique is presented in Appendix II. The key aspects are summarised below.

If South African society is represented as n households deriving income from K different sources (i.e. K different income components), then Appendix II.1 shows that the *Gini coefficient* (G) for the distribution of total income within the group can be derived as:

$$G = \sum_{k-1}^{r} R_k G_k S_k$$

where:

S_K is the share of source k of income in total group income (i.e. $S_k = \mu_k/\mu$), G_k is the Gini coefficient measuring the inequality in the distribution of income component k within the group, and R_k is the Gini correlation of income from source k with total income.[3]

This equation tells us that the effect of source k income on total income inequality can be broken down into three components:

- The share of income component k in total income (captured by the term S_k).
- The inequality within the sample of income from source k (as measured by G_k).
- The correlation between source k income and total income (as measured by R_k).

The larger the product of these three components, the greater the contribution of income from source k to total income inequality.

However, it must be noted that while S_k and G_k are always positive and less than one, R_k can fall anywhere on the interval $(-1, 1)$. When R_k is less than zero, income from source k is negatively correlated with total income and thus serves to lower the overall Gini measure for the sample.

Now, suppose that there is an exogenous increase in income from source j, by some factor σ_j; Appendix II.2 shows that the derivative of the Gini coefficient with respect to a change in income source j is:

$$\frac{\partial G}{\partial \sigma} = -S_j(R_j G_j - G)$$

If $\partial G / \partial j$ is negative then a marginal increase in income component j will lessen income inequality. This will be the case when either:

1. income from component j has either a negative or zero correlation with total income ($-1 \leq R_j \leq 0$); or
2. income from source j is positively correlated with total income ($R_j > 0$) and $R_j G_j < G$.

Alternatively, in order for a marginal increase in source j income to worsen income inequality it is necessary that $G_j > G$ (i.e. income from source j must be more unevenly distributed than total income).

However, this condition alone is not sufficient for a change in income component j to worsen the overall income distribution, as the sign of $\partial G / \partial \sigma_j$ will still be influenced by the strength of the Gini correlation between source j income and total income (Stark *et al.*, 1986: 260).

Table 2.1 presents the results of this decomposition for the total South African sample.[4] A few illustrative features of Table 2.1 will be highlighted. It can be seen that wage income has a dominant share of income (69%) but makes an even larger contribution to inequality (73.5%). The reason for this is the high R of 0.92, implying that a household's rank in the distribution of wage income is strongly correlated with that household's rank in the distribution of total income. This strong correlation is more than enough to compensate for the fact that the Gini coefficient for wage income (0.69) is the lowest of all income sources.

The Gini coefficient for a particular income source (G_k) is driven by the inequality among those earning income from that source (G_A) and the proportion of households who have positive income from that source (P_k), or, changing the focus, *the proportion of households with no access to* particular income source $(1 - P_k)$. Then we see that, for example:

$$G_{\text{wage}} = 0.69 = P_{\text{wage}} G_A + (1 - P_{\text{wage}}) = 0.35 + 0.34$$

Table 2.1 Decomposition of total national income by income sources

Income source	Proportion of households receiving income source (P_k)	Mean income from source (Rands)	Share in total income (S_k)	Gini for income source for households receiving such income (G_A)	Gini for income source for all households (G_k)	Gini correlation with total income rankings (R_k)	Contribution to Gini coefficient of total income ($S_k G_k R_k$)	Percentage share in overall Gini	Effect on overall Gini of a 1% change in income component
Remittances	0.27	68.07	0.03	0.52	0.88	-0.08	0.00	-0.40	-0.021
Wage income	0.66	1,427.94	0.69	0.53	0.69	0.92	0.44	73.50	0.021
Capital income	0.67	285.55	0.13	0.82	0.87	0.81	0.09	15.20	0.015
State transfers	0.23	97.38	0.05	0.26	0.83	0.00	0.00	0.00	-0.029
Agriculture	0.18	79.68	0.04	0.92	0.99	0.79	0.03	4.70	0.008
Self-employment	0.11	123.47	0.06	0.75	0.97	0.97	0.04	7.00	0.006
Total		2,082.04	1.00				0.60	100.00	

Notes

1. G_A is the Gini for the income source when we only consider households with positive income from that source.

2. G_k is the Gini for the income source when we consider all households. Lerman and Yitzhaki (1994) show that $G_k = P_k * G_A + (1 - P_k)$.

This brings us part of the way to apportioning the 'blame' for Gini inequality between the inequality among earners and the inequality between those with some wage income and those with none. It would appear that almost half of what we have termed 'wage inequality' is in fact driven by the 34% of households with zero wage income.

Remittance income has the smallest share of total income (3%) and makes a small, negative contribution to inequality (-0.4%). This negative contribution arises because of the small negative correlation ($R - 0.08$) between the rank ordering of remittance income and the rank ordering of total income. This negative correlation would seem to imply that the fairly high Gini coefficient for remittances arises because remittance income is disproportionately distributed to those at the bottom of the total distribution relative to those at the top. In essence, this analysis suggests that factors that boost remittance income for current recipients would lower overall inequality.

The last column of Table 2.1 shows that effects of a 1% increase in a particular income component. A change in state transfers, remittances or wages will have the greatest effect on the overall Gini. In the last case the Gini increases, but in the other two cases it decreases. The components that increase inequality correlate highly with total income rankings (i.e. R_k is high), which implies that an increase in these sources will primarily benefit the better-off and thus aggravate the Gini. The sum of the absolute changes in the Gini coefficient is zero. This follows because increasing all components of income by 1% has no effect on the income distribution and therefore no effect on the Gini.

From the point of view of government policy, state transfers are of special interest. A well-targeted, redistributionist state expenditure programme would be evidenced by a strongly negative R. State transfers do not quite achieve this negative correlation, but the fact that $R = 0$ ensures a zero contribution to inequality for these transfers. Moreover, we see that an increase in state transfers of 1% will reduce the Gini by 0.03 (0.05%), a more significant impact than is achieved by changing any other component.

While G_k is the coefficient needed to calculate the contribution to inequality, a look at G_A is instructive. G_A is the Gini coefficient when considering only those households actually receiving income from that particular source. There are large disparities in the incomes being earned from agriculture, self-employment and capital income. This points to the dichotomous nature of the South African economy, where there is an immense gap between those engaged in commercial versus subsistence agriculture, those in formal versus informal self-employment, and those earning income from interest and dividends versus those accruing a small capital benefit as a result of owning their dwelling.

However, while the aggregate analysis of any of the income sources presented in Table 2.1 is usefully indicative, it does not really reveal enough about what is going on at the lower end of the distribution relative to the top end. So, for example, it is quite possible for the same aggregate picture to result from an income source that is contributing exclusively to the very poor and very rich or exclusively to the middle of the distribution. Any aggregate picture therefore needs to be complemented by some sensitivity analysis. A particularly useful exercise would seem to be one that splits the population by a poverty line. This was done for the South African case, and the results are presented in Table 2.2.[5]

Inspection of Table 2.2 shows that the aggregate picture presented previously is only a rough average of very different processes taking place above and below the poverty line.[6] As agriculture is a consistently low contributor to average income and to inequality in both the above and the below group, it will not be discussed further at this point.

We will consider wage income first. In the group above the poverty line, this income source makes a large and stable contribution to average income (72%) and to the distribution of income (70.7%) within the group. The distributional effect is the result of a low Gini coefficient (0.57) being offset by a high R of 0.88. For the group below the poverty line, the share of wage income in total income is far lower (38%) but, even within the poor, higher wage income is strongly correlated with higher total income ($R = 0.69$) and this income source therefore still makes a high contribution to inequality (51.3%). It is clear from this breakdown of above and below groups that access to wage income is central to determining which households are able to avoid poverty and, even, the depth to which poor households sink below the poverty line.

On the other hand, it is encouraging to see that state transfers are a much smaller part of the total income for the above group (3%) than for the below group (27%). Moreover, $R = -0.11$ in the above group reveals that this income is not going to the higher income households in society. However, the fairly high Gini coefficient for state transfers in the below group (0.75) and rank correlation ($R = 0.55$) implies that it is the relatively better-off within the poor who are receiving state transfers.

There are two possible explanations for such an outcome. The first is that the targeting of state assistance is not that successful. The second is that the depth of poverty in South African society is so acute that access to some state assistance is sufficient to move a household away from the bottom of the poverty ranking. Apartheid-derived racial biases in welfare allocations are

Table 2.2 Decomposition of total national income by income sources below and above the poverty line

a. Below poverty line

Income source	Proportion of households receiving income source (P_k)	Mean income from source (Rands)	Share in total income (S_k)	Gini for income source for households receiving such income (G_A)	Gini for income source for all households (G_k)	Gini correlation with total income rankings (R_k)	Contribution to Gini coefficient of total income ($S_k G_k R_k$)	Percentage share in overall Gini	Effect on overall Gini of a 1% change in income source
Remittances	0.42	80.62	0.18	0.44	0.75	0.19	0.03	6.71	-0.044
Wage income	0.35	171.56	0.38	0.36	0.76	0.69	0.20	51.57	0.051
Capital income	0.72	32.53	0.07	0.67	0.75	0.42	0.02	5.84	-0.005
State transfers	0.30	119.78	0.27	0.21	0.75	0.55	0.11	28.42	0.006
Agriculture	0.31	18.19	0.04	0.61	0.87	0.34	0.01	3.08	-0.004
Self-employment	0.11	23.97	0.05	0.50	0.94	0.34	0.02	4.39	-0.004
Total		446.65	1.00				0.39	100.00	

b. Above the poverty line

Income source	Proportion of households receiving income source (P_k)	Mean income from source (Rands)	Share in total income (S_k)	Gini for income source for households receiving such income (G_A)	Gini for income source for all households (G_k)	Gini correlation with total income rankings (R_k)	Contribution to Gini coefficient of total income ($S_k G_k R_k$)	Percentage share in overall Gini	Effect on overall Gini of a 1% change in income source
Remittances	0.16	57.42	0.02	0.52	0.92	-0.11	0.00	-0.41	-0.012
Wage income	0.83	2049.90	0.72	0.48	0.57	0.88	0.36	70.70	-0.006
Capital income	0.63	379.86	0.13	0.75	0.84	0.75	0.08	16.61	0.017
State transfers	0.19	88.85	0.03	0.29	0.87	-0.11	0.00	-0.60	-0.019
Agriculture	0.12	101.45	0.04	0.94	0.99	0.86	0.03	5.92	-0.012
Self-employment	0.11	173.22	0.06	0.72	0.97	0.68	0.04	7.82	-0.009
Total		2850.71	1.00				0.51	100.00	

certainly a cause of inefficient allocation.[7] However, there is also some recent econometric evidence (Deaton, 1995) that state pensions are not badly targeted. In addition, studies of rural poverty (see May *et al.*, 1995) have made it clear that 'claims against the state' are central to rural livelihoods. Thus, on balance, the second explanation is more likely to be true.[8] What can be said with more certainty is that the analysis of wage income and state transfers serves to confirm that in South Africa, the poorest of the poor are those households that lack access to either wage income or state transfers.

The low share of remittances in total income (2%) and the negative correlation for remittances ($R = -0.11$) in the above group along with the very much higher share of remittances (18%) in the income of the below group indicate that remittances are much more important on average in the below group. In South Africa remittances generally flow from urban to rural areas and, to a large extent, this result merely confirms that a large component of South Africa's poor are located in the rural areas (Whiteford *et al.*, 1995). However, there is additional information to be gleaned. The low, positive rank correlation ($R = 0.2$) in the below group results in a small contribution to inequality (6.9%). This implies that remittance income is well disbursed within the poor. So, while remittances are not important enough to be a major discriminator of who lies above or below the poverty line, factors that might cause an increase in remittances would have a generalised positive impact on the poor. The converse is true for capital income. This income source is far more important to the above group than to the below group, both as an average share (13% and 8%, respectively) and as a contributor to inequality (16.6% and 6.5%, respectively).

A look at the 'actual' Gini (G_A) for the components when considering only those households actually receiving such income reveals much the same picture as the analysis for the total population. We would, perhaps, have anticipated lower Ginis in the below group, which might be expected to be fairly homogeneous since everyone is, after all, technically 'poor'. This is not the case, however. There are considerable deviations in the incomes earned from capital income and agriculture in both the above and below groups. Self-employment in the below group, however, produces less inequality among those engaged in these activities than in the above group. This is to be expected, since, as we show later, all those in the below group are likely to be involved in informal marginalist activities.

Although the decomposition by income components offers a useful feel for what is driving national inequality, it does not highlight any of the major categorical stratifiers of the South African income distribution. In particular, for policy purposes it is essential to superimpose a racial breakdown onto the analysis; we focus now on this issue.

3.   The importance of race in national inequality

The literature on the decomposition of total inequality by subgroups has a longer lineage than the income source analysis given in the previous section.[9] If the population is divided into mutually exclusive exhaustive subgroups, then there is a degree of inequality both *within* and between these subgroups. It is desirable to decompose a measure of overall inequality into the 'within' and the 'between' portion.[10] The value of decompositions is that 'they gauge the relative importance of various sources and sectors in respect of overall inequality, and thereby direct attention to potentially fruitful areas of research' (Fields, 1980: 438).

The Theil coefficient

The most commonly cited additively decomposable measure is the *Theil T-statistic*, derived directly from the notion of entropy in information theory (Fields, 1980: 103). The definition of the *Theil-T* is given in Appendix II.3.

The *Theil-T* can be decomposed as follows:

$$T = T_B + \sum q_i T_i$$

where T_i is the *Theil-T* inequality measure within the ith group, q_i is the proportion of income accruing to the ith group and T_B is the between group contribution. T_B is calculated the same way as T, but assuming that all incomes within a group are equal.

Theil-*L* statistic

The Theil-*L* (defined in Appendix II.4) decomposes in a similar way to the Theil-*T*, except that the group statistics are weighted by the proportion of households (not income) in each group, i.e.:

$$L = L_B + \sum p_i L_i$$

where p_i is the population share of the ith group.

Atkinson's measure

As shown in Appendix II.5, Atkinson starts from an additive social welfare function in order to derive the following inequality index:

$$I = 1 - \left(\frac{1}{N} \sum_{i-1}^{N} (y_i/\mu)^{i-\varepsilon} \right)^{1/1-\varepsilon}$$

which may be decomposed into between- and within-group inequality so that:

$$I = I_B + I_W + Residual$$

The measure can be interpreted as the proportion of the present total income that would be required to achieve the same level of social welfare as at present if incomes were equally distributed (Atkinson, 1977: 48). Atkinson explicitly introduces distributional objectives through the parameter $\varepsilon \geq 0$, which represents the weight attached to inequality in the distribution. By specifying different values of ε one can vary the importance society attaches to mean living standards versus equality. If society is indifferent about the distribution, we will set ε equal to zero. Increasing ε gives more weight to inequality at the lower end of the distribution. At ε equal to infinity, society is concerned only with the poorest household.

Applying the measures to South Africa

Given the importance of racial breakdowns in South Africa, all three of the decomposition techniques would seem to have obvious relevance. Yet, it is only recently that such decompositions have begun to be used in South Africa.[11] Table 2.3 presents the results of the decomposition of South Africa's total national income by race using the three decomposition techniques discussed above.[12]

All the indexes point in a similar direction, i.e. that the 'within' and 'between' components are both important contributors to overall inequality. This result is at odds with the finding in McGrath and Whiteford (1994)

Table 2.3 Comparison of distribution measures

Measure	Between component	Within component	Residual	Total
Theil-T	0.340	0.365		0.705
	(48.2)	(51.8)		
Theil-L	0.293	0.425		0.718
	(40.8)	(59.2)		
Atkinson	0.149	0.148	0.001	0.299
$E = 0.5$	(50.0)	(49.7)	(0.3)	
Atkinson	0.322	0.373	0.006	0.701
$E = 1.5$	(46.0)	(53.2)	(0.8)	
Atkinson	0.393	0.566	0.0001	0.959
$\varepsilon = 2.5$	(41.0)	(59.0)	(0.01)	

Note: The figures in parentheses show the percentage contribution to total inequality.

that 'within group' inequality accounts for 77% of overall inequality as measured by the Theil-*T*.

The high Theil-*L* index can be explained by the use of population shares as weights. The African group displays the highest degree of income inequality, as measured by the Theil indexes for the individual race groups (Table 2.4). A weighting in accordance with population shares naturally makes a large contribution to the 'within' component of inequality.

Table 2.4   Within-race contribution to overall inequality

Measure	African	Coloured	Asian	White
Theil-*T*	0.414	0.276	0.491	0.326
	[0.159]	[0.023]	[0.028]	[0.156]
	(22.6)	(3.3)	(4.0)	(22.1)
Theil-*L*	0.463	0.325	0.390	0.295
	[0.345]	[0.025]	[0.011]	[0.045]
	(48.1)	(3.5)	(1.5)	(6.3)

Note
1. The first row of figures shows the measure when considering only the particular race group.
2. The figures in brackets show the absolute contribution to total inequality.
3. The figures in parentheses show the percentage of the total inequality.
4. Atkinson's index is *generally* but not *additively* decomposable, hence we cannot apportion the within contribution among the race groups.

The more value placed on equality – i.e. the larger *E* in Atkinson's index – the more significant is within-group inequality in causing overall inequality. Since most of the poor are African, it follows that inequality at the lower end of the income distribution will tend to be 'within-group'.

It is immediately evident that the choice of the Theil-*L* versus the Theil-*T* index paints a very different picture of the contribution of different races to overall inequality. The Theil-*T* suggests that inequality among the white group is almost as large a contributor to overall inequality as inequality among the African group, yet the Theil-*L* suggests that African inequality contributes 48.1% to total inequality *vis-à-vis* a contribution of 6.3% from white inequality. Again, the reason can be found in the use of income as opposed to population weights. This stresses the importance of considering the nature of the decomposition measure before relying on any one statistic. Appendix II.6 discusses the choice of decomposition technique in greater detail.

Notwithstanding the ambiguities resulting from the use of different techniques, it is clear that between-race inequality continues to make a significant contribution to overall inequality and needs to be studied further. Secondly, regardless of the measure used, the inequality that exists between African households emerges as an area that could be fruitfully scrutinised. We take this up later in the chapter.

4. The labour market and racial inequality

Rather than using the decomposition techniques to divide inequality into ever finer gradations, this chapter will use the key aggregate features generated by the previous analysis as a framework for a more focused discussion of the factors undergirding both the between-racial-group inequality (this section) and the within-African-group inequality (the following section). The income source decomposition analysis outlined above showed that wages are the most significant contributor to overall income inequality. In addition, the Gini coefficient for wage income was driven both by the fact that only 69% of households have access to wage income and that this wage income is unevenly distributed ($G_A = 0.53$) within those wage earning households. Thus, wage inequality operates at two levels. The first level concerns the significant income gap that exists among those currently employed. The second layer of inequality is between those earning wages from employment and those individuals who are unemployed. An attempt is made here to understand the dimensions of between-racial-group inequality that exists among the employed and the unemployed.

Employment rates and trends

The population of working age (15 years or older) is approximately 25.7 million people (CSS, 1995).[13] Of these about 56%, or 14.4 million, are economically active. In other words, the employed and the unemployed who want to work constitute just over half of the population of working age. The number of those considered employed is approximately 9.6 million.

A racial division of the employed reveals the first basic level of between-group inequality among the employed. Table 2.5 shows the number of employed by race and the corresponding employment rate. It is quite clear that the probability of being employed is highest for white workers in the labour market. In contrast, the employment rate for Africans is only 58.9%. This is lower than the total mean employment rate of 67.4%. Hence, while employed Africans have realised substantial gains in the last 20 years, the number affected has been disproportionately small, when compared with other race groups.

Table 2.5 Employment levels and rates by race

Race	Employed	Rate (%)
Asian	338 480	82.9
Coloured	1 144 929	76.7
White	2 321 385	93.6
African	5 836 177	58.9
Total	9 640 972	67.4

Source: Adapted from CSS (1995).

Employment by sector and occupation

Inequality among the employed has been primarily due to an aggressive apartheid labour market policy. The most obvious manifestation of this inequality is the persistence of a racial division of labour. This division has ensured that positions for those in middle management and upwards remain the preserve of whites. Black workers, on the other hand, predominate in blue-collar occupations from semi-skilled to unskilled work.

An analysis of recent data reveals that 42.1% of employed African workers are in unskilled occupations (Table 2.6). The next largest category is services and sales. While Asians and whites are rarely labourers, African and coloured workers are concentrated in this category. Of all employed white workers, 40.3% are found in the top three occupations – managers, professionals, associate professionals and technicians. The corresponding figure for Africans is 14.4%, which is also lower than the national mean of 20.6%.

Table 2.6 reveals a second layer of inequality among the employed. Not only are employment rates lower for Africans relative to whites, but also there is a distinct parallel between occupation and race. Hence, for those African workers who are employed, their position is most often at the bottom of the job ladder. Notably, it is also coloured workers who reveal this skills disadvantage.

As an indicator of the source of the demand for labour, it is necessary to examine the relative shares of formal sector industries in the employment of labour (Table 2.7). The largest employer, for all races except Africans, is the manufacturing sector. This is consonant with the sector's contributions to export earnings and more generally its dominance in GDP. The sectors where African workers have a high representation are agriculture, fishing and forestry, and domestic services. Notably, these are industries

Table 2.6   Employment by occupation and race (%)

Occupation/ race	Asian	Coloured	White	African	Total
Managers	9.0	2.4	13.2	2.9	5.5
Professionals	5.9	3.3	11.4	5.1	6.5
Tech., Associates Professionals	10.4	5.5	15.7	6.4	8.6
Clerks	21.6	12.6	23.6	6.9	12.1
Service Sales	15.0	10.6	9.7	10.4	10.5
Agric. fishing	0.4	1.9	2.8	0.8	1.4
Craft, trade	14.1	14.8	15.6	10.3	12.2
Machine operators, assistants	16.8	13.8	4.1	14.1	11.7
Labourers	6.3	34.6	1.8	42.1	30.3
Armed forces	0.0	0.2	1.0	0.4	0.5
Other	0.5	0.3	1.1	0.6	0.7
Total	100.0	100.0	100.0	100.0	100.0

Source: CSS (1995).

Table 2.7   Regular employment shares by sector and race

Sector	Asian	Coloured	White	African	Total
Agriculture, fishing	n.a.	13.4	3.1	16.7	12.2
Mining	0.6	1.0	5.4	9.7	7.3
Manufacturing	36.3	25.0	13.0	15.1	16.6
Electricity & water	0.9	1.9	3.0	1.6	1.9
Construction	4.6	5.3	5.8	5.6	5.6
Wholesale & retail	16.4	13.5	11.5	9.8	10.9
Restaurant	1.2	2.3	2.5	2.7	2.6
Transport	5.7	6.0	12.0	4.7	6.7
Finance	4.6	2.7	11.8	1.2	4.2
Education	12.0	7.3	8.3	7.3	7.8
Medical	4.8	5.6	6.6	5.2	5.6
Legal	2.7	1.2	3.2	1.5	2.0
Domestic	0.3	3.6	0.6	13.4	8.5
Armed forces	3.3	2.4	2.2	2.3	2.3
Other services	6.6	8.1	10.0	3.2	5.6
Other	n.a.	0.6	0.8	0.0	0.3

Source: SALDRU (1994).

intensive in the use of unskilled labour. The sector with the lowest share in African labour is finance. This sector employs predominantly skilled labour. Coloured workers, too, are over-represented in agriculture and wholesale and retail. The dominance of Africans in agriculture and domestic services is in itself another form of inequality among the employed, as these two sectors offer very low wages to unskilled workers. In addition, these workers are unorganised, thus lacking any formal bargaining power. This is in contrast to all other formally employed workers. The latter are relatively well paid and are represented by trade unions. It will be shown later that this presents as a form of within-group inequality.

What the analysis above reveals is that the occupation–race overlap is further manifested in the sectoral shares of employment by race. Sectoral employment biases further contribute to inequality among wage earners. It would appear that whites are likely to be employed in more skilled occupations and better paying sectors. The sectors in which Africans are found in greatest disproportion to the number of whites are also the sectors that pay the least. This leads to the next axis of between-group inequality – inequality in earnings among race groups.

Wage differentials by race

Until very recently the Central Statistical Service collected only rudimentary data on wage rates. The aggregate wage bill and level of employment, by subsector, are available for years past. These may be divided to yield an approximation of the average hourly rate of pay in each subsector. For most industries the data are available by race. However, in 1985 the mining industry stopped providing the racial breakdown, making analysis by population group impossible at the aggregate level.

The striking feature of a breakdown by race is the continued existence of a racially determined wage structure. In 1993, for example, the average wage for whites was R3,063.00, while that for Africans was R1,118.00. In this recent period, there has been a slight narrowing of the white to African wage differential; in 1989, the African wage was 32% of the average white wage and by 1993 this figure had risen to 37% (CSS, 1995).

Despite these advances in African real wage growth, the strict racially determined earnings profile has been retained. These wage inequalities are a legacy of the racial division of labour that made race a predictor of occupation in the workplace. It is therefore desirable to compare wage differentials by both race and occupation.

The ratio of African to white wages may be calculated on the assumption that three basic occupational categories exist – unskilled, semi-skilled and skilled. Table 2.8 illustrates a rapid closing of the wage gap after 1993. Controlling for occupation, the data suggest that the last vestiges of official racially based pay scales are being eroded. Hence, in 1994, the median African wage was 94% of the white wage for those in the unskilled category. The corresponding figure for the other two categories was 95%.

An analysis of average wage rates by sector reveals the sectoral inequality alluded to in the previous section. Table 2.9 presents the average wage by sector, assuming a 40-hour week. The poor earnings in both agriculture and domestic services are clear. The mean wage in agriculture is only 13% of the mean wage in finance. In domestic services, workers' average wage is 8% of that in finance.

Clearly, while inequality is manifest in the occupation–race overlap, it is also evident in sectoral employment and earnings. Those predominantly African workers in agriculture and domestic services are grossly disadvantaged in formal employment, given their very poor remuneration levels.

To gain clarity on the relative importance of occupations, sectors and races, there have been a number of attempts to estimate South African earnings functions. These models also allow educational differences to be considered as an important source of pre-market discrimination. Moll (1995) finds that, even after adjustment for education, a 14% pure discrimination differential still remained in 1993. This differential had declined from 20% in 1980. However, Hertz (in Bhorat and Hertz, 1995) finds that there is a 100% pure race premium for whites relative to Africans even after controlling for education, gender, age, language, location and even unionisation.[14]

Unemployment and between-group inequality

All of the foregoing notwithstanding, the fundamental labour market division remains the gap between the employed and unemployed. This section attempts to illustrate that among the unemployed, Africans – relative to other race groups – are severely disadvantaged.

In calculating unemployment levels the definition of the unemployed person is crucial. The CSS uses the following definition of unemployment: Any persons 15 years and older who:

1. were not in paid or self-employment;
2. were available for paid employment or self-employment during the seven days preceding the interview;

Table 2.8 Median pay levels by skill category and race

Year	Unskilled (R/month)	Unskilled (ratio)	Semi-skilled (R/month)	Semi-skilled (ratio)	Skilled (R/month)	Skilled (ratio)
1992						
White	1706	100	2546	100	3974	100
African	1267	74	1956	77	3290	83
1993						
White	1673	100	2930	100	4738	100
African	1447	86	2484	85	4086	86
1994						
White	1692	100	2992	100	4951	100
African	1590	94	2482	95	4703	95

Source: information from PE Corporate Services in 1995.

Table 2.9 Mean monthly wages for selected sectors

Sector	Mean wage (pounds)
Agriculture	526
Mining	1653
Manufacturing	1988
Construction	2148
Wholesale & retail	1957
Finance	4050
Domestic Services	357
All sectors	1904

Source: Bhorat and Hertz (1995).

3. took specific steps during the four weeks preceding the interview to find paid employment or self-employment; or
4. had the desire to take up employment or self-employment.

The strict definition of the unemployed includes 1, 2 and 3 above. In other words, persons who did not take specific steps in the last month to find a job would not be considered unemployed. The expanded definition of the unemployed includes 1, 2 and 4. In other words, those persons who have not been seeking work but would like to work are classified as unemployed. Option 4 therefore captures the all-important category of the 'discouraged' work seeker. (See Table 2.10.)

Indications are that the expanded definition alters unemployment rates dramatically. The CSS only began to use the expanded definition from 1987 onwards; this definition was accepted as the official rate in 1993.

Table 2.10 Strict and expanded unemployment by race (%)

	Asian	Coloured	White	African	Total
Expanded definition					
Rate	17.1	23.3	6.4	41.1	32.6
No.	69 995	348 414	159 922	4 077 745	4 656 076
Strict definition					
Rate	14.1	19.2	25.8	25.8	20.3
No.	55 740	272 283	2 024 742	2 024 742	2 452 783

Source: CSS (1995).

Under the expanded definition the CSS reports a total unemployment rate of 32.6%.[15] This drops to 20.3% when the strict definition is used. African unemployment stands at 41.1%; if discouraged workers are excluded this figure drops to 25.8%. Coloureds are the most likely group to be unemployed, after Africans. Whites are least likely to be without a job. It is clear, though, that African unemployment rates, for both the expanded and strict definitions, are higher then those of other racial groups. This represents the most basic form of between-group inequality among the unemployed.

It is also possible to group the unemployed according to their period of job search. The period of search is indicative of the extent of long-term structural unemployment as opposed to joblessness of a more temporary nature as in the case of, for example, cyclical unemployment. Table 2.11 divides the unemployed into three categories – those who have been searching for a job for less than 6 months, for between 6 and 12 months, and for a period longer than 12 months.

Table 2.11   Period of search by unemployed according to race (%)

Period/race (months)	Asians	Coloureds	Whites	Africans	Total
< 6	26.0	24.4	45.7	15.5	17.3
6–12	21.7	19.4	15.0	14.5	15.0
> 12	52.3	56.2	39.3	70.0	67.7

Source: CSS (1995).

It is evident that a search period greater than 12 months dominates among all racial groups except whites. Of the African unemployed, for example, 70% have been searching for employment for longer than one year. Only among white workers is the period of search predominantly for less than six months. Africans feature disproportionately in the more-than-one-year cohort. This is indicative of a significant level of between-group inequality

5.   African inequality

It is clear from the analysis in the previous sections that there are lingering racial dimensions to the South African labour market. However, the between-group and within-group decompositions explored earlier revealed that no matter which technique is used, within-group inequality is an equally important contributor to total inequality. This balance adds broad support to a small but growing set of studies in South Africa that have begun to draw attention to movements within the African income distribution.[15]

The complexity of the African income distribution is illustrated in Table 2.12, where African income is broken down into income sources. In comparing this table with the equivalent national decomposition by the poverty line of Table 2.2, it is clear that the African situation is not a simple replication of the below poverty line group. Rather, the emerging picture is consistent with a very much lower African mean income relative to the national mean, but with an overlapping tail. Given this, it is important to discuss the processes that drive within-group African inequality, with a clear perspective on how important these divisions are in the national schema. At the same, time it is clear that most of the policy initiatives of the new South Africa are to be targeted at the poorest elements of the African group. This provides the rationale for examining the importance of gender, age and location within the African group.

From Table 2.12 it can be seen that the aggregate dominance of wage income in driving inequality for the African group is more acute than in any of the previous classifications discussed in this chapter. However, an inspection of Table 2.12 also reveals that only 60% of households receive any wage income and the Gini coefficient for wage income rises from 0.44, if only earners are considered, to 0.66, if all households are considered. To flesh out this distinction a little further, the African population can be divided into two groups: households where at least one person is employed and households where no one is employed. The mean income of the first group is R1,409 compared with R535 in the latter group. Using the Theil-*T* index, 51% of overall African inequality can be attributed to the employed group, 24% to the unemployed group and 25%, to the between-group component. When using the Theil-*L*, however, these percentages change to 32%, 43% and 25% respectively. This again reflects the bias in the choice of inequality measure, but it is clear that very little of the inequality comes from the unemployed group, regardless of how we measure it.

It is therefore important to broaden the discussion of the processes in the formal labour market to the factors determining which groups of the African labour force do not even get into formal employment. We will first look at inequality within formal employment and then contrast the formally employed with the informally employed before concluding with a focus on the unemployed.

Formal employment

Moll (1995) has already been referred to as saying that pure wage discrimination the labour market declined between 1980 and 1993. In

Table 2.12 Decomposition of African total income by income sources

Income source	Proportion of households receiving income source (P_k)	Mean income from source	Share in total income (S_k)	Gini for source for households receiving such income ($\hat{G}_A$)	Gini coefficient for income source ($\hat{G}_k = P_k^* G_A + (1 - P_k)$)	Gini correlation with total income rankings (R_k)	Contribution to Gini coefficient of total income ($S_k G_k R_k$)	Percentage share in overall Gini	Effect on overall Gini of a 1% change in income source
Remittance	0.32	R74.41	0.07	0.49	0.84	0.03	0.00	0.48	-0.033
Wage income	0.60	R689.79	0.68	0.44	0.66	0.89	0.39	82.25	0.069
Capital income	0.67	R57.67	0.06	0.71	0.81	0.57	0.03	5.44	-0.001
State transfers	0.28	R108.51	0.11	0.24	0.79	0.16	0.01	2.82	-0.037
Agriculture	0.25	R21.29	0.02	0.71	0.93	0.33	0.01	1.36	-0.004
Self-employment	0.12	R63.94	0.06	0.65	0.96	0.61	0.04	7.69	0.007
Total		R1015.61	1.00				0.48	100	

much the same spirit as the work described in our chapter, Moll goes on to decompose earnings inequality into between – and within – racial group contributions over time using the Bourguignon *L* technique, concluding that 'in 1980, between-group inequality accounted for 65% of all earnings inequality; by 1993 this contribution had fallen to 42%' (Moll, 1995: 5). The corollary of this is that inequality within African earners had risen over the same period. The factors undergirding this within-group discrimination remain largely elusive. Moll manages to ascertain that there were more than sufficient appropriately educated African workers in 1993 for the upward occupational mobility of many African employees to be higher than the *de facto* mobility situation. African occupational mobility had been rationed and, as such, constituted a source of within-group discrimination.

It is possible, then, to present a summarised composite of the layers of inequality among the formally employed. There would seem to be three types of formally employed workers. First, there are those, predominantly white, workers employed in occupations above the C-Upper grades. Second, there are predominantly African workers in grades below C-Lower. The final category are unskilled African workers in agriculture and domestic services. The three segments suggest the presence of inequality in various forms. Workers in the C-Upper and above categories are predominantly white, while those in blue-collar jobs are predominantly African. Hence, between-group inequality prevails here. However, a significant degree of within-group inequality also exists. This within-group inequality is manifest in the division between Africans in blue collar occupations and those in the farm and domestic sectors. African workers in the latter group are employed as menial labourers, earn very low wages and are unprotected by legislation. These three factors – occupation, earnings and coverage – are the content of the within-group inequality among the formally employed.

While there is both within- and between-group inequality among the formally employed, there is a distinction to be made: among the employed in general, and between the formally and the informally employed. It is to the last that the following section turns.

Employment in the informal sector

The employment data presented above include individuals in both the formal and the informal sectors. Given the importance of the informal sector for soaking up some of the work force, and its longer-term potential to contribute to economic development, it is essential to investigate the nature of employment and the degree of inequality in this sector. The informal sector includes, predominantly, workers involved in survivalist activities. Employment in this sector is viewed as a second-best alternative to formal employment. For this reason the informal sector represents those who, although employed, are severely disadvantaged in the labour market.

The informal sector data presented here will be captured as those individuals who reported themselves as self-employed. It is estimated that about 1.1 million people are self-employed. This is close to the CSS estimate of 1.2 million informally employed individuals. The racial division of the self-employed is provided in Table 2.13. Africans account for 86% of the self-employed and Asians have the smallest representation at 4.4%.

Table 2.13   Self-employment by race

Race	Number
African	944 624
Asian	48 629
Coloured	83 640
Whites	20 877
Total	1 097 770

Source: SALDRU (1994).

The activities undertaken by the self-employed are numerous and varied; the five main activities are retail and service-oriented. Shopkeepers or street sellers constitute 36% of the self-employed. It is perhaps only those employed as artisans who are applying a specific skill to their work tasks. Notably, only 0.77% of the self-employed are located in manufacturing. This has bearing on policy interventions designed to promote the small, medium and micro-enterprise sectors.

In developing countries, the preponderance of women in the labour market is often an indication of women-headed households. This, in turn, is a predictor of the feminisation of poverty. For example, of the total number of African self-employed, 61% are women. What this indicates is that women, not gaining access to formal employment, move into the informal sector. Among Africans, then, gender is the first maker of within-group inequality. It is only for Africans that the number of women present is greater than the national mean, indicating a disproportionate number of self-employed African women.

Another disadvantaged group highly represented in the informal sector is the youth. Table 2.14 illustrates that of the total African self-employed, 40% are below the age of 34 and 16% are in the age cohort 15–24. For the coloured self-employed, 20% are in the youngest age cohort. In contrast, only 5% of self-employed whites are between the ages of 15 and 24.

Table 2.14 Self-employment by race and age (%)

Age	African	Coloured	Asian	White
15–24	15.67	19.62	7.2	5.38
25–34	24.34	14.93	12.97	25.92
35–44	26.73	36.31	39.87	38.55

Source: SALDRU (1994).

Once again the data suggest that the youth, who are unable to gain access to employment in the formal sector, derive income from the informal sector. Age therefore presents as the second marker of within-group inequality among the informally employed.

The distribution of self-employment by region completes the picture of a sector that is essentially survivalist in nature. As shown in Table 2.15, the majority of the African self-employed are found in rural areas.[17]

The composite reflects an informal sector consisting of a disproportionate number of African women and youth who reside in rural areas. In addition, the activities undertaken are not manufacturing related work. The informal sector can therefore be identified as a distinct and marginalised component within the labour market. In developing a representation of within-group inequality, the analysis reveals that gender, age and location are important determinants of within-group inequality. The final and perhaps conclusive evidence of the dualist nature of the employed workforce is found in the income earned by those in self-employment.

Approximately 68% of the self-employed earn less than R500 per month. This is significantly below the average wage earned by those in formal employment. Of the African self-employed, 76% earn less than R500 per month, while only 31% of whites earn in this range. Hence, the informal sector does not truly represent gainful and long-term employment.

Table 2.15 Self-employment by race and region (%)

Race/region	Rural	Urban	Metro	Total
African	54.90	21.36	23.75	100.00
Coloured	1.07	31.18	67.75	100.00
Asian	1.83	59.50	38.66	100.00
White	7.41	31.18	61.41	100.00

Source: SALDRU (1994).

The unemployed

The same three markers of inequality among the informally employed also characterise the African unemployed.

In the first instance, when unemployment is analysed by gender, it is clear that women are disproportionately represented. Table 2.16 shows that African unemployment rates are higher than the national mean for both males and females. Moreover, within the group of African unemployed, female unemployment is 16.6 percentage points higher than that of males.

Table 2.16   African unemployment rates by gender and race (%)

Gender	African	Total
Male	33.6	26.2
Female	50.2	40.6
Total	41.1	32.6

Source: CSS (1995).

Another important marker of unemployment is African youth unemployment. The high levels of African youth unemployment in South Africa have been noted in the recent *World Development Report* (World Bank, 1995: 28). The data indicate a negative correlation between age and unemployment, an effect that is confirmed by Table 2.17.

Of the economically active African population in the 16–24 age group, 64.8% are unemployed. Age then enters as the second indicator of between-group inequality. Given this conclusion it is possible to combine the two markers of inequality and to estimate the effect on unemployment rates. In other words, it is possible to predict unemployment rates for African women for different age cohorts. Table 2.18 indicates that young African females are those most likely to be disadvantaged in the labour market. The unemployment rate for African females is higher than that for males in four of the five age categories.[18] The all-ages African

Table 2.17   African unemployment rates by age (%)

Race/age	16–24	25–34	35–44	45–54	55–64
African	64.8	41.2	28.4	23.2	19.9
Total	53.0	32.6	21.2	17.3	15.3

Source: SALDRU (1994).

Table 2.18 African unemployment rates by age and gender (%)

Sex/age	16–24	25–34	35–44	45–54	55–64	Total
Male	59.1	34.9	24.1	20.3	20.1	33.6
Female	71.2	48.4	33.2	26.8	19.7	44.2
Total	64.8	41.2	28.4	23.2	19.9	38.5

Source: SALDRU (1994).

female unemployment rate of 44.2% is also higher than the total African male rate of 33.6%.

Within-group inequality is present among the unemployed when calculated according to settlement type. If a breakdown into metropolitan, rural and urban areas is taken, the results shown in Table 2.19 are obtained.

Table 2.19 African unemployment rates by race and settlement type (%)

Settlement	African	Total
Rural	41.8	41.0
Urban	34.6	25.7
Metropolitan	34.3	21.5

Source: SALDRU (1994).

Not surprisingly, the African unemployment rate in rural areas of 41.8% is greater than the corresponding rate in both urban and metropolitan areas. Given these data, we can conclude that an economically active African woman between the age of 16 and 24, who lives in a rural area, has the highest probability of being unemployed. The three variables – age, gender and location – remain as the characteristics of inequality in the labour market among the African unemployed and indeed the informally employed.

Conclusion

The analysis in this chapter was restricted to the generation, arrangement and discussion of a set of empirical data on South African inequality. It needs to be clearly stated, however, that the analysis has not attempted to deal with the importance or the macroeconomic viability of specific policies or policy scenarios. Such work would require the formal integration of the statistical representations into a macroeconomic model of the South African economy. Although the decomposition of the Gini coefficient by income source would seem to hold great possibilities for this type of integration, such an exercise is much more ambitious than the scope of this chapter.

The importance of wage income in driving inequality was highlighted. Attention was focused on inequality among wage earners and the gap between wage-earning households and those households without any wage income. Race is still an important discriminator of inequality at both of these levels and, even within the African group, inequality is being driven by a household's labour market entitlement.

All of this draws attention to the importance of facilitating economic growth in order to create employment, forge healthy linkages between the formal and informal sectors, and open up a dynamic climate within the formal labour market that allows racial inequities to dissipate. Finally, broader, more equitable growth is necessary to provide the tax base for the state to target support at those within the African group (women and youth predominantly in the rural areas) who have been shown to be particularly disadvantaged within the African group.

It is therefore heartening that South Africa is once again exhibiting strong growth performance. Of course, growth is always only a necessary but not sufficient condition for the removal of inequities. Employment trends over the last 20 years reveal a steady decline in the labour absorption capacity of South Africa's economic growth path. Growth in employment reached a high of approximately 4% in the early 1970s, but has been falling since.[19] There are dangerous signs that the current growth phase is no different. Although it is making a significant difference to inequities within the formally employed through deracialisation and an increasingly productive use of those already in employment, there is no evidence of the creation of new employment opportunities. The net outcome is likely to be a widening of the gap between the formally employed and the unemployed. Over the longer term, such a growth path will also fail to absorb the beneficiaries of state health and education policies into the labour market and will therefore lower the return to such social investment in the poor.

Appendix I   Household wage income in South Africa

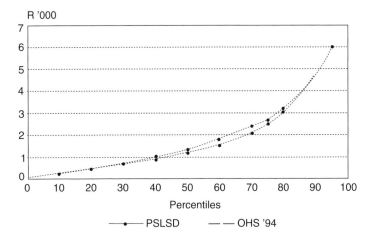

R '000

Figure AI.1   Distribution of household wage income (household with at least one wage-earner) in 1993 prices; net monthly earnings

Appendix II   Inequality measures

1.   'Decomposing' the Gini coefficient

Assume that within the chosen sample there are n households deriving income K different sources (i. e. K different income components). Let y_i denote the total income of household i, where $i = 1, \ldots, n$ and y_{ik} the income of household i from source k where $k = 1, \ldots, K$ (thus $y_i = \sum_{k=1}^{K} y_{ik}$). Also, let the distribution of total household income be represented by $Y = (y_1, \ldots, y_n)$ and the distribution of income component k be represented by $Y_k = (y_{1k}, \ldots, y_{nk})$.

Using this notation, the Gini coefficient (G) for the distribution of total income within the group can be defined as:

$$G = \frac{(2\text{cov}[Y, F(Y)])}{\mu} \tag{1}$$

where μ denotes the mean household income of the sample and $F(Y)$ the 'cumulative distribution' of total household income in the sample. That is, $F(Y) = [f(y_1), \ldots, f(y_n)]$ where $f(y_i)$ is equal to the rank of y_i divided by the number of observations (n)).

Equation 1 can be rewritten and expanded into an expression for the Gini coefficient that captures the 'contribution to inequality' of each of the K components of income:

$$G = \frac{2}{\mu n} \sum_{i=1}^{n} (y_1 - E(y_i))(f(y_i) - E(f(y_i)))$$

$$\rightarrow G = \frac{2}{\mu n} \sum_{i=1}^{n} \sum_{k=1}^{K} (y_{ik} - E(Y_{ik}))(f(y_i) - E(f(y_i)))$$

$$\rightarrow G = \frac{2}{\mu} \sum_{k=1}^{k} \text{cov}[Y_k, F(Y)]$$

$$\rightarrow G = \sum_{k=1}^{k} \left(\frac{\text{cov}[Y_k, F(Y)]}{\text{cov}[Y_k, F(Y_k)]} \right) \left(\frac{2}{\mu_k} \text{cov}[Y_k, F(Y_k)] \right) \left(\frac{\mu_k}{\mu} \right)$$

where μ_k is the sample mean of income from source k and $F(Y_k)$ is the cumulative rank distribution of income from source k; i. e. $F(Y_k) = [f(y_{1k}), \ldots, f(y_{nk})]$ where $f(y_{ik})$ is equal to the rank of y_{ik} divided by the number of observations (n).

Thus, the Gini coefficient can be written as:

$$G = \sum_{k=1}^{K} R_k G_k S_k \tag{2}$$

2.   The effect of a change in income on the Gini

Assume that there is an exogenous increase in income from source j by some factor σj; i.e. $y_{ij}(\sigma_j) = (1 + \sigma_j) y_{ij}$ for $i = 1, \ldots, n$. The distribution of income from source j becomes $Y = ((1 + \sigma_j) y_{1j}, \ldots, (1 + \sigma_j) y_{nj}$. Let G be the Gini coefficient before the change in income and $G(\sigma_j)$ the Gini coefficient after the change in income. Equation 2 gives the expression for G. However, in order to derive an expression for $G(\sigma_j)$ after a change in income from source j by factor $(1 + \sigma_j)$ it is necessary to look at how the change affects each of G_k, R_k and S_k for $k = 1, \ldots, K$:

1. Since we are dealing with a $(1 + \sigma_j)$ times increase for in y_{ij}, G_j does not change. Thus, G_k for all $k = 1, \ldots, j, \ldots, K$.
2. Assuming that the change in income from source j is small enough to leave the ranking of both total income and source j income unchanged, R_k, as a function of ranks of income, will remain unchanged.
3. Since S_k measures income component j's share in total income, S_k for $k = 1, \ldots, K$ will obviously change if income from source j changes. Let us call each income component's new share in total income after the change in income component $jS_k(\sigma_j)$.

Thus, we can write the Gini coefficient after the change in income component j as:

$$G(\sigma_j) = \sum_{k=1}^{K} S_k(\sigma_j) R_k G_k$$

By definition, for $k \neq j$:

$$S_k(\sigma_j) = \frac{\mu_K}{\sum_{k=1}^{K} \mu_k + \sigma_j \mu_j}$$

while for income component j:

$$S_j(\sigma_j) = \frac{(1+\sigma_j)\mu_k}{\sum\limits_{k=1}^{K}\mu_k + \sigma_j\mu_j}$$

thus, the change in the Gini coefficient (ΔG) stemming from the exogenous change in income from source j can be written as:

$$G = G(\sigma_j) - G = \sum_{k=1}^{K}[S_k(\sigma_j) - S_k]R_k G \qquad (4)$$

For $k \neq j$, the bracketed term in Equation 4 can be rewritten as:

$$\sigma_j - S_k = \frac{\mu_k}{\sum\limits_{k=1}^{k}\mu_k + \sigma_j\mu_j} - \frac{\mu_k}{\sum\limits_{k=1}^{K}\mu_k} = \left(\frac{-\sigma_j\mu_k\mu_j}{[\sum\limits_{k=1}^{K}\mu_k]2}\right) / \left(\frac{\sum\limits_{k=1}^{K}\mu_k + \sigma}{\sum\limits_{k=1}^{K}\mu_k}\right)$$

which simplifies to:

$$S_k(\sigma_j) - S_k = \frac{-\sigma_j S_k S_j}{1 + \sigma_j S_j} \qquad (5)$$

Similarly, for $k = j$ it can be shown that:

$$S_j(\sigma_j) - S_j \frac{\sigma_j S_j - \sigma_j S_j^2}{1 + \sigma_j S_j} \qquad (6)$$

Substituting equations 5 and 6 into 4, a more detailed expression for ΔG is obtained:

$$\Delta G = \sum_{k \neq j}\frac{-\sigma_j S_k S_j}{1 + \sigma_j S_j}R_k G_k + \frac{\sigma_j S_j - \sigma_j S_j^2}{1 + \sigma_j S_j}R_j G_j$$

$$\rightarrow \Delta G = \sum_{k=1}^{K}\frac{-\sigma_j S_k S_j}{1 + \sigma_j S_j}R_k G_k + \frac{\sigma_j S_j}{1 + \sigma_j S}\qquad (7)$$

In order to find the derivative of the Gini coefficient with respect to σ_j, it is necessary to take the limit of Equation 7 divided by σ_j as σ_j tends to zero:

$$\lim_{\sigma_j \to 0}\frac{\Delta G}{\sigma_j} = -S_j \lim_{\sigma_j \to 0}\sum_{k=1}^{K}\frac{S_k}{1 + \sigma_j S_j}R_k G_k + \lim_{\sigma_j \to 0}\frac{S_j}{1 + \sigma_j S_j}R_j G_j$$

Hence, it can be shown that the derivative of the Gini coefficient with respect to a change in income source j is:

$$= -S_j \sum_{k=1}^{K}S_k R_k G_k + S_j R_j G_j = S_j(R_j G_j) \qquad (8)$$

3.   Theil's entropy index (T)

This is given by:

$$T = \frac{1}{N}\sum_{i=1}^{N}(y_i/\mu)\log(y_i/\mu)$$

which may be decomposed into between- and within-group inequality

$$T = T_B + T_W$$

where

$$T_B \sum_j q_j \log(\mu_j/\mu)$$

and

$$T_W \sum_j q_j T_j$$

4.   Theil's second measure (L)

This is given by:

$$L = -\frac{1}{N}\sum_{i=1}^{N}\log(y_i/\mu)$$

This may also be decomposed into between- and within-group inequality:

$$L = L_B + L_W$$

where:

$$L_n = -\sum_j P_j \log(\mu_j/\mu)$$

and:

$$L_W = \sum_j P_j L_j$$

5.   'Decomposing' Atkinson's index

Atkinson's measure starts from the additive social welfare function:

$$W = \frac{1}{N}\sum_{i=1}^{N}\frac{y_i^{i-\varepsilon}}{1-\varepsilon}$$

or, when $\varepsilon = 1$,

$$InW = \frac{1}{N}\sum_{i=1}^{N}In\, y_i$$

Atkinson explicitly introduces distributional objectives through the parameter $E \geq 0$, which represents the weight attached to inequality in the distribution. By specifying different values of ε one can vary the importance society attaches to mean living standards versus equality. If society is indifferent about the distribution, we will set ε to zero. By increasing ε we give more weight to inequality at the lower end of the distribution. At ε equal to infinity society is concerned only with the poorest household.

In other words, the ratio of marginal social utilities of two individuals is then given by:

$$\frac{\partial W / \partial y_i}{\partial W / \partial y_j} = (y_j / y_i)^{\varepsilon}$$

Hence, if $\varepsilon = 0$, marginal utility is the same for everyone. As ε tends to infinity, the utility of the poorest dominates.

The inequality index (Atkinson's I) associated with this is given by:

$$I = 1 - \left(\sum_{i=1}^{K} \frac{1}{N} (y_i / \mu)^{(1-\varepsilon)} \right)^{1/(1-\varepsilon)}$$

It can also be written in terms of the indexes for the individual groups, I_j:

$$I = 1 - \left(\sum_j p_j (\mu_j / \mu)^{(1-\varepsilon)} (1 - I_j)^{(1-\varepsilon)} \right)^{1/(1-\varepsilon)}$$

Atkinson's index may be decomposed into between- and within-group inequality, so that:

$$I = I_B + 1_W + \text{Residual}$$

where:

$$I_B = 1 - \left(\sum_j p_j (\mu_j / \mu)^{(i-\varepsilon)} \right)^{1/(1-\varepsilon)}$$

and:

$$I_W = \left(\sum_j p_j (\mu_j / \mu)^{(1-\varepsilon)} A_j^{(1-\varepsilon)} \right)^{1/(1-\varepsilon)}$$

6. Choice of decomposition technique

Different techniques are better suited to particular problems than others. The Theil, for example, gives a clear picture of the importance of each explanatory variable in determining inequality but lacks intuitive appeal. The Gini, while well-known and easily conceptualised, is not additively decomposable and is therefore of limited use if one wishes to avoid being overly technical.

Three issues need to be considered in determining which technique is most useful: the properties (or basic nature) of the measure itself; the value of the information derived from the decomposition; and the suitability of the measure to the problem.

In terms of the 'basic nature' of the measures, the Gini coefficient is popular since it is easily conceptualised in terms of the Lorenz curve. The Theil entropy indexes, on the other hand, have no clear intuitive justification and are somewhat arbitrary formulas from the point of view that they say little in terms of welfare implications. The Atkinson index has easily interpretable welfare implications, but is, of course, derived from a particular welfare framework that is open to criticism.

In terms of their usefulness, the Gini, Theil and Atkinson measures all satisfy Sen's axioms of *scale independence*, *symmetry* and *weak principle of transfers*:

- *Axiom of income scale independence*: this means that measured inequality should not depend on the magnitude of total income, i. e. if everyone's income changes by the same proportion, the measure of inequality should not change.
- *Axiom of symmetry (or principle of population)*: this requires that inequality should not depend on the number of income receivers. If we measure inequality in a particular economy with n people in it and then merge the economy with another identical one, then the combined economy with $2n$ people must have the same measure of inequality.
- *Weak principle of transfers*: consider two individuals, one with income y and the other with income $y + \delta$ where δ is positive. Then transfer a positive amount of income $1/2x$ from the richer to the poorer person, where x is less than $1/2\delta$. Inequality should then definitely decrease.

Another consideration is the sensitivity of the different measures to income changes at various points in the distribution. If our value judgement is that we should give greatest weight to the economic position of the poor, then we require a measure that is more sensitive to inequality at the lower end of the income distribution. The Theil indexes are most sensitive to inequality among the very rich, while the Gini is most sensitive to inequality in the middle of the income distribution. By altering the value of E the Atkinson measure can be easily manipulated to concentrate on different parts of the distribution.

Notes

1. See Deaton (1994) and Cowell (1995) for recent reviews of this literature.
2. The literature starts with Shorrocks (1983) and is most recently extended by Lerman and Yitzhaki (1994).
3. R_k is a form of rank correlation coefficient as it measures the extent to which the relationship between Y_k and the cumulative rank distribution of total income coincides with the relationship between Y_k and its own cumulative rank distribution.
4. It should be noted that the overall Gini coefficient in the table is 0.60 as opposed to the earlier 0.65 quoted from McGrath and Whiteford (1994) from the same data. McGrath and Whiteford re-weighted the sample to coincide with 1991 census population shares, thereby giving more weight to white

incomes and accentuating inequality. In our calculations we used the survey enumeration weights and used a slightly refined data set taking account of the errors in the social pensions data discovered by Pieter le Roux (University of the Western Cape).

5. The Institute for Planning Research publishes poverty lines for rural and urban households of specified age composition. Following Deaton (1994), these lines were converted to an adult equivalence scale of the form:

$E = (A + 0.5K)^{0.9}$, where:
E = number of adult equivalents
A = number of adults
K = number of children

6. For ease of expression, this chapter refers to those above the poverty line as the above group and those below the poverty line as the below group.

7. See Bhorat (1995) for the historical details of racial biases in pension allocations.

8. The one clear contribution made by this analysis of state transfers is the illustration of how careful one has to be in adding interpretation to the empirics of the income decomposition analysis.

9. See Fields (1980) for a review.

10. A *generally decomposable* or *aggregative* index is defined as one where the overall inequality level can be expressed as some general function of the subgroup means, population sizes and inequality measures. The most useful type of decomposability is *additive decomposability*. A measure is additively decomposable if it can be tidily expressed as the sum of a 'between-group' term and a 'within-group' term. The between-group component is the value of the measure were every member assigned the group mean (i. e. there is assumed to be no inequality within the group). Similarly, the within-group component is the value of the inequality measure when all the between-group inequalities are suppressed.

11. See McGrath and Whiteford (1994) and Moll (1995).

12. The PSLSD data set includes 33 households (0.4%) with zero income. For technical reasons, the Theil-*L* measure cannot be calculated for a sample that includes households with zero income. Consequently, all three measures in Table 2.3 are calculated after dropping these 33 households. It is easily shown that this does not influence the results.

13. The CSS omit several hundred thousand workers living in hostels as well as those in defence force camps, hospitals, hotels and old-age homes. The SALDRU estimate of the size of the working age population is 21,095,100, but this counts those aged 16–64 and applies to 1993.

14. This huge differential in estimates is clearly something requiring interrogation.

15. The SALDRU data yield similar but not identical results for 1993 as CSS reports for 1994. They report an overall unemployment rate (including discouraged workers) of 30.1%, with Africans at 38.5 and whites at 4.5%.

16. See Hindson and Crankshaw (1990), McGarth and Whiteford (1994) and, for rural areas, May *et al.* (1995) and Leibbrandt *et al.* (1996).

17. Metropolitan areas, in the SALDRU definition, refer to the major cities, namely Cape Town, Johannesburg and Durban. Urban areas are all other cities and towns.

18. Women are entitled to pensions (and hence leave the economically active population) at age 60, while men must wait until they reach 65. This may affect the comparison of unemployment rates in this age group.
19. Using a basic linear regression, it is possible to regress the logarithm of employment on the logarithm of GDP. An output elasticity of employment of 0.42 was found. In other words, for every 1% increase in economic growth, employment rose by 0.42%.

References

Atkinson, A. B. 1977. *The Economics of Inequality*. Oxford: Clarendon Press.

Bhorat, H. 1995. 'The South African social security net: past present and future'. *Development Southern Africa*, 12 (4): 595–604.

Bhorat, H. and T. Hertz. 1995. 'Statistical overview of the South African labour market'. Input paper for the Presidential Labour Market Commission.

Cowell, F. 1995. *Measuring Inequality*, 2nd edn. London: Prentice Hall.

CSS (Central Statistical Services) 1995. *The October Household Survey*. Pretoria: Government Printer.

Deaton, A. 1994. 'The analysis of household surveys: microeconometric analysis for development policy'. Draft manuscript. Princeton.

Deaton, A. 1995. 'Large transfers to the elderly in South Africa'. Unpublished paper, Research Programme in Development Studies, Princeton University.

Fields, G. S. 1980. *Poverty, Inequality, and Development*. Cambridge: Cambridge University Press.

Hertz, T. 1995. 'Jobs, farms, discrimination and education in South Africa: simulations and regressions on household survey data'. Unpublished paper. Department of Economics, University of Massachusetts at Amherst.

Hindson, D. and O. Crankshaw, 1990. 'New jobs, new skills, new divisions: the changing structure of South Africa's workforce'. *South African Labour Bulletin*, 15 (1): 23–31.

Liebbrandt, M., C. Woolard and I. Woolard. 1996. 'The contribution of income components to income inequality in South Africa: a decomposable Gini analysis'. Living Standards Measurement Study Working Paper No. 125, The World Bank.

Lerman, R. I. and S. Yitzhaki. 1994. 'Effect of marginal changes in income sources on U. S. income inequality'. *Public Finance Quarterly*, 22 (4); 403–16.

May, J., M. Carter and D. Posel. 1995. 'The composition and persistence of poverty in rural South Africa: an entitlements approach'. *Land and Agriculture Policy Centre Policy Paper*, No. 15, Land and Agriculture Policy Centre.

McGrath, M. and A. Whiteford. 1994. 'Inequality and the size distribution of income in South Africa'. *Occasional Paper No. 10*, Stellenbosch Economic Project.

Moll, P. 1995. 'Discrimination is declining in South Africa, but Inequality is not'. Unpublished paper. Chicago.

SALDRU. 1994. *South Africa Rich and Poor: Baseline Household Statistics*. Project for Statistics on Living Standards and Development.

Shorrocks, A. 1983. 'The impact of income components on the distribution of family income'. *Quarterly Journal of Economics*, 98: 311–26.

Stark, O., J. Taylor and S. Yitzhaki. 1986. 'Remittances and inequality'. *Economic Journal*, 96: 722–40.

Whiteford, A., D. Posel and T. Kelatwang. 1995. *A Profile of Poverty, Inequality and Human Development*. Human Sciences Research Council.

3
Fiscal Policy in Post-Apartheid South Africa

Newman Kusi and Lungisa Fusile

1. Introduction

There is little doubt that one of the primary causes of fiscal imbalance in South Africa over the past two decades has been the excessive expansion in government expenditure brought about mainly by the apartheid-required duplication of government services and functions. The high growth in government spending amid a narrow and weakening tax base placed the government in the difficult position of facing growing fiscal deficits, which in recent years reached disturbingly high levels.

The government of national unity (GNU), on coming into power in April 1994, declared its commitment to the eradication of the problems of poverty and gross inequality evident in all aspects of South African society through a growth-oriented reconstruction and development programme (RDP). The GNU also committed itself to the progressive reduction of the overall fiscal deficit, recognising that the sustainability of the RDP hinges crucially on the maintenance of fiscal discipline. Excessive fiscal deficits will result in higher inflation, higher real interest rates, balance of payments disequilibrium and lower economic growth, thereby putting the RDP at risk (Government of South Africa, 1994). A major area of concern, however, relates to how the goal of fiscal sustainability can be achieved in the face of the anticipated increases in the claims on the fiscus arising from the expansion of the social and economic functions needed to redress the poverty and inequality in the society. This is an issue requiring a detailed analysis of the role and macroeconomic implications of the government's fiscal policy, which are the subject of this chapter.

The chapter examines the fiscal policy stance of the GNU in order to establish its potency in addressing (1) the short-term goal of reducing the budget deficit and the implications of this for the much-needed delivery of social and economic services; and (2) the medium- or longer-term goal of keeping the growth of expenditures in line with the expected growth in revenue, removing market distortions that lead to inefficiencies in resource use, and restructuring capital expenditure to support the growth of the economy's productive capacity.

2.   Economic performance and fiscal policy

For the past two decades, the South African economy has been characterised by downswings and upswings in real domestic output. Figure 3.1 shows that major downswings occurred in 1982/83 and 1985, with a protracted one in 1990–92. The upswings occurred in 1975/76, 1978–8l, 1986–89 and the current one that began in 1993. In consequence, real GDP grew by an average of 1.6% per annum between 1975 and 1994. With population growth exceeding GDP growth, the real GDP per capita declined throughout the period, except in the upswing periods of the late 1970s and 1980s.

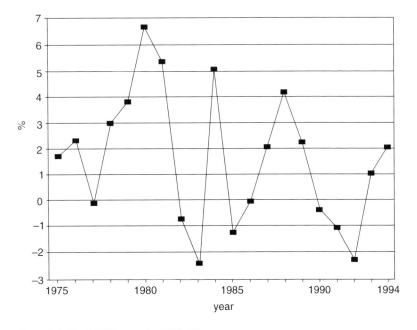

Figure 3.1   Real GDP growth, 1975–94

The downswings that occurred during the period under review were due to a host of factors, ranging from the purely economic to the purely political. The downswing of 1982/83, for example, reflected the effects of the recession in the world economy during that period, while the downswing in 1985 was due mainly to the political turmoil that plagued the country. The latter downswing coincided with the widespread threat of sanctions on trade, disinvestment and the refusal of foreign banks to defer repayments of short-term loans. Consumer boycotts and workers' strikes were also common occurrences during the period. These events resulted in a marked decline in domestic production and deterioration in the external accounts, leading to the most serious balance of payments crisis that the country had ever experienced. Access to external financial resources was substantially reduced, while capital outflows (associated with the uncertain domestic environment that had developed) increased to an alarming extent (Kusi, 1993). The imposition of exchange controls, including the reintroduction of the financial rand (abolished for the second time in March 1995), could not stem capital outflows.

The third, and longer, downturn (1990–92) coincided with the beginning of the process of political transformation, which affected production in both the primary and secondary sectors, and a drought, which had a marked negative impact on agricultural production. The lifting of the ban on political parties and the release of political prisoners, which began in 1990, created uncertainty about the political and economic future of the country.

The conflicting policy pronouncements by the leadership of some of the political organisations and the belief by their supporters that the socioeconomic backlogs created by the apartheid system could effectively be addressed through nationalisation of certain industries and/or sectors fuelled the uncertainty about the future direction of the country. There were also the effects of the rising level of violence and numerous strikes and work stoppages in many parts of the country. Together, these developments produced negative effects on both domestic production and investor confidence.

The low level of economic growth for most of 1975–94 was also due to the low level of domestic investment. On average, gross domestic investment as a percentage of GDP stood at 18.8% in 1985–94, well below the 27% that the IMF estimated necessary to ensure a GDP growth rate in excess of the 3.5% required to sustain the employment creation to meet the growing number of job-seekers in the country (Lachman and Bercuson, 1992). Of course, the IMF stressed the need for 'a major domestic saving effort', particularly by the public sector, to support the desired level of investment. Unfortunately, the government has been a net dissaver for most of the past three decades. After averaging about 2.7% of GDP between 1960 and 1983, net government saving turned negative after 1984 and has since remained negative. Besides, domestic savings were used to finance capital outflows over much of the past decade, contributing to the low level of domestic investment and productivity in all sectors of the economy. In terms of capital, the growth capacity of the economy declined from an average of 6.5% per annum in 1973–78 to an average of 1.3% per annum in 1985–91 (Central Economic Advisory Service, 1993).

Apart from the low level of domestic savings, the decline in domestic investment was also attributable to the increases in interest rates, which were kept very high for most of the 1980s and early 1990s. Until the late 1970s, credit ceilings, hire purchase controls, and liquid asset and cash reserve controls were the commonly used instruments of monetary policy, with interest rates playing a minor role. During the late 1970s, however, controls were relaxed and interest rates were brought into play in a way unprecedented in the country's monetary history. For example, the prime lending rate rose from 18% in 1982 to a record of 25% in May 1985, before falling steadily to 12.5% in April 1987 as the authorities tried to stimulate demand. The authorities argued that inflation at that time was essentially 'cost-push' – arising from the slump in the rand – and not a result of excess money supply or demand. However, as the upward phase of the period put pressure on the balance of payments, interest rates were pushed higher again, reaching 21% in 1989 through 1990, before falling to 15.25% in 1993 (Economist Intelligence Unit, 1988; Nedcor, 1993). As the spectrum of interest rates kept rising, it became increasingly difficult for investors to finance investment by borrowing from the domestic banking system.

The past two decades also saw the country's public finances experience increasing strain. Figure 3.2 shows that although both government expenditure and revenue exhibited similar trends for most part of the 1970s and 1980s, revenue remained consistently below expenditure, leading to a persistent deficit before borrowing, with the deficits widening in the late 1970s, late 1980s and early 1990s of fiscal expansion. Between 1975 and 1993, for example, nominal government revenue increased by an average of 17.3% per annum. Over the same period, nominal government expenditure expanded by an average of 18.9% per annum (South African Reserve Bank, 1994), implying that the deficits persisted not because of any significant stagnation in revenue but mainly because of the surge in expenditure growth. Although the government preached

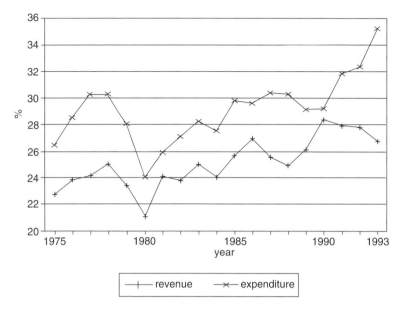

Figure 3.2 Government revenue and expenditure, 1975–93 (in % of GDP)

fiscal discipline throughout the 1980s, it consistently failed to practice it. The consistent excuse of actual expenditure over budgeted expenditure for most of the 1980s and early 1990s points to the failure of the government to maintain fiscal discipline (Mohr, 1989). Attempts to contain expenditure growth were concentrated rather severely on the curtailment of capital spending, which was cut from 23.7% of total general government spending in 1975 to 11.1% in 1993 (GSA, 1995), with adverse effects on the growth capacity of the economy.

The rise in government expenditure in the 1980s and early 1990s was due to the rapid increases in consumption expenditure. As a percentage of GDP, government consumption expenditure rose from 13.1% in 1975 to 20.5% in 1993. Over the same period, the share of government capital spending in GDP declined from 5.4% to 3.8% (SARB, 1994), causing the ratio of capital investment to consumption expenditure to fall from 41% in 1975 to 18.5% in 1993. The disheartening aspect of the increases in government consumption spending was that they were financed mainly through borrowing, which was facilitated by the unification of the revenue account and the loan account of the budget into a single state revenue account in 1976. Prior to the unification of the two accounts current expenditure was financed from current revenue, while loans were only used to finance capital expenditures (Mohr, 1989). Consequently, interest payments on government debt became an important budget item, increasing from 7.2% of total general government expenditure in 1975 to 14.3% in 1993 (SARB, 1994).

Although the deficits before borrowing in the early 1990s were partly a result of cyclical influences and exogenous factors (such as the severe drought), their levels were more disconcerting than the deficits in the late 1970s for two reasons. First, the average growth rate of the economy was considerably higher in the 1970s than in the early 1990s. In the earlier period the real growth rate of the economy averaged some 4.5% per annum compared with the average growth rate of –0.6% per annum in 1990–93. Thus the actual deficits in the early 1990s were considerably larger than those of the late 1970s. Secondly, in the 1970s when the deficits were recorded, the general government was a net saver. After 1984, however, the government became a net dissaver, with the rate of dissaving increasing sharply from 1.5% of GDP in 1985 to 6.4% in 1993 (GSA, 1995).

The fiscal imbalances that beset South Africa during the period under review can be viewed as a pincer movement. On the one hand, government expenditure escalated as the cost of administering the apartheid system increased. On the other hand, the economic inequality engendered by the apartheid system produced an economy with a very narrow tax base (McCarthy, 1991). The effect of this development was that the government found itself in the difficult position of facing persistent shortfalls between current revenue and current expenditure, with the deficits reaching as high as 6.4% of GDP in 1993 (GSA, 1995)

In an attempt to make its presence strongly felt in all spheres of the economy, the government initiated a segregated but intricately woven administrative network that sought to provide public goods and services along racial lines. This culminated in the creation of separate political and administrative structures for blacks, whites, Indians and coloureds. The immediate impact of this arrangement was a massive duplication of government services and extensive bureaucratic redundancies as each race pursued independent policies but had one thing in common: the source of funding.

Apart from the escalating cost of the duplicated administrative structures, the absence of a proper system of checks and balances to coordinate and control the activities of the inter-racial 'own affairs' departments in order to ensure an integration of their activities with the central government agenda also created an incentive for uncontrollable spending. Most importantly, the multiplication of services called for increased public employment levels, with serious implications for the public sector wage bill. For example, employment levels in the central government, local administration and the homelands together rose from 632,000 in 1980 to 938,000 in 1988, representing an increase of 48% over the eight-year period (Jammine, 1990). The 1991 census showed that almost 15% of the country's entire economically active labour force was absorbed by the public sector (CEAS, 1993). The result of this was that general government expenditure on wages and salaries as a percentage of GDP rose from 8.4% in 1980 to more than 35% in 1988 and to over 40% in 1991/92 (Lachman and Bercuson, 1992; GSA, 1995).

The development of the separate political and economic structures along racial lines not only led to an explosion in the direct costs of duplicate government services and functions, it also led to substantial increases in expenditures on security, education, health and housing. Defence expenditure became more important as the government and indeed the whole country became increasingly isolated from the international community. Although defence expenditure's share in total general government expenditure declined somewhat, from 14.2% in 1982 to 8.1% in 1993, in absolute terms defence spending more than trebled from R3.5 billion to Rl0.7 billion over the period. Together with spending on public order and safety, expenditure on protection services declined marginally from 19.7% of total general government expenditure in 1982 to 16.9% in 1993, while expenditure on education increased from 17.7% to 20.8% over the same period (SARB, 1994, 1995b), with more than two-thirds of these expenditures devoted to the payments of wages and salaries.

As with many developing countries, the dominant proportion of the government revenue in South Africa consists of tax revenue, while transfers and income from the sale of goods and services are comparatively insignificant. Furthermore, the tax revenue was derived from a narrow and shrinking base. Between 1980 and 1992, for example, over 55% of the total government tax revenue originated from personal and corporate incomes, with the share of personal income tax in total tax revenue increasing from 20.1% to 40.3%. Besides, only a small proportion of the population, some 25%, contributed to this source of revenue (Loots, 1991), and although the top marginal tax rate for individuals was more or less in line with the rates that existed in other countries, the income level at which South Africa's top rate was levied was relatively low by international standards.

The tax base also weakened as the country's growth capacity deteriorated. First, the relatively high growth of government consumption expenditure crowded out capital expenditure, causing a switch in the expenditure mix against investment goods, especially after the mid-1980s. Secondly, the net outflow of capital following the foreign debt crisis of 1985 had a devastating effect on the country's capacity growth. Expressed in real terms, the outflow of capital as a percentage of GDP amounted to an average of 2.9% per annum in 1985–91. In addition, since 1984, the government had been financing part of its increased current spending by loans from domestic sources. The country, therefore, had to depend on domestic funds in the form of personal and corporate savings, not only for financing domestic investment but also for financing the capital outflow and inefficient use of savings by the public sector. Meanwhile, personal savings were declining gradually from an annual average of 4% of GDP in the mid-1970s to 1.8% in 1985–91, while the corporate savings rate increased from 3.8% to 5.6% over the same period (CEAS, 1993). Thus, while government investment declined over the period, the private sector's resources for financing domestic investment also dwindled. Consequently, the share of gross fixed investment in GDP declined, with severe implications for the growth of the economy and thus tax revenue.

In addition to the economic inequality brought about by the apartheid system and the poor growth performance, many aspects of the tax system itself also contributed to the erosion of the tax base and waste of scarce resources. Broadly, the tax system was viewed as complicated, unfair and interfering with economic choices. In the business sector, for example, taxes levied on companies and non-residents on equity investment, until the 1995/96 fiscal year, consisted of four elements: the basic corporate income tax of 35%; the secondary tax on companies (STC) of 25% on any distributed dividend declared; the transitional levy of 5%; and the non-resident shareholders tax at the normal rate of 15% or reduced by treaty in some cases to 7.5% or 5%. For individuals, separate income tax systems with different income brackets and marginal rates and different degrees of progressivity existed side-by-side for men and women.

This unsatisfactory tax system developed through piecemeal and *ad hoc* reforms over the years in response to the technical and policy needs of the time. Particular difficulties were introduced by the high levels of inflation, which complicated the measurement of income on one hand and led to bracket creep on the other (Margo Commission,[1] 1987). The measures introduced to rectify these problems resulted in frequent alterations in the tax rates and the imposition of additional taxes, in response both to the requirements of economic policy and to the needs of the fiscus for revenue. Moreover, the constant need to close loopholes in the tax system contributed to the complication of the structure and impaired the fairness and economic neutrality of the tax regime. Consequently, many decisions that ought to have been taken by businesses and individuals on purely economic or commercial grounds were taken on the basis of tax considerations. Hence, the country's scarce resources were often directed to where after-tax rather than economic returns were the highest, a situation that led to a less than optimal allocation of resources. The decline in simplicity, caused partially by exemptions, deductions and other considerations, for its part, undermined certainty in the tax system, thus diminishing efficiency by complicating the decision-making process of businesses and individuals. These defects in the tax structure generated a widespread belief that the tax system was inequitable. The consequences of this were many: a decline in tax morality, high incidence of tax avoidance and evasion, the growth of a skilled tax avoidance industry, and the proliferation of tax shelters. Together, these tax malpractices led to both an eroded tax base and the use of resources in unproductive activities (Margo Commission, 1987).

3. Fiscal policy in the post-apartheid era

When it came into office the government of national unity (GNU) declared as its vision for post-apartheid South Africa 'the pursuit of policies which will lead to accelerated investment and employment creation, sustainable economic growth and social development within a framework of macroeconomic stability' (GSA, 1995). The RDP provides the broad outlines of this vision for socioeconomic development.

Government economic vision and fiscal objectives

Fiscal aspects of the government's broader economic vision have been central to the design of the RDP. Within this vision the prime objective of fiscal policy is to gradually reduce the budget deficit before borrowing and debt repayment to a more manageable level over the next five years. With economic growth at an average rate of 3% per annum or higher during the second half of the 1990s, the government envisages the fiscal stance will reduce the budget deficit to about 4% of GDP in 1998/99. Thereafter, the objective is to achieve fiscal sustainability, including establishing new priorities for government expenditure to increase allocations for social services, capital expenditure and the RDP (SARB, 1995a). To achieve these objectives the government intends to conduct fiscal policy within several tight constraints:

- avoiding permanent increases in the overall tax burden;
- reducing consumption expenditure relative to GDP, which translates into the containment of non-interest recurrent expenditure in real terms;
- keeping overall wages and salary increases within inflation limits;
- strengthening government contribution to gross domestic fixed investment to ensure the maintenance of social and economic infrastructural development (GSA, 1995).

On the revenue side, 25% of GDP has been set as the ceiling on tax revenue of the consolidated central and provincial governments. This implies that the present level of taxation in the country leaves little scope for deficit reduction in the short term. In the medium term, however, revenue growth associated with economic expansion and achievement of a lower borrowing requirement relative to GDP will facilitate a reduction in both the overall deficit and the tax–GDP ratio. In broad terms, the overall growth performance of the economy will determine the increase in revenue that will accrue to the budget each year given the existing tax structure and the extent to which either an increased tax burden or borrowing will have to be used to finance additional outlays. Revenue and deficit targets thus constrain the overall government expenditure levels that the economy and the fiscus can sustain (GSA, 1995).

On the expenditure side, three broad guidelines shape fiscal policy. First, the government envisages that the main burden of the fiscal adjustment would have to be a phased reduction in the ratio of recurrent expenditure to GDP. This phased approach to deficit reduction is dictated in part by considerations related to inflation. Although the recent reduction in the inflation rate should in time lead to lower inflation expectations and lower interest rates, the accumulated public debt (on which fixed coupon interest is paid) will continue to impose a rising interest burden on the budget for several years. The increased real burden of accumulated debt liabilities is an unavoidable cost to the budget, while the maturity structure of this cost sets limits to the feasible pace of the deficit reduction. To this end, revenue gains associated with economic growth are to be channelled into deficit reduction rather than increased expenditure on recurrent goods and services. Since interest payments are a statutory first charge on the fiscus, this translates into a target of a constant level of real non-interest recurrent expenditure of the con-solidated national and provincial governments. A substantial reduction in the deficit will also occur if the planned restructuring of state assets results in capital receipts that are applied to the lowering of the public debt. The benefits of the debt reduction will, in due course, be seen in lower interest payments relative to GDP and the release of these future streams of resources to increase allocations for social services and capital expenditure.

Secondly, as economic growth proceeds, the government aims to reduce general government consumption expenditure from the present level of 21% to about 17% of GDP. Thirdly, it is the policy of the government to ensure that the contribution of the public sector to social and economic infrastructure development is maintained at adequate levels. Accordingly, a modest increase in capital expenditure from the present level of 2.1% of GDP is envisaged during the second half of the 1990s (GSA, 1995).

Specific fiscal measures

The broad fiscal objectives of the government have been designed to underpin economic growth and social development, which will, in the longer term, facilitate more and extensive provision of public services. In order to ensure efficient application of fiscal policy, the government has undertaken several specific initiatives,[2] ranging from tax issues to restructuring of state assets.

Tax issues

Tax administration has been chaotic for the past two decades. As at September 1994, for example, R9.0 billion tax was outstanding, 150,000 VAT audits were in arrears and VAT refunds of Rl.0 billion had been made in error. The tax handbook was six years out of date, while losses in tax through inefficiencies were between R5.0 billion and R15.0 billion a year (Katz Commission,[3] 1994).

Enhancing the efficiency of the tax administration has, therefore, become a critical issue in the government fiscal adjustment. Steps have been taken to train and retrain revenue officials, enhance customer services, and counter tax avoidance and evasion. A uniform personal income tax structure with new rate adjustments and base broadening has been introduced, while child rebates have been eliminated. The income tax systems of the former homelands and self-governing territories have also been harmonised with those of the Republic of South Africa and a once-off tax amnesty to persons who were not previously registered as taxpayers has been granted. On corporate taxation, the government has maintained the basic company income tax at 35% and STC at 25% (reduced to 12.5% in the 1996/97 fiscal year) but has scrapped non-resident shareholders' tax and removed surcharges on all capital and intermediate goods.

As a further boost to the efficiency of the tax administration, the government has announced that the Inland Revenue and Department of Customs and Excise are to be amalgamated into an autonomous service to be known as the South Africa Revenue Service (SARS), with a board of directors that will develop and monitor the administrative policy of the service and a chief executive who will control its management. The SARS will be run along business lines to ensure greater efficiency and professional service, but will remain within the discipline and control of the public service and will be subject to audit by the Auditor General.

Expenditure restructuring

The government recognises that the redirection of public expenditure in keeping with changing needs and priorities requires a long-term planning framework alongside the annual budgetary process. To this end, the government has convened a Macroeconomic Policy Group to formulate long-term expenditure guidelines in accordance with its aims and requirements for a consistent macroeconomic framework.

Policy issues that fall under responsible ministries and expenditure allocations assessed by the various function committees will also yield inputs into the longer-term planning process. The budgetary process has also undergone a thorough overhaul. As a point of departure, the government has accepted the principle of budgeting from zero and all spending agencies are expected to continually reassess their activities with this principle in mind. Accordingly, the Department of State Expenditure has revised the planning stage of the budgetary process to effect this goal. A RDP Fund has also been established to give a maximum impetus to the redirection of government spending towards capital expenditure and new priorities and to assist in the restructuring of the budgetary process.

Sectoral programmes

The expenditure restructuring process has also affected many functions of the government. In the area of social services, for example, the government has launched a process to provide quality education to all. Underpinning this vision is the principle that basic educational entitlement should be free. Financial and other resource constraints, however, limit the ability of the state to fund all schools at the level of per capita expenditure prevailing in those schools that had higher levels of funding in the past. The government has thus agreed that many schools will have to continue to charge fees consistent with the capacity of the school community to pay and with the costs of such schooling that exceed the minimum acceptable standard to be supported from public funds. The government also intends to promote new funding partnerships between education departments and institutions, stakeholders in education and training, and other organisations of civil society.

For social security and welfare payments, where the growth of unemployment compensation and race-based disparities in the levels of social pensions and other social grants have contributed to a sharp increase in spending during the 1990s, the government has taken steps to review the current system and will develop an integrated social security network for the country. The national welfare department and the welfare departments of the nine provinces are in the process of developing a coordinated and cost-effective social grants system. The task involves a rationalisation of the 14 systems used by the provincial governments to administer social grants, implementation of a central database and introduction of improved information technology. These initiatives are expected to streamline the administration of social grants and help eliminate fraud and duplication in payments.

Defence spending and subsidies to industry and trade sectors have also come under the spotlight of the new fiscal initiatives. The share of government spending allocated to the protection services, reflecting a reduction in defence spending, has declined in recent years. The government recognises that the financial cost of the integration of non-statutory forces into the South African National Defence Force (SANDF) is not likely to make a drastic cut in defence spending possible in the short run. In the medium term, however, it is the objective of the government to rationalise the SANDF, reduce personnel numbers to affordable levels and adapt defence spending to new priorities.

Subsidies applied to industry and trade sectors have increased substantially over recent years, reflecting the shift towards an outward oriented strategy. Expenditure on export promotion schemes, for example, increased from R850 million in 1990 to R1.27 billion in 1992 (GSA, 1995), due largely to the revision of the general export incentive scheme (GEIS) in 1992. Partly in view of efficiency considerations and in order to reduce the overall impact of the scheme, GEIS payments were made taxable in March 1995. The medium-term strategy is to replace the GEIS with targeted supply-side and export support measures consistent with acceptable international practices.

Civil service restructuring

This initiative intends to provide an efficient and effective public administration and programmes. The task involves rationalising and reorganising the civil service departments, employment and remuneration. To this end, a special adviser to the Minister of Finance was appointed to assist government departments in the design and implementation of the restructuring programmes. A uniform civil service salary structure including allowances and benefits was established in 1994, while the reorganisation of the departmental structures and integration of provincial administrations was completed in October 1995. Given the large and growing share of remuneration of employees in the consolidated national and provincial expenditure (35.9% in 1992 and 38.1% in 1994), restraint on both increased employment and the rate of remuneration was seen to be critical in the civil service restructuring process. Negotiations with employee representatives in this regard have taken place, and several task teams have been appointed to investigate issues relating to conditions of service, including the improvement of salaries and wages, to be addressed within a three-year plan. Progress is also underway to rationalise the various pension funds at the national and regional levels of government into a single new pension fund to which all public servants will belong.

Restructuring of state assets

The government recognises the need to restructure state assets and associated liabilities to reflect the new reconstruction and development priorities. The task of restructuring state assets and enterprises is being pursued by task groups at cabinet level. The first official report on this issue was tabled in August 1994 by the Ministry of Public Enterprises. The main thrust of the report is that the restructuring of state enterprises should be used to increase competition and guard against monopolistic behaviour, unlock currently under used resources to meet the basic needs of the poor, and contribute to the empowerment of disadvantaged communities and sectors. The report groups state-owned enterprises into socioeconomic service delivery, strategic and non-public policy categories (Table 3.1). The report is not in favour of full-scale privatisation of parastatals in the socioeconomic service delivery category because these enterprises are expected to play a crucial role in meeting the new development priorities. To the government, a change in the ownership of these enterprises from public to private without regulatory protection could lead to the inability to realise RDP targets. While the report does not rule out a minority shareholding by a private partner who could offer financial, technical and managerial support, only parastatals that are loss-making and/or do not have an impact on socioeconomic delivery would be put up for outright sale.

Table 3.1 Restructuring of state enterprises, 1995

Enterprise	Total assets (R'000)	Total liabilities (R'000)	Turnover (R'000)	Profit before tax (R'000)	Number of employees
Category 1 – Public policy value					
Airports Company	846 566	87 575	150 811	33 823	1 531
Air Traffic & Navigation Serv.	211 556	13 463	89 817	12 706	467
Eskom	49 761 000	30 162 000	12 891 000	2 601 000	39 173
Portnet	4 138 000	2 652 894	2 539 000	687 684	11 005
SABC	1 285 883	467 673	1 393 297	108 461	4 397
SA Post Office	2 576 417	2 316 398	1 457 472	22 704	24 183
SARCC	4 788 155	1 370 797	474 228	1 051 030	10 815
Spoornet	21 583 000	5 204 472	7 624 000	618 261	65 452
Telkom	16 464 387	11 387 603	8 365 412	1 206 032	60 000
Category 2 – Public policy/strategic value					
Armscor	681 700	342 000	311 400	5 000	1 016
Atomic Energy Board	515 686	746 319	745 401	15 406	2 623
Denel	4 078 500	1 337 900	3 014 500	324 900	11 523
Mosgas	11 219 840	10 504 026	1 188 276	516 703	1 290
Petronet	1 432 417	911 504	446 000	141 685	653
SAA	4 355 000	2 377 622	3 999 000	217 000	10 367
Soeker	199 268	1 356 210	5 657	(52 996)	310
Strategic Fuel Fund	3 689 233	731 264	2 641 536	1 030 027	320
Category 3 – No public policy value					
Profitable					
Alexkor	257 970	41 862	228 005	46 409	1 661
Autonet	234 000	142 849	399 000	3 664	1 883
Safcol	691 541	201 307	448 921	56 798	5 433
Sun Air	86 252	26 597	46 253	(4 047)	257
Non-profitable					
Abakor	314 344	95 060	338 769	(15 429)	2 600
Aventura	100 731	54 516	109 586	(6 772)	1 585
PX (Express Airways)	593 000	981 543	557 000	(297 000)	8 757
Transkei Airways	6 743	7 838	9 244	(6 240)	45
Transnet – Other	6 085 966	3 091 116	359 631	194 487	47 810
Total	**138 343 722**	**76 612 408**	**49 632 585**	**6 409 275**	**315 156**

Source: Ministry of Public Enterprise, August 1995.

State enterprises falling under the second category are those having a national security or strategic role. These enterprises will not be privatised. Enterprises in the third category are those considered by the government as playing no visible role in the RDP. Loss-making enterprises in this category that are being supported by either cross-subsidisation or state subsidies would be sold off or liquidated. In December 1995, the government announced plans to sell part of South African Airways, Telkom and the Airport Company and fully divest from Autonet, Sun Air and Transkei Airways. The announcement immediately drew a threat of work stoppage and strikes from the trade unions, who fear that the process will cost jobs and deny black empowerment and access to services. The unions' reaction led to a negotiated agreement in which the government is bound to consult the unions before any further decision on privatisation can be taken.

Intergovernmental finance

Act 200 of the Interim Constitution of 1993 establishes the Financial and Fiscal Commission (FFC) and gives it the task of making recommendations to the legislative authorities regarding financial and fiscal policies, equitable allocations to the national, provincial and local governments from revenue collected nationally, the power of provincial governments to levy taxes and surcharges, the raising of loans by lower-tier governments, and the criteria to be used for these purposes (FFC, 1995). The FFC was appointed by the President in August 1994. In June 1995 the FFC released a draft framework document for intergovernmental fiscal relations for discussion by the relevant and interested parties. The framework document explores how the FFC's role and responsibilities are envisaged in the Interim Constitution and how they may be realised.

   In the meantime, the Minister of Finance has been authorised to take over government debt of both the former TBVC states and the self-governing territories as national government debt until such time that final decisions are made on the apportionment of the debts and liabilities between the provinces and the national government. An inter-departmental steering committee has been created to identify and reconcile the debts and liabilities of the affected regions, to determine debts and liabilities directly linked to specific assets, and to submit proposals to the relevant decision-making authorities. Government has agreed that spending on local government services will continue to be charged to the budgets of the respective provinces until replaced by other mechanism still to be determined. It is envisaged, however, that the overall increase in local government expenditure would be broadly consistent with the government's commitment to no real increase in non-interest current expenditure.

Public debt management

The 1994 budget noted that the maturity structure of government debt indicates an accumulation of redemptions scheduled for the 1996/97,

1998/99 and 2000/2001 fiscal years. The strategy of the government is to explore the possibilities of shifting the redemption structure in order to avoid imposing excessive refinancing pressure on the market in any single year, as part of the ongoing effort to improve the efficiency of public debt management. In addition, the government intends to review the practice of issuing long-term government bonds at a large discount as this has had an adverse impact on the transparency of the fiscal accounts and impaired the market's ability to assess the actual extent of the government borrowing requirement.

The policy of the government is not to rely to a large extent on external debt as a means of financing the national budget deficit. Government foreign borrowing is thus not to be seen as an attempt to find additional sources of finance, thereby enabling a larger deficit to be maintained, but rather as a substitute for domestic finance depending on cost considerations and pressure on the domestic financial markets.

4. Fiscal policy issues in a growth-oriented RDP

The RDP is to be implemented within the institutional framework of a mixed economy in which the public sector plays a significant role in determining the broad directions of development, as well as by acting as a counter-force to the concentration of wealth in private hands.[4] This framework has been consciously adopted to promote growth along with social justice. While growth is emphasised, it is the aim of the RDP to change the composition and, more importantly, the distribution of services to benefit the poorer sections of the society. The achievement of these objectives calls for several measures to be in place. We discuss the fiscal measures that would be required in a growth-oriented reconstruction programme to regulate domestic absorption, increase domestic savings and investment, promote efficient resource use, and channel an acceptable share of the benefits of economic growth to the poor and disadvantaged communities and sectors.

Short-term fiscal policy

Where public finances have gone off track and the government is incurring a deficit on its current account and on the total of current and capital accounts, efforts must be made to reduce the current account deficit so as to bring down government borrowing from the banking system. But significant changes in the composition of revenues and expenditures and in the tax structure cannot be brought about instantaneously – or even in the short run. How then is the task of reducing the deficit to be accomplished?

In general, and particularly where inflationary pressures have built up, reduction in the actual level of government expenditure would be a more effective way of bringing down the budget deficit in the short term. But this will not be an easy task since, in the short run, several items on the expenditure side of the budget are likely to be rigid. Nevertheless, there should be some room to manoeuvre. First, expenditure increases could be contained through a short-term freeze on public sector employment and on wages for government employees. Secondly, action could be taken to reduce subsidies other than those on exports and on essential goods for the poorer and disadvantaged sections of the society. Thirdly, the introduction of zero-base budgeting for all but key development-related areas would enable savings in current expenditure and redeployment of staff from non-developmental to developmental departments. Fourthly, there could be some pruning of inefficient capital expenditure.

On the revenue side, where the tax ratio is already high (tax ratio of 25% and above of GDP) and/or wages and salaries are indexed, it will be difficult to increase revenue through rate increases in the short run. If some increase becomes imperative in order to reduce the deficit, it would be better to do so by levying a uniform surcharge on all taxes other than the corporate tax. In that way, the basic tax structure will not be altered hastily and the extent of rate increase will be the minimum needed since all taxes but one will be covered by the increase. Where the tax ratio is lower, short-term increases in revenue would be more feasible through rate increases, although the low tax ratio may not be attributed to low rates but to an inadequate structure and inefficient administration.

Medium-term fiscal policy

In the medium term, the fiscal system should be used to produce the desired supply-side effects. The most important of these is the increase in the efficiency of resource use and in the rate of growth of productive capacity. To achieve efficiency in resource use there should be a minimum of undesired distortions in relative prices of factor inputs and of producer choices. For productive capacity to be expanded, savings and investment must increase and investment directed to more productive activities. At the same time, the fiscal system must mobilise sufficient resources to be used for development purposes.

In the medium term, tax revenue must rise substantially to bring the overall budget deficit under control and, at the same time, the tax structure must exert a favourable influence on the economy. This favourable influence, which would lead to higher growth, would in turn be reflected in higher revenue. Thus, the level of revenues and the structure of the tax system are both important in the medium term.

It is important that indirect taxes do not produce distortions in the relative prices of factors of production or lead to any significant degree of cascading. For economic reasons as well as for ease of administration, there should be a general tax with few rates. This could be supplemented by a selective consumption tax, such as taxes on petroleum products, levied at a higher rate so that the indirect tax structure, taken as a whole, would be progressive with respect to consumption expenditure. The general tax could take the form of a value added tax and would have to apply to domestically produced goods as well as to imports. If it is desired that the indirect tax system should be used to support investment, then taxes paid on capital and intermediate goods may be eligible for set-off or levied at lower rates.

The promotion of savings and investment can also be achieved through direct taxes on companies and on the richer sections of the community. Ideally, given the limitations of income taxation, which contains bias against savings and which can only be levied on a realization basis, direct taxation should take the form of a tax on personal income supplemented by some variant of cash flow tax on companies. First, for equity reasons, a progressive income tax would be the appropriate choice. However, it is necessary to ensure that the rates be moderated and that the number of marginal rates be kept to the minimum. It would also be necessary to provide for incentives for savings under the tax. Deductions from taxable income should also be granted for certain forms of financial investments, such as insurance premiums and provident/pension fund contributions. Secondly, even if a progressive income tax is retained for equity reasons, company income must be taxed at low or, at most, the same rates as personal income. A relatively low rate of tax on companies would induce greater risk-taking and leave enough resources for financing additional investment. Along with the lowering of the rate of company tax, many of the exemptions that erode the tax base should be removed. It would be necessary, however, to provide for accelerated depreciation to encourage and facilitate capital formation. Thirdly, taxation of capital gains should be simplified and made more equitable: after adequate indexation, capital gains can be included as part of income and there would be no need to make any distinction between short-term and long-term gains.

In a number of developing countries, the informal and non-monetary sectors constitute a substantial part of the economy but taxes fall mainly on the formal monetised sector. Hence, a 'limit to taxation' has to be decided in terms of the conditions prevailing in the country. Clearly, if taxation proceeds beyond the limit in relation to GDP, growth is likely to be retarded. Hence it is important to control expenditure. Strenuous efforts would have to be made in the medium term to bring the growth of expenditure in line with that of revenue. Priority should be given to the elimination of government dissaving, which emphasises reducing current spending. As a rule it is safe to proceed on the principle that all current spending should be covered by current revenues. This means that the growth of the components of current expenditure, other than interest payments, should be regulated to bring down the level of total current spending to the level of total current revenue within a reasonable period of time. Thereafter, the rate of growth of current expenditure must be made to keep pace with that of revenue.

Expenditure on subsidies is a significant component of public expenditure in a number of countries. In general, subsidies that involve disincentives to production or lead to significant distortions in the allocation of resources should be eliminated. Equally objectionable are subsidies to cover losses by inefficiently run public enterprises. Even for the efficiently run enterprises, losses would occur if prices of their products are kept below costs and these losses are covered by budgetary subsidies. Such subsidies also tend to mitigate against efficient allocation of resources. Export subsidies and subsidies in favour of the poor must be allowed. Even then, the total of these subsidies in the budget should reflect growth in GDP and government revenue.

It is necessary to categorise loss-making public enterprises into those in the core sector, such as infrastructure, and those in non-core sector. In the medium term, enterprises in the latter category that are making losses must be closed down or sold off to the private sector. Public enterprises in the former category must be made to work out time-bound programmes for making their operations profitable; provided they are working efficiently and wages are not rising faster than labour productivity, they must be allowed price increases justified by increases in the costs of inputs.

5.   Is government fiscal policy in good company?

To address the question of whether the GNU's fiscal policy is adequate and on track, it is important to know whether the budget really was suffering from fiscal stress before the new government came into office in April 1994. The reason is that it is common practice to select the budget balance and to view it and its movements as direct indicators of the stance of fiscal policy. But, for a given tax and expenditure structure, a different budget balance will result when the economy is booming, for example, than when it is in recession. It could, therefore, be erroneous to infer directly from the size and movements in the budget deficit that fiscal policy is expansionary or contractionary; a weakening economic situation could cause a widening deficit, and is important to take into account the underlying structural conditions of the economy in any assessment of government fiscal stance. For this reason, we begin our assessment of the stance of fiscal policy prior to 1994 on the basis of the estimates of the real cyclical effect of the budget.[5] This indicator measures the difference between the actual budget balance and the cyclically neutral balance, with the latter taking into account the effects of the business cycles on the budget. If the cyclical effect of the budget is positive, then fiscal policy is deemed expansionary; the converse is also true. In the former case the actual budget deficit gives cause for concern. The cyclical effect of the budget is, however, highly sensitive to the choice of the base year balance. A more robust indicator is provided by the year-to-year changes in the cyclical effect of the budget. This measure of the fiscal impulse indicates the initial contribution to the annual fluctuation in the aggregate demand (Chand, 1984).

Taking 1975 as base period, Table 3.2 shows that fiscal policy was largely expansionary from the perspective of the conventional budget balance, with the rate of expansion increasing rapidly in the late 1980s. The conventional budget balance, adjusted for the cyclical effects of the

Table 3.2 Consolidated general government fiscal data, 1975–93[a] (period average in % of GDP)

	1975[b]	1976–79	1980–84	1985–89	1990–93
Conventional balance					
Actual balance	3.4	4.7	2.9	3.9	4.3
Cyclically neutral balance	3.4	3.5	1.9	2.4	3.2
Cyclical effect of the budget[c]	–	1.2	1.0	1.5	1.1
Fiscal impulse[c]	–	0.3	0.1	0.4	0.8
Structural balance	3.4	4.6	4.4	4.9	4.5
Primary balance					
Actual balance	1.9	2.7	0.6	0.4	–0.1
Cyclically neutral balance	1.9	2.2	0.5	0.9	1.7
Cyclical effect of the budget[c]	–	0.5	0.1	–0.5	–1.8
Fiscal impulse[c]	–	0.2	0.1	–0.3	0.6
Structural balance	1.9	2.4	2.0	1.4	0.1

Notes
[a] All budget figures represent deficits in real terms.
[b] Base year.
[c] Negative values represent contractionary effect and otherwise.

economy, expanded by an average of 1.0% of GDP per annum in 1980–84 and rose to 1.5% of GDP per annum in 1985–89, before dropping to 1.1% in 1990–93, causing considerable fluctuations in the level of domestic aggregate demand. For example, the contribution of the budget to the changes in the domestic aggregate demand (as measured by the fiscal impulse) increased from an average of 0.1% of GDP per annum in 1980–84 to 0.8% of GDP per annum in 1990–93. From the perspective of the primary budget balance, there was a relatively small expansion in the fiscal policy in the 1976–84 period. Fiscal policy contracted thereafter, with the level of contraction reaching an average of 1.8% of GDP per annum in 1990–93. The contribution of the primary budget deficit to changes in aggregate demand was also negative throughout the 1980s. Two things thus emerge from this assessment. First, fiscal policy was generally expansionary during the period under review, and particularly in the period after 1984. Secondly, the expansion in fiscal policy was attributable to the large and growing interest component of the budget. These findings suggest that a reduction in the public sector debt and the associated interest payments is crucial to the maintenance of a sustainable fiscal deficit.

Is the government's fiscal policy adequate to deal with the fiscal stress? The discussions in the previous two sections indicate that the new regime's fiscal policy and the underlying measures are broadly in line with those perceived to be necessary in a growth-oriented reconstruction and development programme. Government fiscal policy has been designed to reduce the budget deficit to an acceptable level in the short term through the containment of non-interest recurrent expenditure in real terms. In the medium term, growth in government expenditure is to be kept in line with the growth in revenue to ensure fiscal sustainability. New priorities will be set for capital expenditure, and expenditures increased to strengthen the infrastructural development that will support the growth of productivity of private investment.

Despite the numerous measures introduced, certain aspects of the government's fiscal policy are still problematic. First, and particularly disturbing, is the continuing reliance on direct taxation as the major source of government revenue. At 52% of total government receipts in fiscal year 1994/95 (SARB, 1995), income tax remains the largest revenue source, and in tapping this source the government has relied increasingly on tax on individuals. Consequently, personal income tax as a proportion of GDP has increased from 4.5% in 1981/82 to 9.7% in 1994/95, while company tax revenue has declined from 6.5% of GDP to 3.3% of GDP over the same period. This has led to an increase in the total tax burden on individuals (mainly wage earners and those with private sector pensions) to very high levels, with negative effect on private savings. It has also limited the scope for further tax increases in the short term since the tax is paid by only a small proportion of the population.

There is consensus that the fiscal burden has already reached its ceiling and that substantial increases in tax revenue cannot be achieved without faster economic growth. This suggests that the government is likely to be locked into a vicious circle, whose exit is to be found only in the medium term through sustained growth in GDP. A resort to growth-retarding taxes for a purely short-term solution to the problem of the fiscal deficit might, therefore, make no economic sense in the long run. In the country's circumstances, it might even be necessary, as part of tax reform, to encourage changes that could produce less impact on the fiscal deficit in the short term but would have desirable supply-side effects on the economy over the medium term. The Katz Commission's (1994) observation deserves consideration here: that the economic growth and international competitiveness the country so vitally needs to enhance the prosperity of all its people and to create employment opportunities for the growing number of job-seekers requires a reduction in most of the marginal rates for personal income tax, a reduced direct personal income tax burden and reduced nominal rates of corporate tax. Although a reduction in the income tax rates will lead to a loss in revenue to the fiscus, we believe that the loss could be recouped through the benefits of efficient tax administration and better tax collection, an increased tax base from economic growth, and a movement towards a greater reliance on indirect taxes, particularly on VAT and excise taxation.

Secondly, the delayed action by the government on capital gains tax is causing considerable uncertainty in the minds of some investors. As the Katz Commission pointed out, the absence of any capital gains tax is seen by some foreign investors as an incentive to invest in the country. However, the more recent speculation that capital gains tax will be introduced in the near future has eroded that perception, because the details of such a tax are presently unknown. Many investors, therefore, see the situation as negative because they have no certainty about the potential effect of such a tax on their investment (Katz Commission, 1994). The fear of a future capital gains tax affecting existing investment has become a real deterrent to many investors, requiring the government to make its stand on the issue known. In view of the critical need for economic growth we feel that the introduction of capital gains tax in the next three to four years will make no economic sense, particularly when there are numerous calls for making the effective tax on companies as low as possible. Capital gains tax can be introduced in the medium to longer term. Even then it should be indexed and included as part of income for the purposes of taxation. It should also be made to apply to assets acquired after the date on which the tax is to come into effect. That way the fears of foreign investors that they may be subjected to a punitive capital gains tax on their investment now would be allayed.

The third problematic issue relates to the government's capacity to contain non-interest expenditure increases, particularly expenditures relating to public sector employment and remunerations. As part of the government's strategy to reduce civil service employment numbers, a special initiative, whereby serving officials who complied with specified criteria could volunteer for early retirement,[6] was introduced in 1994. Although the actual number of civil servants who took advantage of this arrangement is not known, the total public sector (including all tiers of government, parastatals and public sector corporations) employment level rather than contracting increased from 1.63 million in March 1994 to 1.89 million[7] in March 1995. The original plan of the government was to draw up a three-year plan to address the issue of salaries and remunerative allowances in the civil service (GSA, 1995). However, to put a stop to the wave of industrial actions by some civil servants (police, municipal council workers, nurses, etc.) and loss of skilled professionals to the private sector, the government was forced to come out quickly with a salary improvement plan. In this plan, the government wage bill for the 1995/96 fiscal year, excluding the public sector corporations, is expected to reach R59 billion; this figure is set to rise to about R68 billion in 1996/97. The plan thus adds over R9 billion to the total public sector wage bill in 1996/97 but it also envisages a staff cutback of some 60,000, mainly from the former homeland bureaucracies. Already several public servants' organisations have declared that they are not party to or committed to the government's salary aims. These organisations regard the government's salary plan with mistrust and, therefore, they cannot guarantee industrial peace in the country. With the threat of industrial action, there is every possibility that the government will commit itself to significant increases in wages and salaries in the 1997/98 fiscal year, seriously undermining its ability to restrain increases in the rate of remuneration.

Fourthly, a major area of concern relates to the privatisation of the non-core public enterprises. It is estimated that disposing of R50 billion of state assets could reduce the public debt/GDP ratio to 45% from the current level of 50% and generate savings of R5 billion in terms of interest payments (*Financial Mail*, 1995). Given the critical need to attract direct foreign investment, promote economic efficiency,[8] and reduce the size of the public sector and thus bureaucratic redundancies – as well as to generate resources to finance the RDP and/or reduce public sector debt and its crippling interest burden – privatisation of the non-core state assets should not only be seen as timely. More importantly, it has to be bold – a few portfolio disposals will be pointless and loss-making enterprises will attract no private interest. While the political commitment to privatisation is not in doubt, the process had failed to get off the ground because of a number of practical constraints including the slow process on the part of the government of identifying the assets it wishes to divest. There is also the opposition to the process by the trade unions for fear of labour retrenchments. Labour's fears of job losses are entirely legitimate. Most of the state enterprises are overstaffed, so privatisation will inevitably lead to cuts in employment numbers. Even privatisation on a limited scale as announced by the government will create temporary unemployment. The government has as yet to outline how far it will go to protect the jobs of the existing workers in the enterprises targeted for divestiture and how employees will be compensated if large-scale retrenchments become necessary. If these anxieties are not handled sensitively, the privatisation process will encounter avoidable resistance. As part of the privatisation package, government needs to outline measures that will help to create jobs and/or redeploy workers whose jobs will be lost.

It must also be pointed out that the sale of state assets will lead to a once-for-all reduction in the fiscal deficit if the proceeds are treated as capital revenue or debt repayment in the government account. The change in the deficit may not reflect a fundamental change in the fiscal policy stance. Privatisation can permanently improve the fiscal performance only if large efficiency gains, both productive and allocative, result from the transfer of ownership from the public to the private sector. In such a case, the government will benefit from the process to the extent that it can capture part of the expected efficiency gains in its sale price and/or additional taxes (Hemming and Miranda, 1991).

The seeming lack of coordination between fiscal and monetary policy is another disturbing issue. From Table 3.2, the conventional deficit suggests that fiscal policy was expansionary throughout the period under review. The primary deficit, on the other hand, suggests that fiscal policy was expansionary in the second half of the 1970s and the early 1990s but contractionary in the entire decade of the 1980s. The difference between the conventional deficit and the primary deficit is affected by the size of both the public debt and the nominal interest rate. In an inflationary environment, variations in the conventional fiscal deficit/GDP ratio might be caused mainly by changes in the nominal interest payments on the stock of public debt with floating interest rates. The rise in the conventional deficit in the 1970s was mainly due to the increase in the public debt, whereas in the 1980s it was the rise in the nominal interest rate that caused the rising trend in the deficit (Abedian, 1992). This makes apparent the fiscal impact of the reserve bank's interest rate policy. The changes in the bank's monetary policy in the 1980s in favour of higher interest rates seem to have thrown the fiscal budget into a crisis. The bank's philosophy of high interest rate policy continues to jeopardise both the fiscal and the growth efforts of the new government. For example, the bank rate was raised three times, from 12% to 15%, within the ten months from September 1994 to June 1995, causing the prime rate to reach 18.5% in June 1995. This action was meant to contain the rapid expansion in the money supply and thus reduce inflation. While the reduction in inflation is very necessary, one finds it difficult to justify the current levels of interest rates given that the inflation rate has stayed below 10% since June 1995. Moreover, the current high levels of interest rates have caused the cost of capital and thus investment costs to rise. Although South Africa does not have variable interest on public debt issues, the changes in the term structure of the stock of public debt, from long-term to short-term debt, have equivalent effects in terms of the interest cost of the debt (Abedian, 1992). For the sake of economic growth, either the rate of increase in the public debt should be arrested or the monetary philosophy of high interest rates policy should change.

Finally, the issue of dominance of government in the RDP has been frowned at and indeed considered objectionable by many, as government interventions are usually held responsible for budget deficits and inefficient allocation of resources. Notwithstanding the realities of the negative impact of government interventions, the fact is that given the history of the country and the extent of poverty and gross inequality evident in all spheres of economic and social life, the only feasible institution with the integrity to articulate, inspire, guide and direct the reconstruction and development process in a socially desirable direction is the state. Because private initiative is not always forthcoming in vital areas of long-run socioeconomic development owing to the inherent difference between the way potential investors read cost–benefit signals of the future and the way in which public authorities may read the signals, the government may be justified in maintaining its dominance over the broad direction of the development process. That way the pursuit of social justice and equity will not be unduly sacrificed in the operation of fiscal policy for the purposes of reducing the budget deficit.

6. Conclusion

This chapter examined the fiscal policy of the government in the post-apartheid era, to assess the potential for achieving the short-term objective of reducing the budget deficit to a more acceptable level and the medium- to longer-term objective of achieving fiscal sustainability along with economic growth.

The chapter showed that the government's fiscal policy is broadly in line with that perceived to be necessary in a growth-oriented reconstruction and development programme. Fiscal policy is being conducted within tight constraints, involving the avoidance of permanent increases in the overall tax burden, the containment of non-interest recurrent spending in real terms, and the strengthening of government contribution to gross domestic capital formation to ensure the maintenance of social and economic infrastructure development.

Despite the numerous programmes and measures undertaken to achieve these objectives, certain aspects of the government's fiscal policy still pose problems for long-term economic growth and thus tax revenue. Particularly disturbing is the continuing reliance on personal income tax as the main source of tax receipts; this has caused the tax burden on individuals to rise to very high levels, with adverse implications for personal savings and further increases in tax revenue. The continuing existence of such taxes as the marketable securities tax and the secondary tax on companies, coupled with the extension of the period of depreciation write-off and uncertainty surrounding the introduction of capital gains tax as purely a short-term solution to the problem of the fiscal deficit, poses a great disincentive to entrepreneurship, domestic and foreign investment, and thus economic growth. Added to this are the seemingly ineffective application of a short-term freeze on public sector employment and the government's ambivalence toward privatisation of non-core state-owned enterprises. These are critical issues requiring immediate and serious attention if the short- and medium-term fiscal objectives of the government are to be achieved together with economic growth and social justice.

If the design of the government's fiscal policy could lead to a simplified tax structure, introduce moderate tax rates and improve the tax administration – as well as determine the proper choice of fiscal instruments that take into account socio-political sensitivities and flexibility in the fiscal ceiling – then the policy's growth-promoting role would be greatly enhanced. It is also important to remember that fiscal policy is only one element of economic policy and needs to be seen in the overall context as it complements monetary policy, trade and industrial policy, labour market policy. In particular, the close relationship between fiscal and monetary policy carries with it the possibility of conflict and sub-optimal policies should their implementation be at cross-purposes. On the other hand, a coordinated monetary-fiscal policy may be mutually reinforcing and therefore more effective.

Notes

1. The Margo Commission was appointed by the government in November 1984 to inquire into the tax structure of the Republic of South Africa.
2. The details of these measures are well documented in the SA Government Budget Review (1995) and the SA Reserve Bank *Annual Economic Report* (1994; 1995).
3. The Katz Commission was appointed by the government in June 1994 to inquire into certain aspects of the tax structure in South Africa.
4. This discussion draws largely on Chelliah (1987).
5. To determine the effect of the budget on the economy (i.e. aggregate demand), first determine a cyclically neutral balance (CNB). $G_0 - T_0$ (where G and T refer to government expenditure and revenue, respectively, in base year, 0) denotes the balance in some base year of satisfactory performance. The CNB for each subsequent year is determined by applying the base year revenue to GDP ratio (t_0) to that year's actual output level and the base year expenditure to GDP ratio (g_0) to that year's potential (trend) output level; the difference is the CNB. Next, the computed CNB is substracted from the actual budget deficit for that year to determine the cyclical effect of the budget (CEB) in real terms, i.e., $\text{CEB} = G - T - [g_0\text{GDP}^p - t_0\text{GDP}]$, with GDP representing gross domestic product and GDP^p its potential level. A positive CEB indicates an expansionary budget effect; the converse is also true. This value is zero for the base year. The 'structural' or underlying budget balance is equal to the sum of the base year balance and the CEB (Chand, 1984).
6. The government cannot resort to outright cuts in personnel numbers because the interim constitution guarantees job security for all civil servants during the restructuring process.
7. The figure includes almost 500,000 bureaucrats from the former homelands and self-governing territories, whose inclusion in central government lifted the staff complement of national and provincial numbers from 764,000 in March 1994 to 1.26 million in June 1994.
8. Enterprises whose inefficiencies are subsidised by the taxpayer can afford to continue operating inefficiently. But organisations financed by the private sector have to account regularly and relatively transparently to shareholders for their performance.

References

Abedian, I. 1992. 'Fiscal policy and economic growth'. In I. Abedian and B. Standish, eds, *Economic Growth in South Africa: Selected Policy Issues*. Cape Town: Oxford University Press.

Central Economic Advisory Service (CEAS). 1993. *The Restructuring of the South African Economy: A Normative Model Approach*. Pretoria: Government Printer.

Chand, S. 1984. 'The stabilizing role of fiscal policy'. *Finance and Development*, March. Washington, DC: The International Monetary Fund.

Chelliah, R. J. 1987. 'Growth-oriented adjustment programs: fiscal policy issues'. In V. Corbo, M. Goldstein and M. Khan, eds, *Growth-Oriented Adjustment Programs*. Washington, DC: The IMF.

Economist Intelligence Unit. 1988. *South Africa: Country Profile*. May. London: Economist Intelligence Unit.

FFC (Financial and Fiscal Commission). 1995. *Framework Document for Intergovernmental Fiscal Relations in South Africa*. June. Halfway House: Financial and Fiscal Commission.

Financial Mail, 15 Dec. 1995.

GSA (Government of South Africa). 1994. *White Paper on RDP*. Cape Town: Office of the Minister without Portfolio.

GSA (Government of South Africa). 1995. *Budget Review*. Cape Town: Government Printer.

Hemming, R. and Kenneth Miranda. 1991. 'Privatisation'. In Ke-Young Chu and Richard Hemming, eds, *Public Expenditure Handbook*. Washington, DC: The IMF.

Jammine, A. 1990. 'Monetary and fiscal policy'. In B. Godsell and others, eds, *Economic Alternatives*. Kenwyn: Juta and Co. Ltd.

Katz Commission. 1994. *Interim Report of the Commission of Inquiry into Certain Aspects of the Tax Structure of South Africa*. Pretoria: The Government Printer.

Kusi, N. K. 1993. 'External imbalance and structural adjustment: South Africa in the 1980s'. *The South African Journal of Economics*, vol. 61 (4): 255–65.

Lachman, D. and K. Bercuson. 1992. 'Economic policies for a new South Africa'. *IMF Occasional Paper*, No. 91. Jan. Washington, DC: IMF.

Loots, L. 1991. 'A tax strategy for redistribution'. In P. Moll, N. Nattrass and L. Loots, eds, *Redistribution: How Can it Work in South Africa?* Cape Town: David Philip.

Margo Commission. 1987. *Report of the Commission of Inquiry into the Tax Structure of the Republic of South Africa*. Pretoria: The Government Printer.

McCarthy, C. 1991. 'Stagnation in the South African economy: where did things go wrong?'. *Stellenbosch Economic Project Occasional papers*, No. 1. Cape Town: Stellenbosch Economic Project.

Mohr, P. J. 1989. 'Fiscal policy in South Africa'. In P. A. Black and B. Dollery, eds, *Leading Issues in South African Macroeconomics*. Johannesburg Southern Book Publishers pty.

Nedcor. 1993. *Guide to the Economy*, quarterly, Johannesburg: Nedcor Economic Unit.

SARB (South African Reserve Bank). 1994. *Public Finance Statistics of South Africa 1946–1993*. March. Pretoria: South African Reserve Bank.

SARB (South African Reserve Bank). 1995a. *Annual Economic Report*. Various issues Pretoria: South African Reserve Bank.

SARB (South African Reserve Bank). 1995b. *Quarterly Bulletin*, Dec. Pretoria: South African Reserve Bank.

4
Public Policy and Private Investment in South Africa: An Empirical Investigation

Kupikile Mlambo and Kevin Nell

1. Introduction

The performance of private investment is central to the success of any growth strategy that South Africa will follow. First, this is because achieving the goals of the Reconstruction and Development Programme (RDP) and setting the economy on a sustainable growth and development path to meet the basic needs of the mass of the population will require strong participation and response from local private investors in South Africa. A second reason is that a strong response from domestic private investors will not only contribute to growth and development, but will also act as a catalyst to attract direct foreign investment. A major policy challenge facing the architects of the new South Africa is therefore to design policies that will increase private sector investment from the (1994) level of 12% of gross domestic product (GDP).

The challenge is compounded by the fact that domestic investment has borne the brunt of the contraction in aggregate demand following the energy crisis in the 1970s, political instability since the mid-1970s and the debt crisis of the 1980s. Between 1974–80 and 1988–92, gross domestic investment as a percentage of GDP fell from 28.5% to 20.6% and reached 17.6% in 1992. Simultaneously, gross domestic savings (GDS) rates declined from 32.4% in 1974–80 to 25.0% in 1988–92. The sharp drop in investment and domestic savings accompanied a severe fall in real GDP growth from 4.7% in 1965–73 to –0.3% in 1988–92 and –2.0% in 1992. These trends in South Africa are similar to those elsewhere in sub-Saharan Africa (SSA) where investment rates declined from a 1974–80 peak of 22.2% to 16.7% and 17.5% in 1981–87 and 1988–92, respectively. Real GDP growth rates also declined from 4.7%

in 1965–73 to 1.7% in 1981–87 and improved slightly to 2.5% in 1988–92.

Within this overall perspective, two important questions with policy implications arise: Why did investment rates fall in the late 1970s and 1980s and, secondly, what role could public policy play in reviving private investment in South Africa? Regarding the first question, a number of explanations have been offered to explain the sharp drop in domestic investment. Poor growth performance, foreign debt, worsening terms of trade, and a host of domestic policy errors and political instability have been identified as contributory factors (Bleaney, 1994). The second question is more difficult to answer and, in part, depends on the answer we provide for the first question. If low investment is believed to be a result of shortage of capital in the economy, then policy will concentrate on making financial markets work better. If, on the other hand, the problem of low investment is viewed as a consequence of low demand, maintaining a stable macroeconomic environment will be the main policy response.

The purpose of this chapter is to identify the major determinants of private investment in South Africa and to explore its response to income growth, real exchange rate depreciation, external shocks, changes in public investment, and macroeconomic and political instability. This investigation is intended to shed light on the policies needed to promote higher investment rates to achieve high and sustainable growth. The chapter is divided into five further sections. The next section traces investment trends in South Africa since 1960. In the third section a number of hypotheses to explain investment behaviour in South Africa are proposed. The main focus is on the role of economic policy. Econometric estimation results are discussed next, and the conclusion offers policy implications.

2. An historical overview of investment flows in South Africa: 1960–94

Judged purely in terms of South Africa's growth performance as shown in Table 4.1, the period 1960–76 was one of economic prosperity. A high and sustainable economic growth rate of 4.7% per annum was matched by relatively high investment and saving levels. However, between 1977 and 1984 the reversal in South Africa's growth performance was dramatic. At the same time, the record high GDS and GDFI to GDP ratios defy the basic proposition that high saving and investment levels automatically and unconditionally translate into higher growth rates. According to Fallon

Table 4.1   Macroeconomic indicators in South Africa (average annual %s)

	1960–76	1977–84	1985–94
Real GDP[c] growth	4.7	2.7	0.7
Foreign financing of			
GDI[b]	6.4	0.2	–11.0
GDS[d]/GDP	23.7	27.2	20.5
GDFI[a]	23.6	26.7	18.7
Private investment/GDP	12.9	14.3	12.0
Public investment/GDP	10.7	12.4	6.7
Average annual			
inflation	5.1	12.9	14.0
Real interest rate[e]	2.92	1.7	3.5
Nominal interest rate	7.6	14.6	17.5
Fixed capital stock			
(growth rate):			
Private	4.8	3.8	4.7
Parastatals	6.6	5.6	–0.3
General government	7.3	3.8	3.4
Total	6.2	4.4	2.6

Notes:
[a] GDFI: gross domestic fixed investment.
[b] GDI: gross domestic investment.
[c] GDP: gross domestic product.
[d] GDS: gross domestic saving.
[e] Real interest rate = nominal lending rate – inflation (average % increase p.a. in the CPI).
Sources: SARB (1994b/c, 1995); IMF (1995).

and de Silva (1994) the wide disparity between growth rates and investment levels during the 1970s and early 1980s was largely driven by South Africa's pursuit of external independence and self-sufficiency. During this period deliberate policy measures ensured that capital intensive parastatals faced a lower user cost of capital than the private sector.[1] Consequently, capital was misallocated from the private sector with high capital productivity levels to parastatals with below average capital productivity levels. Although public investment has historically played an important role in stimulating domestic aggregate demand for private investment, the misallocation of capital during the 1970s and early 1980s accounted for much of South Africa's poor growth performance.

Figure 4.1 shows that private and public investment closely followed each other until 1980, suggesting that some complementarity exists between the two forms of investment. However, since 1980 public and private investment have substantially diverged, with private investment maintaining a remarkably stable trend since 1960. By contrast, the sharp

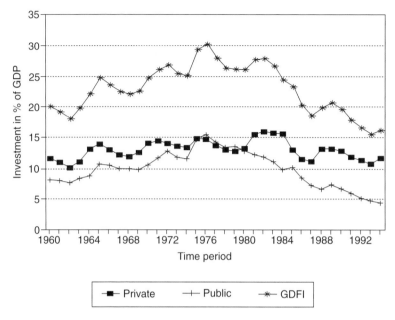

Figure 4.1 Private and public investment rate

drop in public investment accounted for much of the overall decline in GDFI during the 1980s and 1990s.

A decomposition of public investment in Figure 4.2 indicates that both parastatal and general government investments peaked during the mid-1970s. Since then, general government and parastatal investment has been declining. The decline in parastatal investment became more pronounced during the early 1980s and thereafter, while general government investment has gradually declined since its peak in 1975.

According to Van de Walt and De Wet (1993), 1985 was, in economic terms, a watershed year in South Africa. By then, the political situation in South Africa had deteriorated to such an extent that foreign creditors showed reluctance to extend further credit facilities to domestic enterprises and other financial institutions. Disinvestment campaigns, mainly by Western nations, accompanied by stricter trade and financial sanctions, forced the government to declare a moratorium on foreign debt in 1985. Disinvestment together with the repayment of foreign debt contributed to net capital outflows of around R5 billion per annum after 1985.

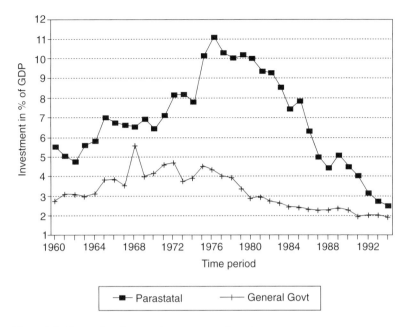

Figure 4.2   Parastal and general government investment

The cyclical pattern of the balance of payments (BOP) that characterised the South African economy before 1985 was abruptly disrupted by net capital outflows from 1985 onwards. Van der Walt and De Wet (1993) have used Weiskopf's 'two-gap analysis' to show that from 1985 the BOP placed an effective ceiling on growth of around 0.9% to 2.7% per annum. A higher growth rate would not be attainable, since capital outflows necessitate a continuous surplus on the current account. Whereas in the past current account deficits were financed by capital inflows, net outflows since 1985 implied that the current account had to be transformed into a surplus through an excess of exports over imports, a decrease in the country's propensity to import or an excess of saving over investment.

Developments in the BOP constraint have had important implications for investment in South Africa since 1985. Despite a trade regime of import substitution, South Africa relies heavily on imported capital and intermediate goods. According to De Wet (1994), real growth, which implies more imports, cannot increase further when the value of imports equals the value of exports because capital outflows necessitate a surplus on the current account.[2] As a means to finance capital outflows from 1985, deflationary policy – primarily through restrictive monetary policy – has been based on restricting investment, or realigning investment with domestic saving (Kahn, 1989, 1991). It is further illustrative to note (Table 4.1), that high positive foreign financing of GDI (or positive capital inflows as a percentage of GDI) generally corresponded with higher growth rates. Positive capital inflows thus allowed a deficit on the current account, which in turn allowed the business cycle to run its normal course.

Table 4.1 also shows that the gross domestic saving to GDP ratio of 20.5% in the period 1985–94 was significantly lower than the preceding subperiods. Saving was therefore not enough to preserve a current account surplus; consequently a restrictive monetary policy was entirely aimed at restricting investment and consumption demand. Restrictive monetary policy during 1985–94 primarily involved a higher average real interest rate level of 3.5%, as opposed to lower real interest rate levels recorded in the preceding two subperiods. Compared with 1960–76 and 1977–84, GDI as a percentage of GDP declined in all its different components, with public investment showing the sharpest drop from the relatively high levels attained before 1985.

Although private investment as a percentage of GDP varied within a narrow ranger over the sample period, a major policy objective would have been to reverse South Africa's low and declining GDFI trend. A crucial question is whether the initial impetus should come from private investment or whether a reversal in public investment would reinforce the complementary relationship that existed before 1981.

3.   The determinants of private investment in South Africa

This section largely draws from theoretical literature coupled with some preliminary evidence in South Africa. The section investigates the relationship between private investment and changes in macroeconomic variables, as well as the impact of macroeconomic and political uncertainty on private investment. It also considers the response of private investment to macroeconomic policy and whether an improvement in public investment would complement private investment in the desired fashion.

The most popular model used in empirical investment literature, especially in developing countries, is undoubtedly the neoclassical model, which identifies accelerator and cost of capital effects as the major determinants of private investment.[3] However, given the institutional factors (e.g. underdeveloped capital and financial markets, a large informal sector, etc.) and data availability problems (especially on depreciation costs and net investment), the application of theoretical investment models has concentrated mainly on listing different hypotheses about private investment behaviour (see Greene and Villanueva, 1991; Oshikoya, 1994; Hadjimichael *et al.*, 1995). The benchmark model nevertheless remains the neoclassical accelerator type model, which assumes that because of various lags, firms may not be able to adjust capital levels instantaneously in accordance with profit maximisation, but that adjustment does occur over time. The theory then defines net investment as the difference between the desired capital stock and the existing capital stock:

$$\Delta K_t = I_t^n = \alpha(K^* - K_{t-1})$$

where

K_t = actual capital stock in the current period,
K_t^* = desired capital stock in the current period,
K_{t-1} = actual capital stock lagged one period,
α = adjustment coefficient.

The desired capital stock is assumed to depend primarily on neoclassical investment behaviour, and is therefore derived from the long-run equilibrium condition where expected marginal benefits of an additional unit of capital or the value of the marginal product of capital (VMP_k) is equal to the cost of an additional unit of capital (MP_k). This condition is transformed so that K^* depends on expected profits, which in turn depend on prices, output and other autonomous shocks.

Empirical work has proceeded by listing some of the price and autonomous shock variables that affect expected profits, and therefore private investment. The subsections that follow explore some of the policy variables on which K^* is considered to depend and that therefore determine private investment in South Africa.

Changes in macroeconomic variables and private investment

A number of empirical studies (e.g. Greene and Villanueva, 1991; Morriset, 1993; Serven and Solimano, 1993; Fallon and de Silva, 1994; Hadjimichael *et al.*, 1995) have offered partial explanations of private investment behaviour in terms of changes in key macroeconomic variables. Neoclassical theory suggests that changes in macroeconomic variables transmit their influence on private investment through the user cost of capital. The macroeconomic variables most commonly used are changes in the real interest rate, inflation, taxes and changes in the real exchange rate. The discussion will proceed by examining the influence of these variables on private investment in South Africa.

Interest rate and monetary policy

Two divergent views have emerged to explain the relationship between interest rate changes and investment. The Keynesian view accentuates the user cost of capital, so that a high nominal interest rate increases the cost of borrowing and hence depresses investment. By contrast, following the influential work of McKinnon (1973) and Shaw (1973), the financial liberalisation school postulates that low or negative real interest rates discourage high saving rates, and furthermore allocate capital to unproductive sectors (see Hunt, 1989). The attainment of high, positive real interest rates would thus increase savings and the volume of credit available for productive investment purposes.

The data in Table 4.1 show that over the sample period, average real interest rates were positive in South Africa, with the exception of the 1970s and early 1980s, when real interest rates were primarily negative. The relatively high real interest rates coincided with a high saving and growth rate in the period 1960–76. However, and surprisingly, the following subperiod indicates that a lower real interest rate corresponded with a high ratio of gross domestic saving to GDP, but a significantly lower growth rate. During the period 1985–94, when restrictive monetary policy was primarily aimed at preserving a current account surplus, a high average positive real interest rate (3.5% per annum) appears to have contributed to a fall in investment demand and eventually resulted in a low economic growth rate. During this period a high real interest rate did not induce a higher saving ratio as suggested by the financial liberalisation school.

For the entire period, the preliminary evidence tends to support some of the underlying assumptions of the Keynesian view as well as the financial liberalisation school. As previously mentioned, a low user cost of capital during the mid-1970s and early 1980s redirected capital away from the private sector to parastatals with low capital productivity levels.[4] Table 4.1 indicates that the negative real interest rates that prevailed during this period seem to have contributed to the high growth of capital stock in parastatals. During the period 1985–94, however, positive high real interest rates redirected capital away from less productive parastatals to the more efficient private sector. Table 4.1 shows that the capital stock of parastatals grew at a negative rate in the period 1985–94, while the growth rate of capital in the private sector showed some improvement compared with the average for the period 1977–84. These developments lend support to some fundamental propositions of the financial liberalisation school, that high, positive real interest rates ensure the allocation of capital to the most productive sectors. Some of their suppositions are questionable, however, since savings and investment declined sharply in the period 1985–94.

Some empirical studies, such as Clarke (1996) and Rittenberg (1991), have shown that setting the interest rate too high or too low may be equally undesirable. What is important is the way in which high, positive real interest rates are achieved. When positive real interest rates are achieved through an exorbitantly high nominal interest rate, the Keynesian view becomes more relevant. This was the case in South Africa between 1985 and 1994 where, to maintain a high positive real interest rate, the monetary authorities set the average nominal rate at 17.5%. In contrast, in the period 1960–76, when South Africa recorded high growth, investment and saving levels, a high positive real interest rate was accompanied by a relatively low nominal interest rate.

Regarding other aspects of monetary policy, it is important to note that before 1979 monetary policy was primarily based on direct control measures that included regulatory measures such as periodic quantitative limits on bank credit and liquid asset requirements (Whittaker, 1992). Following its interim report in 1978 and its final report in 1985, the Commission of Inquiry into the Monetary System and Monetary Policy in South Africa recommended a change in monetary policy based on more indirect control measures. The monetary system envisaged by the Commission, and implemented from 1979 until the present, encompassed a more market-oriented approach, where financial institutions have the option to free and unconditional accommodation at the discount window of the central bank. The stated objectives of monetary policy primarily revolve around price stability and the protection of the external value of the rand. The attainment of these objectives would, in turn, create a stable macroeconomic environment conducive to growth and employment creation.

To guarantee the effectiveness of monetary policy, the South African Reserve Bank (SARB) can exert an indirect influence on short-term market interest rates by maintaining a positive money market shortage (through open market operations and cash reserve requirements), i.e. banks always remain indebted to the SARB (Meijer, 1992). When financial institutions seek accommodation at the discount window, the SARB can charge an interest rate slightly above or equal to its chosen bank rate (Whittaker, 1992). It follows, then, that the SARB's refinancing rate will be closely approximated by short-term market interest rates (Kock and Meijer, 1992).

Monetary policy plays an important role in its capacity to manage outstanding government debt. The SARB's open market operations are primarily aimed at funding a fiscal deficit in the most sagacious fashion (Kock and Meijer, 1992) to ensure a money market shortage that is neither too low, thus rendering their discount policy ineffective, nor one that is too high thus altering market expectations about future increases in interest rates.

A distinction is usually made between a debt-financed government deficit and a money financed government deficit (Dornbusch and Fisher, 1994). It is believed that a debt-financed deficit (i.e. debt issued to the public) is non-inflationary, while a money financed deficit (when the treasury borrows directly from the central bank) is inflationary, since it unequivocally leads to an increase in the money supply. Furthermore, both forms of financing will lead to an increase in interest rates, thus crowding out private investment. In many respects, however, South Africa's monetary system differs from the oversimplified standard version. If, for example, the SARB buys securities directly from the treasury (i.e. a money financed deficit), it credits the treasury's account by the amount of the purchase (Van der Walt, 1992: 396–7). In this interim stage there is no change in the monetary sector's net claims on the government sector and thus no change in the money supply or monetary institutions' cash reserves. As soon as the treasury spends the newly received funds, the monetary sector's net claims on the government sector increases by an amount equal to the decline in government deposits. At this stage it would seem as if the money supply has increased, since the private sector's deposits with monetary institutions have risen. However, because banks always remain indebted to the SARB, excess liquidity will be used to retire previous debt (Kahn, 1991). The money supply and interest rates therefore remain unchanged.

Conversely, when government debt is taken up by the private banking sector, it ultimately leads to an increase in accommodation by commercial banks. When the treasury spends these funds, they re-enter the financial system, which enables banks to repay previous accommodation (Kahn, 1991). Again the money supply remains unaltered. Similarly, when debt is taken up by the non-banking private sector, the money supply will remain unchanged, because money is simply channelled from the private sector to the government sector.

This discussion indicates that it does not really matter whether debt issues are taken up by the SARB or the public. Furthermore, a debt financed fiscal deficit will not necessarily increase interest rates, since the rediscount rate of the SARB is closely approximated by short-term market interest rates. However, the rates could diverge when market participants expect the SARB to change its rediscount rate.

The relevant question, then, is: under what circumstances will interest rates change? Interest rates will ultimately increase when an increase in accommodation is not offset by a decrease in accommodation. According to Kahn (1991), a fiscal deficit will be inflationary when fiscal expenditure causes an increase in the demand for bank credit. Potentially, a deficit financed by bank credit may not be inflationary during a recessionary period (i.e. when aggregate demand is low). However, during an upswing in the business cycle, a fiscal deficit financed through money creation may cause an increase in the demand for bank credit and therefore increased demand for accommodation (Van der Walt, 1992). In this case, an increase in the money market shortage is ineffective to offset a decrease in accommodation, with a resultant increase in the money supply and inflationary pressure. To make the money market shortage more effective, the SARB will react by increasing the cost of borrowing at the discount window, with market interest rates following suit. It follows that changes in interest rates were primarily dependent on the SARB's policy objectives at the specific time and/or for prevailing market conditions.

Fiscal policy

A crucial question concerning fiscal policy is whether budget deficits increase aggregate demand and output, and therefore private investment, or whether excessive budget deficits crowd out private investment. The Keynesian view argues that budget deficits increase aggregate demand and output. That is, even if interest rates increase, and even though some crowding out takes place, the net effect of the deficit on GDP remains positive (Heyns, 1995). A different view, the full-employment hypothesis of the classical approach, indicates that budget deficits completely crowd out investment (Kahn, 1991; Dornbusch and Fisher, 1994).

In contrast to the Keynesian and classical views, the Ricardian equivalence states that fiscal deficits simply do not matter (Kahn, 1991; Standish and Beelders, 1991; Dornbusch and Fisher, 1994). This view asserts that budget deficits imply increases in future tax liabilities. Individuals realise that they or their children will be faced with higher tax payments in the future, and therefore decide to increase bequests to their children through increased private savings. Subsequently, dissaving by the government is completely offset by an increase in private savings; national savings remain constant and aggregate demand (AD) is unchanged.

In the case of fiscal policy in South Africa, Table 4.2 illustrates that current expenditure (as a percentage of GDP) by the general government increased rapidly after 1961, averaging 30.4% per annum in the period 1989–94. The main components of current expenditure show a similar increase, with consumption expenditure averaging 20% per annum 1989–94 and interest payments 5%. Investment expenditure as a percentage of GDP, however, gradually declined after 1971–75, averaging 2.0% per annum in the period 1989–94. A decomposition of consumption expenditure indicates that from 1984–88, remuneration of employees increased sharply compared with expenditure on goods and services (see figures in parentheses). On the revenue side (Table 4.3), direct and indirect taxes as a percentage of GDP displayed a similar increasing trend, averaging 13.4% and 12.0% per annum, respectively, in the period 1989–94.

Table 4.2   General government current and investment expenditure as a % of GDP

	Current expenditure				Invest expenditure
	Consumption expenditure	Interest payment	Other	Total	
61–65	10.5	0.8	3.2	14.5	3.2
66–70	11.3	1.2	3.3	15.8	3.8
71–75	12.6	1.4	3.4	17.4	4.2
76–80	14.3	2.4	3.9	20.6	3.6
81–83	14.8	3.2	4.0	22.0	2.7
84–88	17.6 (10.4) (7.2)[a]	4.1	5.1	26.8	2.3
89–94	20.0 (12.5) (7.5)[a]	5.0	5.4	30.4	2.0

Note:
[a] Decomposition of consumption expenditure: Remuneration of employees, and goods and services, respectively.

Table 4.3   General government indirect and direct taxes (as a % of GDP)

	Indirect tax	Direct tax	Total
1961–65	5.0	8.8	13.8
1966–70	7.0	10.2	17.2
1971–75	7.1	11.3	18.4
1976–80	8.0	12.0	20.0
1981–83	9.0	12.0	21.0
1984–88	11.0	12.7	23.7
1989–94	12.0	13.4	25.4

Sources: SARB (1994b, 1995).

Table 4.4 shows that the fiscal deficit as a percentage of GDP remained fairly stable, averaging around 4% per annum over the entire period. However, it is not the deficit *per se* that matters, but rather whether excessive expenditure is used on productive outlays (Abedian, 1992). Since 1983, government spending has not been growth inducing. The rapid increase in consumption expenditure and the concomitant decline in investment expenditure suggests this. Moreover, Table 4.5 indicates that the government has been a net dissaver since 1984, with current expenditure exceeding current revenue. Dissaving should also not be a problem if borrowed funds from the private sector are used in a productive way. Furthermore, it is also possible, according to the Ricardian equivalence theorem, that government dissaving is negligible since it is completely offset by an increase in private saving.

Table 4.4   Fiscal deficit (as a % of GDP) and total outstanding government debt

	Fiscal deficit	GDP-Debt[a] (% differences)
1961–65	4.0	2.7
1966–70	4.4	0.05
1971–75	3.2	2.9
1976–80	5.0	4.7
1981–83	1.8	0.05
1984–88	4.2	−1.6
1989–94	4.8	−9.3

Note
[a] A negative sign denotes that the growth rate of debt exceeds that of the nominal GDP growth rate.
Sources: SARB (1994a, 1995).

Table 4.5, however, suggests the contrary. Total net saving and private saving began falling in 1981, and gained further momentum in the subsequent periods. The precedence for consumption expenditure, of which wages and interest payments formed a large proportion, implies that private sector saving derived from direct taxes was used inefficiently. This point is illustrated in Table 4.4, where the growth rate in nominal outstanding government debt exceeded the nominal economic growth rate in the period 1984–88, and reached an unprecedented high level in 1989–94. The excessive growth in government debt suggests that the taxable capacity of the economy is diminishing at a rapid rate.

Table 4.5 General government and private net saving as percentage of GDP

	Net government saving	Net private saving	Total net saving
1961–65	3.7	9.8	13.5
1966–70	4.4	8.0	12.4
1971–75	4.0	9.2	13.2
1976–80	2.4	12.4	14.8
1981–83	1.1	8.6	9.7
1984–88	–1.2	8.1	6.9
1989–94	–3.2	7.0	3.8

Source: SARB (1994b).

The implications for private investment are threefold. First, because the composition of government expenditure has not been a function of higher growth, income and savings, private saving that could have been used for private investment purposes was allocated to unproductive outlays. Secondly, as indicated in the previous section, there is no *a priori* reason to believe that fiscal deficits were the underlying cause of high nominal interest rates during the 1980s and 1990s. However, the size of the deficit, the inefficiency of government expenditure and the cost of borrowing, all interact in a cumulative way that will make it increasingly difficult to reduce interest rates in the near future. If the structure and composition of government remain unchanged in the future, the management of public debt in a non-inflationary way will require high interest rates to make money market shortages effective. Finally, although at first sight it would seem as if government borrowing from the private non-banking sector has a negligible impact – where government dissaving is completely offset by an increase in financial saving of the private non-banking sector – in the long term there are potentially significant economic implications. When the newly acquired funds are used to finance dissaving, government's interest burden increases, which in turn could force the government to increase future tax rates. Prudent financing principles therefore require current expenditure to be financed by current income and capital expenditure through borrowing. The government will then be in a position to finance fiscal deficits through returns on investment, or an improvement in the taxable capacity of the economy.

Inflation

The rate of inflation can influence private investment through two possible channels. First, inflation indirectly taxes the return on investment and could lead to an overall reduction in investment and the capital stock (Dowd, 1994). Secondly, during times of explosive inflation rates, economic agents could hedge against inflation by substituting speculative investment for investment in productive assets (Mohr and Rogers, 1988).

Table 4.1 shows that South Africa's inflation rate has not been excessive, and at the same time was not characterised by a high degree of variability. It is nevertheless possible that the sharp increase in the inflation rate during the mid-1970s did induce a substitution effect, although the conclusion reached at this stage is at best tenuous.

From a theoretical point of view the first effect of inflation will be a problem only when real interest rates are negative.[5] However, as indicated earlier, positive real interest rates in South Africa were achieved at the cost of high nominal interest rates. High, positive real interest rates will thus be beneficial to those institutions (e.g. big businesses, wealthy individuals, insurance companies, etc.) who have money that has not been borrowed, irrespective of the nominal interest rate (Botha, 1986). However, the groups most likely to be influenced by a high nominal interest rate are small business enterprises, farmers and homeowners. Even though the inflation rate in South Africa has not exceeded 20% over the sample period, the impact of a higher inflation rate on investment since the mid-1970s is not negligible. Inflationary pressure induces a higher nominal interest rate to keep the inflation rate in check. It follows, then, that if monetary authorities allow a market-oriented interest rate, the impact of inflation on private investment is indirectly felt through a higher nominal interest rate. As indicated, the link between nominal interest rates and inflation is particularly relevant in South Africa.

Exchange rate policy

The effect of real exchange rate changes on investment is ambiguous. It will largely depend on whether the relevant country is export-oriented or whether investment primarily depends on imported capital and inter-mediate goods (see Serven and Solimano, 1993; Hadjimichael *et al.*, 1995). In the case of an export-oriented country, a real depreciation of the exchange rate will increase the profitability of the export sector and concurrently increase private investment in this sector. Conversely, a real appreciation will decrease the profitability of the export sector and hence lead to a decline in private investment. In many developing countries, however, imported capital goods form a large component of investment, which implies that a real depreciation will place an implicit cost on imported goods and therefore lead to a subsequent decline in private investment.

With the breakdown of the Bretton Wood system in 1971, South Africa experimented with various exchange rate systems to accommodate floating exchange rates. Following the recommendations of the 1978 Interim Report of the Commission of Inquiry into the Monetary System and Monetary Policy, South Africa opted for a dual-managed floating exchange rate system in 1979, with substantial intervention by the South African Reserve Bank (Kahn, 1989; Smit, 1991). The high gold price during the 1970s and early 1980s contributed to the exchange rate being over-valued. Given South Africa's high import propensity for capital and intermediate goods (Kahn, 1987), the over-valued exchange rate cheapened the price of capital, with a concomitant increase in capital intensity.

In 1983 SARB allowed the exchange rate to be more market determined. Furthermore, a direct attempt was made to drain the economy of excess liquidity with the liberalisation of exchange control measures. The financial rand mechanism was abolished in February 1983 (De Kock, 1989). These occurrences, coupled with a declining gold price after 1981, political unrest, disinvestment and the eventual debt standstill in 1985, contributed to a sharp depreciation of the exchange rate in 1983 (Kahn, 1993). Capital outflows since 1983, however, necessitated the reinstatement of the financial rand in 1985.

It is possible that the over-valued exchange rate during the 1970s and early 1980s partly contributed to higher private and parastatal investment levels compared with the period 1984–94. The fall in private investment following the exchange rate depreciation in 1983, however, was less pronounced than parastatal investment (see Figures 4.1 and 4.2).

The complementarity between public and private investment

According to Fallon and de Silva (1994), public investment has generally stimulated private investment through the provision of socioeconomic infrastructure. South Africa's trade regime of import substitution since 1922 made private investment dependent on public investment to stimulate domestic aggregate demand. Figure 4.1 shows the high degree of complementarity that existed between public and private investment until 1980. After 1980, however, public investment declined rapidly while private investment remained fairly stable.

High public investment levels during the 1970s and early 1980s were mainly driven by South Africa's pursuit of external independence and self-sufficiency. Despite 'strategic investments' during this period, parastatal investment also benefitted from favourable movements in economically relevant variables (see note 4). Furthermore, fiscal incentives such as lucrative tax concessions, investment allowances and depreciation write-offs were purposefully directed to capital intensive state-related industries (Fallon and de Silva, 1994).

Although public investment stimulated aggregate demand, the low user cost of capital during the 1970s and early 1980s also had an economically undesirable effect. Capital was effectively redirected away from the more productive private sector to less productive parastatals.[6] The turnaround came during the early 1980s, however, when interest rates increased sharply, the exchange rate depreciated and the fiscal incentives were phased out. Since then, capital has been allocated to the more productive private sector. Compared with 1977–84, the growth rate of fixed capital stock increased in the private sector during 1985–94, while it fell sharply in parastatals (Table 4.1). Although other economically relevant variables have played a role, the main contributory factors to the decline in parastatal investment since the early 1980s were probably the completion of strategic investment projects, the cessation of any further strategic investments and the decline in capital outlays by the general government.

It is clear that the complementary relationship between private investment and parastatals had already reached a saturation point during the early 1980s. A major policy challenge facing the government is to reverse its declining investment trend and at the same time to maintain fiscal discipline. Furthermore, in its endeavour to expand private investment in the best possible way, government investment will have to avoid the ill-conceived investment decisions that characterised its past behaviour.

Macroeconomic instability, political uncertainty and policy credibility

According to Pindyck (1991), investment expenditures can be characterised by two distinct features. First, investment expenditures are largely irreversible, i.e. expenditures are sunk costs that cannot be recovered. Secondly, investments can be delayed, giving firms time to wait for additional information and positive market signals. These characteristics introduce three important determinants of private investment: macroeconomic instability, political uncertainty and policy credibility. During times of political turmoil, macroeconomic instability and major policy reforms, investors are likely to postpone investment decisions (Rodrik, 1991; Schmidt-Hebbel *et al.*, 1994). In South Africa, not much empirical work has been done on the problem of uncertainty. The only exception is a study by Bleaney (1994), who uses net capital flows as a proxy for political uncertainty and finds that it played a prominent role in discouraging private investment in South Africa.

4. Econometric analysis

To investigate the role of economic policy in determining private investment in South Africa, we estimated the following investment function:

$$IPY = F \; [\Delta Y_t, \; RIR, \; \Delta DCR, \; GIY, \; GDEFY, \; ULC, \; TOTGR, \; RERGR, \; DUM1, \; IPY_{T-1}, \; \phi]$$

where:

IPY	= private investment to GDP ratio
ΔY_t	= real GDP growth
RIR	= real lending rate
ΔDCR	= real change in domestic credit
GDEFY	= government budget deficit to GDP
ULC	= unit labour costs
TOTGR	= terms of trade growth
RERGR	= change in the real effective exchange rate
IPY_{t-1}	= lagged IPY
DUM1	= dummy variable, 1985–94 = 1, and 0 otherwise
GIY	= public investment to GDP

The measurement of these variables and the data sources are included in the Appendix.

The econometric estimation, carried out for the period 1960–94, proceeded along the following steps. First, the model was estimated by ordinary least squares, which in the case of small samples is less sensitive to misspecification errors than simultaneous methods (Mariano, 1982; Phillips, 1983). Secondly, to avoid the problems of spurious regression and to ensure stationarity, the variables entering the investment equation were expressed as ratios of GDP or in rates of change. Finally, the model was estimated in logarithmic form.

The discussion of the econometric exercises will be grouped under two headings: standard macroeconomic and policy effects and uncertainty effects. No preferred investment function is selected because of possible collinearity among the regressors, which affects the significance levels of individual variables. Before examining each investment determinant, it is important to note that the model explains between 70% and 80% of the variance in investment in South Africa between 1960 and 1993.

Standard macroeconomic effects

Table 4.6 shows the results of the basic model. Real GDP growth is included to capture the accelerator effects. Current and lagged real GDP

Table 4.6   Determinants of private investment in South Africa, 1960–94

VARS	EQN 1	EQN 2	EQN 3	EQN 4	EQN 5
CONST	−1.2273	−1.1987	−1.5783	−1.9302	−1.8175
	(−2.77)	(−2.68)	(−4.54)	(−5.88)	(−4.93)
LPIN	0.3156	0.3085	0.3777	0.6415	0.5877
	(5.08)	(4.79)	(8.76)	(15.47)	(8.69)
ΔYt	0.0001	0.0001	0.0001	0.0001	0.0001
	(5.65)	(5.62)	(5.75)	(4.71)	(2.56)
LGIY	0.3676	0.3833	0.2381	–	–
	(4.17)	(3.20)	(6.16)		
RIR	−0.0082	−0.0075	−0.0051	0.0028	−0.0002
	(−2.05)	(−2.21)	(−1.81)	(0.85)	(−0.14)
ΔDCR	0.0003	0.0002	0.0003	0.0002	0.0002
	(2.50)	(2.65)	(2.51)	(2.09)	(1.70)
INFL	−0.0263	−0.0256	0.0226		−0.0011
	(−5.82)	(−5.87)	(−5.97)		(−0.15)
ULC	−0.0099	−0.0011	–	−0.0012	−0.0020
	(−2.03)	(−1.97)		(−1.95)	(−2.12)
TOTGR	−0.0012	–	−0.0012	–	–
	(−0.90)		(−1.19)		
RERGR	−0.0001	–	–	–	–
	(−0.17)				
DEFY	−0.0213	−0.0213	−0.0171	–	−0.0105
	(−4.76)	(−4.94)	(−3.76)		(−1.77)
INFR	–	–	–	0.1887	0.1671
				(7.83)	(4.63)
NINFR	–	–	–	−0.2330	−0.0873
				(−2.84)	(−0.65)
DUM1	0.1432	0.1364	–	0.0229	0.0575
	(2.62)	(2.52)		(0.52)	(1.20)
R^2	0.926	0.9249	0.9221	0.9427	0.9493
Likelihood	68.90	68.60	67.95	73.31	75.44
F-test	26.26	34.24	32.90	45.69	44.92
DW	1.34	1.32	1.18	1.33	1.25

Note
The dependent variable is the log of real private investment: GDP.
T-statistics are in parentheses.

growth were experimented with, and the latter selected principally to reduce the problem of simultaneity – that investment also affects growth in the current period. The results confirm what has been found in the empirical literature, that there is a solid and positive relationship between private investment and real income growth (see Shapiro, 1986). Although positive and significant, the effect is not that large. The estimated coefficient of the lagged real GDP growth rate indicates that a 10 percentage point increase in real income growth would result in an increase in the private investment ratio of 0.001%.

The lagged private investment to GDP ratio ($LPIN_{t-1}$) was also included; it captures investment inertia. The coefficients of this variable are positive and significant, suggesting the presence of strong inertial forces.

The effects of financial policy are captured by the real interest rate (RIR) and the growth of real domestic credit (ΔDCR). The latter accounts for the quantity effects of financial policy. For the real interest rate, bank lending rates corrected for inflation were used. As pointed out earlier, the theoretical literature on the effect of the interest rate on private investment makes ambiguous predictions. The financial repression literature stresses that positive real interest rates will encourage more savings, and therefore higher investment, while negative real interest rates have adverse consequences for capital accumulation. This is based on the classical assumption that savings preceed investment. Keynesian literature, however, emphasises the user cost of capital effects: that high interest rates discourage private investment. The results shown in Table 4.6 indicate that the real interest rate has a negative and statistically significant effect on private capital accumulation. On the other hand, growth of real domestic credit has a positive and statistically significant impact on private investment.

Fiscal policy variables used in the estimation include the ratio of public investment and government budget to GDP. From theory, the effect of public investment on private investment is ambiguous. On the one hand, public investment may, depending on how it is financed, result in higher interest rates and credit rationing, and crowd out or substitute for private investment. On the other hand, public investment may, depending on where it is concentrated (as for example in physical and social infrastructure), improve the productivity of private investment. The estimation results reported in Table 4.6 provide support for the complementarity hypothesis that public investment increases the marginal product of capital, and the coefficient of public capital is consistently positive and statistically significant at the 5% level. The results show that the effect is not small, either. A 10 percentage point increase in the rate of public capital induces an increase in the share of private investment to GDP of between 3% and 6%. We also experimented with different functional components of public investment, and decomposed it into infrastructural (*INFR*) and non-infrastructural investment (*NINFR*). The former includes economic and social infrastructural investment, while the latter is calculated as a residual. The estimation results are reported in

Table 4.6 in the fifth and sixth columns. Infrastructural investment has a positive and statistically significant impact on private investment.

Another fiscal policy variable included is the government budget deficit, which captures the crowding out effect of government. An increase in government spending financed by money creation lowers real money balances and raises the real interest rate. The government budget deficit ratio has a negative and significant effect on private capital accumulation. Like public investment, the effect of the government budget deficit is also robust, even when included with the uncertainty variables. This suggests that it has an independent effect on private capital accumulation.

To investigate the extent to which the long-run effects of government spending on private investment depend on the government's financial policy, we have decomposed *FDEFY* into bond financed deficit and money financed deficit. The money financed deficit (*MDEFY*) is measured as the ratio of reserve money to GDP, while the bond financed deficit is calculated as a residual. The data on *MDEFY* were obtained from the International Financial Statistics (*IMF*, 1990–95). The OLS estimation yielded the following results:

$$LPIYt = 0.599 + 0.234LPINt + 0.0001Yt + 0.503LGIYt - 0.011RIRt$$
$$(1.49) \quad (3.29) \qquad (5.31) \qquad (6.39) \qquad (-3.19)$$
$$+ 0.0004DCRt - 0.001TOTGRt - 0.0001RERGR - 0.001ULC$$
$$(2.34) \qquad (-0.98) \qquad (-0.12) \qquad (-2.85)$$
$$- 0.029INFL - 0.238DUM - 0.043MDEFYt - 0.067BDEFYt$$
$$(-7.47) \qquad (-5.46) \qquad (-0.34) \qquad (-4.51)$$

$$R^2 = 0.9466 \qquad F_{(12,22)} = 32.48 \qquad DW = 1.486$$

The results show that the bond financed deficit has a significant coefficient, while the money financed deficit does not appear to have a significant effect on private investment. Both negatively affect private investment. Some support for the long-run money neutrality of the monetarists is therefore found, but not for the debt-neutrality of public debt literature. Bond financed debt not only has a larger *t*-ratio, it has a larger coefficient. A 10 percentage point increase in *BDEFY* will result in a 0.67 percentage print decline in private investment to GDP ratio. Bond financing thus appears not only to have been an important source of deficit financing, but also to have significantly affected private investment.

To capture the role of exchange rate policy on private investment in South Africa, we have used the rate of change in the real exchange rate

(*RERGR*). As mentioned earlier the exchange rate affects private investment through several channels (see Serven and Solimano, 1993). First, the exchange rate affects the supply price of capital goods, especially in countries where a significant portion of capital is imported. A depreciation or devaluation of the exchange rate also raises the cost of imported inputs, and is thus likely to have an adverse effect on private capital accumulation. Another negative impact of exchange rate changes on private investment works through the interest rate. A depreciation of the domestic currency raises the nominal and real interest rates, which affects the profitability of private investment. On the other hand, a depreciation increases the price of tradeables relative to non-tradeables, and may therefore stimulate private investment, especially in exportables. If there is a positive correlation of profits across sectors, an investment boom in the exportable goods sector may spill over into other sectors. Our results show that for South Africa, the exchange rate change has a negative but insignificant impact on private capital accumulation. Cardoso (1993) finds a similar result for a group of Latin American countries.

In addition to the real exchange rate change, changes in the terms of trade as a determinant of private investment in South Africa have also been included. Cardoso (1993) argues that for developing countries, terms of trade changes affect private investment through two channels. The first, which she calls the 'Manaus Opera House effect', is where a deterioration of terms of trade reduces real income and the profitability of the export sector, thereby negatively affecting private capital accumulation. Secondly, adverse terms of trade will worsen the current account, forcing the government to react by devaluation or tightening money supply. For South Africa, terms of trade changes have a positive impact on private investment, suggesting that deterioration of the terms of trade would reduce private investment. The result is not robust, however, and is sensitive to specification error. In a similar study for South Africa, Bleaney (1994) used the logarithm of terms of trade and found the current terms of trade to have a positive and significant effect on private investment.

Unit labour costs (*ULC*) have a strong, negative impact on private capital accumulation in South Africa. It is generally believed that high labour costs and low labour productivity contribute substantially to South Africa's economic problems. The regression results show that a 10 percentage point increase in the unit cost of labour will reduce the ratio of private investment to GDP by about 0.02%.

A post-1981 dummy was also included to capture the effects of a number of policy shifts. First the interest rate was sharply increased, reversing the negative real interest rate trends of the 1970s. Secondly, the market was let to largely determine the exchange rate. Last, in the 1980s, there was also an accentuation of political uncertainty and instability. The dummy variable is generally positive and statistically significant, though this result is not robust.

Uncertainty and private investment

Recent studies have shown that uncertainty plays a very important role in private sector investment decision-making. This is because of the nature of the investment process, that investment takes time to build and that it is partly irreversible. Where the future is uncertain, firms delay taking decisions to invest, waiting until the source of uncertainty is resolved, or choose to invest in an information gathering process to reduce or eliminate the source of uncertainty (Bernanke, 1983; Pindyck, 1991; Rodrik, 1991). In the econometric estimation, we will concentrate on two sources of uncertainty. First is the uncertainty associated variability of volatility of standard macroeconomic variables that affect private investment, such as inflation or GDP growth. The proxies used to represent macroeconomic uncertainty are the rate of inflation (*INFL*) and its variance (*VARINF*). The rate of inflation is measured as a percentage change in the consumer price index, while inflation variability is the average squared deviation of values from the mean.

The second source of uncertainty arises from time or dynamic inconsistency problems. This is because investment depends a great deal on what Keynes called the 'animal spirits' of investors. A belief by firms that current policy will not be sustainable may cause them to postpone their investment decisions, resulting in a drop in current investment levels. Rodrik (1991) has studied this problem in connection with the economic reform programmes, and found that those programmes that emphasise policy stability and sustainability are likely to be more successful than those that emphasise only liberalisation measures. To measure the stability, consistency and credibility of public policy, we have used three proxies: exchange rate, terms of trade variability, and the foreign debt scaled down by GDP. The foreign debt to GDP ratio (*FDEBTY*) also captures the debt overhang effect, which acts as an anticipated foreign tax on current and future incomes.

The results show that the macroeconomic and policy uncertainty variables have the expected negative signs, suggesting that uncertainty exerts a negative effect on private investment in South Africa. The level of inflation gives the most consistent result, and when it was omitted from the estimation, a number of variables became insignificant. In a number of studies the level of inflation has been used to indicate macroeconomic uncertainty, since high inflation is usually accompanied by high volatility (Oshikoya, 1994). The regression results in Table 4.7 show that in South Africa, a one percentage increase in the rate of inflation reduced *PIY* by about 0.02%. The results also show that the variance of inflation (*VARINF*) and the variance of the real exchange rate (*VARRER*), although negative, are statistically insignificant. The measure for terms of trade uncertainty is strongly significant compared with the terms trade level. This result suggests that with the exception of the inflation rate, it is the variability or volatility of prices that affects private investment in South Africa.

Table 4.7 Uncertainty and private investment in South Africa

VARS	EQN 6	EQN 7	EQN 8	EQN 9
CONST	–1.8268	–1.6565	–1.8301	1.8008
	(–5.58)	(–4.02)	(–5.47)	(–5.44)
LPIN	0.4208	0.3804	0.4211	0.4174
	(10.89)	(8.21)	(10.56)	(10.48)
ΔYt	–0.0018	0.0036	–0.0017	–0.0011
	(–0.81)	(1.09)	(–0.87)	(–0.55)
LGIY	0.1632	0.2016	0.1628	0.1673
	(4.11)	(4.61)	(3.98)	(4.17)
RIR	–0.0026	–0.0024	–0.0029	–0.0036
	(–0.86)	(–0.55)	(–1.06)	(–1.59)
INFL	–0.0221	–0.0163	–0.0220	–0.0223
	(–6.17)	(–3.04)	(–6.14)	(–6.40)
VARINF	–0.0114	–0.0089	–	–
	(–0.1?)	(–1.82)		
VARRER	–0.0003	–0.0005	–0.0003	–
	(–0.41)	(–0.75)	(–0.57)	
VARTOT	0.0008	0.0014	0.0008	0.0009
	(1.82)	(2.37)	(2.39)	(2.40)
GDEFY	–0.0192	–	–0.0188	–0.186
	(–3.33)		(–3.77)	(–3.80)
LDEBTY	–0.00011	–0.00012	–0.00011	–0.0001
	(–4.99)	(–4.07)	(–5.28)	(–5.19)
DUM1	0.0507	0.0798	0.0532	0.0649
	(1.00)	(1.17)	(1.14)	(1.58)
R^2	0.9211	0.8864	0.9210	0.9203
LogLikelihood	67.71	61.33	67.69	67.55
F-test	24.40	18.7	27.97	32.09
DW	1.09	1.26	1.10	1.15

Notes
The dependent variable is the log of real private investment: GDP.
The *t*-statistics are in parentheses. Definitions of the variables are contained in the Appendix.

As expected, foreign debt and the budget deficit ratio exert a negative effect on private investment in South Africa. The debt ratio is significantly negative, especially when *VARINF* and *VARRER* are excluded. This suggests that both uncertainty and debt overhang effects operate in South Africa. Similar results have been confirmed by other empirical studies (see Ozler and Rodrik, 1992). The effect is small, however, as the results show that for every percentage point increase in the debt ratio, the investment increased by up to 0.0001%. The budget deficit ratio remains significant even when the uncertainty variables are included. This indicates that both policy uncertainty effects and crowding out of private investment operate in South Africa. The high demands placed on the budget, especially in the 1980s and 1990s, and viewed against the backdrop of low and sometimes negative economic growth rates, put a question mark on the ability of fiscal authorities to sustain fiscal deficits without causing serious macroeconomic problems. That is, the negative effect of the budget deficit ratio presents an important policy dilemma: reducing the fiscal deficit would reduce macroeconomic uncertainty and thus improve the private investment climate, but lowering the deficit by cutting government investment spending may be detrimental to private investment.

5. Policy implications and suggestions

The framework used in this study has been useful to analyse investment behaviour in South Africa and has shed some light on the potential determinants of private investment in the future. However, the policy implications and policy suggestions discussed here are based on a more flexible approach, to take full account of South Africa's reintegration into a competitive global economy during the early 1990s. Moreover, reminiscent of the past decade, macroeconomic and political uncertainty will yet again be an overriding factor in determining private investment behaviour. The newly elected government will have to display full commitment to macroeconomic stability and growth-inducing policies that largely conform with international standards. Yet, although commitment is important, uncertainty as a determinant of private investment behaviour will largely depend on the government's ability to implement macroeconomic stabilisation measures on a sustainable basis. The results of this study suggest that sound fiscal and monetary policies create a stable macroeconomic environment necessary for increased private investment and sustainable economic growth. The South African government should therefore avoid policies that result in high inflation, spiralling fiscal deficits, an over-valued exchange rate and unmanageable foreign debt levels.

The policy regime in South Africa is largely dominated by the BOP constraint, so that policies designed to deal with the balance of payments will also influence private investment behaviour and growth. During 1994, the BOP constraint was somewhat eased with net capital inflows, albeit of a more short-term nature. At the time of writing (June 1996), the government announced its macroeconomic policy document, which among others stipulated total commitment to a stable macroeconomic environment. This is an important step in the right direction since it is not necessarily the absolute level of macroeconomic variables that creates uncertainty, but rather political uncertainty that induces perceptions of macroeconomic instability in the future.

If South Africa is seen as an attractive haven for foreign investment, capital inflows will ease the BOP constraint and induce higher private investment levels. A reduction in inflationary pressure emanating from capital inflows will ultimately lead to lower interest rate levels, while at the same time it will be possible to maintain positive interest rates at lower nominal levels. Positive real interest rates attained at lower nominal rates will, in turn, accomplish an important twofold function. First, it will ensure allocative efficiency as stressed by the financial liberalisation school. Secondly, lower nominal rates will reduce the user cost of capital, which is particularly beneficial to small business enterprises.

To support the fundamental propositions in the government's macro-economic policy document, fiscal authorities will have to adhere to sound financing principles. Private saving should be used in the most efficient manner, i.e. as an injection into the income stream rather than an outflow, as has been the case since 1984. As stipulated in the government's macroeconomic policy document, the privatisation of state assets is a high priority. This will undoubtedly contribute to greater fiscal efficiency and at the same time generate more funds for capital expenditure. Additional funds generated from privatisation will enable the government to finance current expenditure with current revenue, thus accumulating more funds available for investment spending. In the process, investment spending will unequivocally stimulate aggregate demand and henceforth comple-ment private investment. Finally, fiscal policy that is bound to prudent financing principles will induce a more manageable public debt burden and hence reduce upward pressure on interest rates.

Although government investment expenditure has a future role to play in stimulating private investment, an improvement in South Africa's export performance is likely to be the driving force behind private investment. During the isolation years, public investment played an important role in stimulating domestic demand for private investment. With South Africa's reintegration into the world economy and affiliation with the World Trade Organisation, the priority is to become more export oriented. A significant and sustainable expansion in private investment will thus ultimately depend on the successful transformation from an inward to a more outward looking economy. Furthermore, with international capital being more mobile than ever, an export-oriented economy can effectively insulate South Africa against external shocks and reduce its dependency on capital inflows, thus avoiding painful internal adjustments such as high real interest rates.

Appendix: definition of variables used in the regression

$LPIY$ = log of real private investment to GDP. Data on private investment were obtained from various issues of the South African Reserve Bank *Quarterly Review* (SARBQR) and consist of private business enterprise investments.

$LGIY$ = log of public investment to GDP. Public investment consists of public business enterprises, public corporations and general government investment. The data were also obtained from the SARBQR.

ΔY_t = average of annual real GDP growth rate, and was obtained from SARBQR and from the *International Financial Statistics (IFS) Year Book*, 1995.

RIR = real interest rate, measured as the difference between the nominal lending rate and the rate of inflation (INFL). Data on the lending rate and inflation rate were obtained from the IFS (1995).

ΔDCR = changes in real domestic credit, and was obtained from the IFS (1995).

$GDFEY$ = fiscal deficit to GDP ratio. The data on the fiscal deficit were obtained from various issues of the SARBQR. In the estimation, the GDFEY ratio was multiplied by minus unity for ease of interpretation.

ULC = log of the yearly indexes of the unit labour costs for the private economy. The data were obtained from the National Productivity Institute Report, 1995.

$TOTGR$ = rate of change of the terms of trade as compiled by the IFS (1995).

$RERGR$ = rate of change in the real exchange rate. The real exchange rate was measured by the US dollar/rand nominal exchange rate index multiplied by the ratio of US to South African price indexes.

$LDEBTY$ = log of total external debt outstanding at the end of the year divided by GDP. Data on external debt were obtained from the SARBQR.

ϕ = macroeconomic uncertainty variables VARINF, VARRER and VARTOT, which measure the coefficient of variation of inflation, the real exchange rate and terms of trade, respectively.

Notes

1. For the purpose of this chapter public investment is divided into two components: investment undertaken by parastatals and investment by the general government. Parastatal investment refers to investment by public business enterprises and public corporations (see Fallon and de Silva, 1994).
2. Kahn (1987), for example, estimated that for every 1% rise in domestic expenditure, manufactured imports will rise by 2.16%.
3. The investment literature can be categorised in different ways. For example, Chirinko (1993) has argued that models appearing in the literature on investment can be divided into two broad groups, depending on whether they treat dynamics implicitly or explicitly. Using a different categorisation, Rama (1993) classified models of private investment into the neoclassical model, the accelerator model and Tobin's Q model.
4. Earlier World Bank research on parastatal investment in South Africa suggests that parastatals also respond to economically relevant variables (see Fallon and De Silva, 1994).
5. A positive real interest rate may ensure that investors earn a return in excess of the inflation rate, while the opposite is true for a negative real interest rate (Botha, 1986).
6. During the period 1961–91 the private sector recorded an output to capital ratio of 0.6, with a corresponding ratio of 0.2 for public sectors (Fallon and de Silva, 1994).

References

Abedian, I. 1992 'Fiscal policy and economic growth'. In I. Abedian and B. Standish, eds, *Economic Growth in South Africa*. Cape Town: Oxford University Press.

Aizenman, J. and N. P. Marion. 1993. 'Macroeconomic uncertainty and private investment'. *Economic Letters*, vol. 41: 207–10.

Barro, R. 1991. 'Economic growth in a cross-section of countries'. *Quarterly Journal of Economics*, vol. 106: 407–44.

Bernanke, B. 1983. 'Irreversibility, uncertainty, and cyclical investment'. *Quarterly Journal of Economics*, vol. 98: 85–106.

Bleaney, M. F. 1994. 'Political uncertainty and private investment in South Africa'. *The South African Journal of Economics*, vol. 62, no. 3: 188–97.

Botha, D. J. J. 1986. 'Interest rates as an instrument of monetary policy in South Africa'. *South African Journal of Economics*, 54 (1): 41–54.

Cardoso, E. 1993. 'Private investment in Latin America'. *Economic Development and Cultural Change*, vol. 41, no. 4 (July): 833–48.

Chirinko, R. S. 1993. 'Business fixed investment spending: modelling strategies, empirical results, and policy implications'. *Journal of Economic Literature*, vol. XXXI: 1875–1911.

Clarke, R. 1996. 'Equilibrium interest rates and financial liberalization in developing countries'. *Journal of Development Studies*, 32(3): 391–413.

De Kock, G. 1989. 'Economic growth and foreign debt: the South African case'. In P. A. Black and B. E. Dollery, eds, *Leading Issues in South African Macroeconomics*. Johannesburg: Southern Book Publishers.

De Wet, G. L. 1994. 'The RDP and a structural problem in the South African economy'. *South African Journal of Economics*, 62(4): 307–32.

Dornbusch, R. and Fischer, S. 1994. *Macroeconomics*. USA: McGraw-Hill.

Dowd, K. 1994. 'The cost of inflation and disinflation'. *Cato Journal*, 14(2): 305–31.

Fallon, P. and de Silva, A. 1994. *South Africa: economic performance and policies*. Discussion Paper 7. Southern Africa Department: Washington, DC.

Greene, J. and D. Villanueva. 1991. 'Private investment in developing countries: an empirical analysis'. *IMF Staff Papers*, vol. 38: 33–58.

Hadjimichael, M. T., D. Ghura, M. Muhleisen, R. Nord and E. M. Ucer. 1995. 'Sub-Saharan Africa: growth, savings, and investment, 1986–93.' *Occasional Paper 118*, IMF, Washington, DC.

Heyns, J. v. d. S. 1995. 'The dimension of government saving in South African fiscal policy'. *South African Journal of Economics*, 63(3): 307–31.

Hunt, D. 1989. *Economic Theories of Development: An Analysis of Competing Paradigms*. London: Harvester Wheatsheaf.

International Monetary Fund (IMF). 1995. *International Financial Statistics (IFS) Yearbook*.

Kahn, B. 1987. 'Import penetration and import demands in the South African economy'. *South African Journal of Economics*, 55(3): 238–48.

Kahn, B. 1989. 'Exchange controls and exchange rate policy in the South African economy'. In P. A. Black and B. E. Dollery, eds, *Leading Issues in South African Macroeconomics*. Johannesburg: Southern Book Publishers.

Kahn, B. 1991. 'Budgeting for a future South Africa: Fiscal policy and the constraints on deficit spending'. Economic Policy Research Project, no. 3, University of the Western Cape.

Kahn, B. 1993. 'An overview of exchange rate policy in South Africa'. In P. H. Baker, A. Borraine and W. Krafchik, eds, *South Africa in the World Economy in the 1990's*. Cape Town: David Philip.

Khan, M. and M. Kumar. 1994. 'Public investment and the growth process in developing countries'. IMF Working Paper Draft, Washington, DC.

Kock, A. D. and J. H. Meijer. 1992. 'Reserve bank accommodation'. In L. J. Fourie, H. B. Falkena and W. J. Kok, eds, *Fundamentals of the South African Financial System*. Johannesburg: Southern Book Publishers.

Mariano, R. S. 1982. 'Analytical small-sample distribution theory in econometrics: The simultaneous equation case'. *International Economic Review*, vol. 23: 503–33.

McKinnon, R. I. 1973. *Money and Capital in Economic Development*. Washington, DC: The Brookings Institution.

Meijer, J. H. 1992. 'Instruments of monetary policy'. In L. J. Fourie, H. B. Falkena and W. J. Kok, eds, *Fundamentals of the South African Financial System*. Johannesburg: Southern Book Publishers.

Mohr, P. and C. Rogers, 1988. *Macroeconomics*. Johannesburg: Lexicon Publishers.

Morriset, J. 1993. 'Does financial liberalization really improve private investment in developing countries?'. *Journal of Development Economics*, 40: 133–50.

Oshikoya, T. W. 1994. 'Macroeconomic determinants of domestic private investment in Africa: an empirical analysis'. *Economic Development and Cultural Change*, vol. 42: 573–96.

Ozler, S. and D. Rodrik, 1992. 'External shocks, politics and private investment: some theory and empirical evidence'. *NBER Working Paper Series No. 3960*.

Phillips, P. C. B. 1983. 'Exact small sample theory in the simultaneous equation model'. *Handbook of Econometrics*, vol. 1. Amsterdam: North-Holland Publishing Co.

Pindyck, R. 1991. 'Irreversibility, uncertainty and investment'. *Journal of Economic Literature*, vol. 29: 1110–49.

Rama, M. 1993. 'Empirical investment equations for developing countries'. In L. Serven and A. Solimano, eds, *Striving for Growth after Adjustment: The Role of Capital Formation*, The World Bank, Washington, DC.

Rittenberg, L. 1991. 'Investment spending and interest rate policy: the case of financial liberalization in Turkey'. *Journal of Development Studies*, 27(2): 151–67.

Rodrik, D. 1991. 'Policy uncertainty and private investment in developing countries'. *Journal of Development Economics*, vol. 36: 229–42.

Schmidt-Hebbel, K., L. Serven and A. Solimano. 1994. 'Saving, investment and growth in developing countries'. *Policy Research Working Paper*, No. 1382. Washington, DC: The World Bank.

Serven, L. and A. Solimano. 1993. 'Debt crisis, adjustment policies and capital formation in developing countries: Where do we stand?' *World Development*, vol. 21, no. 1: 127–40.

Shapiro, M. 1986. 'Investment, output and the cost of capital'. *Brookings Papers on Economic Activity*, vol. 1.

Shaw, Edward S. 1973. *Financial Deepening in Economic Development*. New York: Oxford University Press.

Smit, B. W. 1991. 'The variability of the rand and South African exports'. *Studies in Economics and Econometrics*, 15(2): 19–29.

South African Reserve Bank (SARB). 1994a. 'Public finance statistics of South Africa 1946–1993'. Supplement, SARB *Quarterly Bulletin*. Mar.

SARB. 1994b. 'South Africa's national accounts 1946–1993'. Supplement, SARB *Quarterly Bulletin*. June.

SARB. 1994c. 'Labour, price and other selected economic indicators of South Africa 1923–1993'. Supplement, SARB *Quarterly Bulletin*. Sept.

SARB. 1995. *Quarterly Bulletin*, no. 198. Dec.

Standish, B. and O. Beelders. 1991. 'Do South African fiscal deficits matter?' *Studies in Economics and Econometrics*, 15(2): 1–17.

Van der Walt, S. J. 1992. 'Public debt management'. In L. J. Fourie, H. B. Falkena and W. J. Kok, eds, *Fundamentals of the South African Financial System*. Johannesburg: Southern Book Publishers.

Van Der Walt, J. S. and G. L. De Wet. 1993. 'The constraining effects of limited foreign capital inflow on the economic growth of South Africa'. *South African Journal of Economics*, 61(1): 3–12.

Whittaker, J. 1992. 'Monetary policy for economic growth'. In I. Abedian and B. Standish, eds, *Economic Growth in South Africa*. Cape Town: Oxford University Press.

5
Industrial and Energy Policy: A Partial Review

Ben Fine

1. Introduction

This chapter starts with a review of three firmly established approaches to industrial policy that have been highly influential in South Africa: those from the World Bank, the Industrial Strategy Project (ISP) and the Monitor Group. Paradoxically, although the first of these is probably the least respected, it is almost certainly the most important. For it is like an alter ego, informing even those alternatives that fundamentally break with it. The market is presumed to work unless you can show otherwise; it is more a matter of addressing the balance between the state and the market, and less one of unravelling the formation and representation of economic and political interests through both of these institutions.[1] In practice, if not by necessity, it is suggested that each of these approaches has misjudged the structure and dynamic of the South African economy and each places undue optimism in policies that are liable to have limited impact in generating employment and meeting basic needs.

An alternative assessment of the South African economy as a minerals–energy complex is very briefly outlined in the third section. This is used in the fourth section to emphasise the continuity in industrial policy that has marked the first year of the Reconstruction and Development Programme (RDP), a result of the continuity in institutional structure and functioning. Such a focus also allows some insight into the potential that has existed and, in certain instances, has been taken in making breaks with past policy. The concluding remarks offer some strategic alternatives for industrial policy.

2. Debating industrial policy

Broadly, three different approaches have been most prominent in setting recent debate about South African industrial policy. They emanate from the World Bank, from the Industrial Strategy Project and, most recently of all, from the Monitor Group. While they differ considerably, they do have one common characteristic – each is informed by an analytical framework that was developed without reference to South Africa itself. This might be considered a strength, given the elaboration of general principles without their being unduly prejudiced by their specific application to South Africa. In part, this depends, first, on the validity and usefulness of the principles themselves as well as, secondly, on the extent to which they are, indeed, appropriate in practice to South Africa. Neither of these conditions is met by these approaches. As a consequence, because the fit between the theory and the facts of South African industrialisation has often proved uncomfortable within these approaches; one or the other has often been sacrificed in the examination and formulation of industrial policy. This has implied the necessity for considerable flexibility and ingenuity in the application of the various approaches, giving rise to nuances that the brief overview offered here is incapable of elaborating. In short, we hope to provide a fair if rough review.

The World Bank (1993) approach focuses on two related issues – the need to eliminate distortions in prices whether as inputs (capital costs and labour, for example) or as outputs (protection) and the need to reduce state intervention more generally. It argues that the high level of capital intensity in some sectors of South African industry, such as heavy chemicals, is due to artificially depressed costs of capital and that manufacturing weakness, more generally, is due to protection from international competition. In addition, it otherwise takes the high levels of unemployment as indicative of real wages that are already high enough. But there is an acceptance that inequality in provision of infrastructure, including education and skills, has reinforced other aspects of apartheid and inhibited the emergence of small and medium-sized enterprises (SMEs). Interestingly, the World Bank has not adopted a strong stance on privatisation, especially in the form of denationalisation, and has even accepted that the public sector might crowd in rather than crowd out private sector investment. Its emphasis has been on getting the prices of capital and labour 'right' and eroding protection.

The weaknesses of this approach lie in its central commitment to the notion that the market works and, where it does not, policy should be aimed at conforming with the market. As an explanation for successful industrialisation, as in the East Asian NICs, this has been shown to be woefully inadequate.[2] In the case of South Africa, it is particularly inappropriate since much of the economy's success has been built on state intervention on behalf of, and in coordination with, large-scale corporate capital, as in Escom, Iscor, Sasol, Transnet, Armscor, etc. It is not necessary to argue that these corporations represent an optimal mobilisation and use of resources. But neither can there be a presumption that in their absence, and with appropriate undistorted prices, these huge capital investments would have been replaced by a more labour-intensive and internationally competitive manufacturing sector. The evidence for such a counterfactual is simply non-existent even if sense could be made of it.

In addition, there is a serious neglect in the World Bank approach of the political economy of industrial policy. The growth of capital intensive industry within South Africa has reflected the formation of large-scale private corporate capital and the representation of its interests through the state. These interests and their corresponding economic power cannot simply be wished away by virtue of the election of a democratic government whether it be committed to undistorted prices or not.[3]

The ISP (1995) approach has drawn its inspiration from the idea that we now inhabit a new post-Fordist world of flexible specialisation. While concerned with economy-wide factors such as industrial relations, technology and corporate monopolisation, the ISP focus has primarily been on the restructuring of individual sectors towards best practice in the new forms of flexible production.[4] Rogerson (1994) provides a thorough review of the applicability of the flexible specialisation (FS) paradigm to South Africa. Fine (1995c) presents a critical response, emphasising how little of the South African economy can be understood in these terms and how limited will be the benefits of an FS strategy in terms of employment creation where it is applicable. Fine notes as well that the analysis has deep roots in a reversed dualism between the large-scale and the small-scale sectors, in which the latter is now taken as the harbinger of modernisation, requiring a compromise in principle between capital and labour that in practice is liable to lead to an erosion of wages and working conditions as flexible enterprises struggle to survive.

The focus here, then, is more explicitly on how the ISP approach has unfolded in addressing South African industrialisation. One of its strengths is that it has highlighted the need to examine vertical integration in formulating industrial policy, to consider the filière, to use its vernacular. This has, however, been married to the FS approach of seeking market niches and a corresponding search for international competitiveness through high product quality and variety. It necessarily leads to a pessimistic view of the potential for employment creation through manufacturing – output will come from higher productivity and serve fragmented and competitive markets.

The logic of this approach is questionable, for there is undoubtedly within South Africa an enormous *domestic* market for standardised products to serve the basic needs of the majority of the population – in housing, clothing, food, energy, infrastructure, etc. Many of these products can be based on labour-intensive methods using standardised production and drawing on the existing strengths of the economy. Moreover, insofar as an FS approach is adopted to serve international niche markets, *and* a domestic elite, it can have the effect of crowding out the provision of cheaper, standardised products with the potential to support basic needs including employment.[5] In other words, it is not simply that the FS approach is likely to be of limited scope even where it is worth pursuing to meet market niches and international competitiveness, but it can have the effect of crowding out the potential for more labour-intensive, cheaper, standardised production. Paradoxically, this is precisely what used to be argued about the apartheid economy with its division between white elite consumerism and black impoverishment!

These negative aspects of its policies, were they to succeed, have been recognised by the ISP. Since only an elite of workers can benefit, there is a danger of that elite being unduly rewarded by virtue of their trade union organisation and attachment to profitable firms and sectors. Consequently, a national accord and multi-tier bargaining are necessary to control their wages and conditions and to prevent them from setting standards that would render other employment uncompetitive where levels of quality and productivity are not matched. More positively, the needs of those excluded from the FS strategy are incorporated through a mixture of training and education, promotion of SMEs, and the unbundling of conglomerates that are perceived to have excluded SMEs from access to markets. These initiatives also have the rhetorical advantage of being designed to advance the interests of the black population in both employment and opportunities for entrepreneurship. However, and this is not unique to the ISP approach, the deserved attention to training, SMEs and competition policy cannot serve as a substitute for mainstream employment creation in the economy more generally. Indeed, providing training without employment, promoting SMEs that are not commercially viable and substituting competition for more broadly based industrial policy can, at best, be tokenism and, at worst, counterproductive.

The Monitor Group's analytical framework was previously developed in Porter's (1989) *The Competitive Advantage of Nations*. It has prompted a world-wide business consultancy. It, too, emphasises vertical integration in terms of the focus on industrial 'clusters' of related industries and activities. It rejects the World Bank's exclusive emphasis on relative prices and stresses the importance of creating comparative advantage rather than relying on it. As an approach, it is stronger on terminological innovation than analytical content. It is organised around the notion of the 'diamond' (i.e. four) factors – inputs, demand, firm strategy, structure and rivalry, and relations to related and supporting industries (clusters). Consequently, the approach has been recognised as little more than an extremely flexible descriptive framework.[6]

Not surprisingly, academic response to the Monitor approach has combined a mixture of contempt and envy, with admiration reserved for the wealth of descriptive material. For Miller (1990: 103–6), there is 'codifying the obvious', 'cutesy mnemonics', 'a book devoid of original insights', 'mumbo-jumbo' and by way of the study's conclusion, 'a taxi driver made pretty much the same point to me as I was coming back from the airport the other day'. For Thurow (1990: 95), 'Porter preaches the economic equivalence of the survival of the fittest'; for Jones (1991: 352–4), there is 'oversimplification or even banality' and we are liable to 'shudder at some aspects'. Arndt (1991: 335) notes, 'Unlike an abstract model, limited by its nature to a few causal factors, Porter's explanation of industrial success seems to encompass virtually everything. . . . It would be easy to criticise . . . for describing everything and explaining nothing. This is correct but not surprising given that Porter has chosen an inductive approach.' Also particularly notable is the facile periodisation of industrial development, with its plagiarised overtones of the modernisation teleology adopted from the long since discredited stages of economic growth associated with W. W. Rostow (Monitor, 1995, Appendix, p. 11):

> There are four stages of national competitive development: factor-driven, investment-driven, innovation-driven, and wealth-driven. All nations begin at the factor-driven stage. Here, virtually all the nation's internationally successful industries draw their advantage almost solely from basic factors such as natural resources or low cost labour. In the investment-driven stage, a nation and its firm actively invest in factor upgrading and in modern, efficient plants and methods, normally based on foreign technology. . . . In the innovation-driven stage, all four determinants are in place and work together to foster continuous innovation and upgrading in a wide range of industries in the economy. . . . The fourth, or wealth-driven stage, is a stage of decline. In this stage, vitality ebbs and redistribution of wealth, rather than its creation, becomes the focus.

Despite these apparent analytical deficiencies, the specific application of the approach to South Africa has had some merit. It has exposed the lack of vertical integration and coordination, for example, in a variety of industries, as well as product fragmentation within the car industry. But very rarely have novel insights emerged, with limited original research and ample support to that fastest growing of South African industries, the employment of domestic and foreign consultants. What Monitor (1995: 8) does provide is some ballast against the market-led view, with a designated role for the state to intervene in order to enhance the Diamond:[7]

> Government's role is inherently partial, and it succeeds only when working in tandem with favourable underlying conditions in the Diamond. Government policies that succeed are those that create an environment in which companies can gain competitive advantage rather than those that involve government directly in the process. Government's role is strongest as a catalyst and challenger. It is to encourage, or even push, companies to raise their aspirations and move to higher levels of competitive performance, even though this process may be unpleasant and difficult. Government's job is to make firms feel wanted but in need of improvement, not to forge cozy business-government "partnerships", relax pressures on industry, or seek to eliminate risks.

Despite the evidence to the contrary from the NICs, however, this places the state in a secondary position to private enterprise. What is more important than state or private ownership is 'rivalry', according to Roberts and Green (1995: 38):[8]

> Rivalry triggers product rationalisation, greater manufacturing efficiency, and price competition.

Almost inevitably, despite a cautionary approach to privatisation, the Monitor position is one of reliance on market forces and private profitability and against the state's strategic planning and development of industry.[9] What this fails to recognise is the extent to which the state has been instrumental in creating many of the strengths of the South African economy, even if on the basis of the inequalities and iniquities attached to the apartheid system.

On these latter issues, and those of politics and power more generally, the Monitor approach has been remarkably silent. Although the Diamond is intended to construe the economic performance in terms of a system, it embodies an extremely limited understanding of the socioeconomic system inherited from apartheid. Apart from the deeply embedded and systemic features of racist oppression and inequality – which go far beyond the boundaries even of an unpolished Diamond – the system of corporate power, its global operations and its interaction with a bloated financial system are scarcely recognised.[10] In short, the Monitor approach provides more or less good business advice for enhancing the economic performance of particular sectors. As Thurow (1990: 96) comments on Porter (1989):

> We all know we should consume less and invest more in education, research and development, plants and equipment, and infrastructure. But we don't. We all know that the US financial system places a dangerous emphasis on short-term profits. But we don't change the system.

The same must be said of the Monitor studies of South Africa. Whatever the merits of their proposals, the political economy of implementation is notable for its absence.

3.   Towards an alternative

In the report of the Macroeconomic Research Group (MERG) (1993), the policy stances adopted represented a compromise between inputs from two essentially incompatible positions. The first derived from the work of the ISP. The second position arose from the research of Fine and Rustomjee.[11] It argued against much of the conventional wisdom that informed both the ISP project and the greater part of the literature on South Africa's industrialisation.[12] The latter has almost universally been seen as arising over the past 70 years out of import substituting industrialisation (ISI) as a consequence of freely given protection for consumer goods industries. These have primarily served white consumers and promoted profitable, but internationally uncompetitive, indigenous capitalists, generally presumed to include politically favoured Afrikaners.[13]

By contrast, Fine and Rustomjee (1997) emphasise the presence of what they term a minerals–energy complex (MEC) at the heart of the South African economy. Quite apart from its own core sectors in mining and energy, the MEC has been primarily responsible for the extent and form taken by South Africa's industrialisation. For it is the immediate, downstream activities from mining and energy – in iron and steel, metal processing and heavy chemicals, for example – that have been most prominent. To a large extent, this has been disguised by the traditional way of constructing national statistics in which manufacturing has been separated from primary production even though the two have been intimately connected with one another. This has then led to aggregate figures for primary, non-agricultural production and for manufacturing that give the impression that the latter, easily and erroneously identified with consumer goods, has become relatively more important. Exactly the opposite is the case.

Fine and Rustomjee (1997) also tie their different view of the form taken by South Africa's industrialisation with a broader political economy. They argue that the MEC has been built around the small number of large-scale, corporate capitals that have always dominated the economy over the past century. They have been integrally coordinated through state policy and with the large-scale state corporations such as Escom, Iscor, Sats (now Transnet), Sasol and Armscor. Further, the postwar period has witnessed both the incorporation of Afrikaner-based ownership into the MEC and the extensive conglomeration of corporate capital over the entire economy, with a particularly prominent role played by mergers, acquisitions, interlocking and pyramid forms of ownership, and parallel developments and control in the financial sector.

These differences of interpretation might now only seem to be of academic or historical interest. But this is wrong for three reasons. First, even where there is common agreement about many negative features of the economy – the lack of development of small-scale business, monopolisation, low levels of investment, relative lack of capacity in intermediate and capital goods, poor export performance in manufacturing, the negative impact of sanctions and social instability, the low levels of skills of the workforce, and the inappropriately high levels of capital-intensity in many sectors for a labour surplus economy – these will be interpreted differently in terms of their causes, significance and solutions. Secondly, the Government of National Unity (GNU) is faced with an industrial sector with a particular dynamic and a particular set of economic and political interests with which it is forced to compromise. Thirdly, the GNU has inherited a set of private and public institutions that, in view of the economy's history, are inappropriate for the formulation and implementation of alternative policies.

Against this background, the specific proposals for industrial policy in the Reconstruction and Development Programme itself are extremely weak. Apart from acknowledging the apparent necessity to adjust to a more liberal trade regime without undue disruption, it recognises the excessive concentration of economic power in the hands of a few whites. The main goal is to increase investment and employment. But concrete proposals are few and far between: small, micro and medium enterprises (SMMEs), will be promoted; monopoly pricing in vertically integrated production linkages will be investigated along with antitrust actions; parastatal mandates will be reviewed together with the lines of account-ability to their responsible ministries; and privatisation proposals will be reviewed and reversed where against the public interest.

4. The institutional context

Over the short life of the GNU, these limited policy perspectives within the RDP have, if anything, been even further weakened. It is not simply that the commitment to public ownership, for example, has been further eroded and even reversed, with privatisation erroneously seen as a potential means by which to fund the RDP.[14] Rather, the RDP has been divorced from industrial and other areas of economic policy and increasingly reduced to measures traditionally associated with the welfare state.[15] This raises the issue of who is deciding and making industrial policy if it is not being driven by the RDP. It is here that the institutional structures carried over from the apartheid regime have continued to be important.

But, first, it is necessary to consider what constitutes industrial policy before its practitioners can be identified.[16] At one extreme, industrial policy tends to be reduced to a single issue. This figures prominently in the conventional wisdom concerning South Africa's ISI. According to the Industrial Development Corporation (IDC, 1990: 1), the problems of poor industrial performance have been due to tariff policies:

> For almost 70 years, the industrial development policy of successive governments was based on import replacement.

Accordingly, almost as if as a matter of terminological convenience (p. 1):

> In this report the terms 'trade policy' and 'industrial policy' are used synonymously and interchangeably.

A different example is provided by the *laissez-faire* stance, in which the issue of industrial policy is simply a matter of greater or lesser reliance on the market or the state, especially in terms of private versus public ownership, although many other issues around getting the prices right can also be incorporated. At other times, competition policy, and its counterpart in regulation, have been more prominent in industrial policy debates.

At the other extreme, it is apparent that as industrial performance is potentially influenced by any number of economic policies, the potential scope of industrial policy is more or less unlimited. This is true of specific interventions for particular sectors, for particular types of business (SMMEs for example), and for economy-wide factors whether these concern traditional macroeconomic policies (the level of aggregate demand, interest rates, the exchange rate, etc. all affect industrial performance) or infrastructural provisions (as in technology policy or education and training).

In this light, two important conclusions emerge. First, industrial policy and debate are liable to be profoundly ideological, with any particular definition shifting to accommodate particular policy stances. Thus, at the time that the IDC was defining industrial policy as trade policy, it had itself been responsible, possibly more than any other agency, for industrial policy through the extent of its own industrial investments in heavy industry.[17] Currently, the preoccupation with industrial policy as the promotion of SMMEs has the dual advantages of being associated with affirmative action and of displacing attention from its effective absence in the ownership and control of big business.[18] In short, industrial policy does not simply shift in response to changing circumstances and interests, its very definition is subject to change.

Secondly, this implies, from an analytical point of view, that the attempt should not be made to provide a general definition of industrial policy. Depending on the particular issue concerned, there will be differences in the underlying factors determining industrial performance and the scope of specific policies to influence outcomes. In the case of telecommunications, for example, it is more likely to be an issue of dealing with multinationals, joint ventures and technology transfer than in the case of the clothing industry where the problems concern wages, tariffs, appropriate choice of available technology, product mix and marketing, etc.

It follows that industrial policy will be heterogeneous and, consequently, will draw on a shifting range of policies that affect industrial performance but which do not necessarily fall directly or primarily under its rubric. In some respects, this strengthens the *laissez-faire* case against industrial intervention: this is that government is no better at picking industrial 'winners' than is the private sector. Against this, it has effectively been argued that government must not only pick winners, it must also coordinate highly variable conditions for their success. Indeed, the creation both of winners from which to pick (not just separating out the losers) and of the conditions for them to succeed is a pre-condition for successful industrial performance. Both theoretical and empirical evidence suggest that this is precisely where state intervention has proved essential.[19]

Industrial policy requires, then, both coherent objectives and the coordinated means by which to achieve them on a case-by-case basis. In some respects, postwar industrial development of South Africa can be considered a success in these terms. It was designed to strengthen large-scale Afrikaner capital and, after gold and energy price increases in the 1970s, to take advantage of these through the state-led expansion of economic activity around the MEC. The downside to this has been the continuing absence of long-term, coherent industrial policy in terms of a concerted promotion of a broader industrial base. Consequently, especially with the fall and stagnation of gold prices in the 1980s and the exhaustion of the most productive gold reserves,[20] industrial investment has stagnated alongside the sharp fall in public sector investment in the MEC parastatals.

Apart from these inherited contours in the industrial structure, the GNU has been faced with a corresponding institutional structure and mode of operation appropriate to past policy goals. This is characterised by a number of features. First, there are a number of different ministries whose policies have significant potential impact upon industrial policy, which is not, thereby, the sole preserve of the Department of Trade and Industry. This is so for the policies adopted by the Ministries of Employment, Transport, Public Enterprises, Communications, Mineral and Energy Affairs, and others. In addition, other bodies such as the Industrial Development Corporation (IDC), the Competition Board, and the Board on Trade and Tariffs are of considerable importance. Not surprisingly, given the view adopted here of the complexity and heterogeneity of industrial policy, responsibility for it is widely spread. One index of this is the division of public corporations between the various ministries, with Trade and Industry having no direct power over telecommunications (subject to Department of Post and Telecommunications) or electricity (Department of Public Enterprises).[21]

Secondly, each of these ministries is itself organised on a hierarchical basis with limited scope for rapid reform given the security of employment effectively granted in the constitutional settlement to the existing civil service, limited openings available for new posts and a lack of black employees with the necessary skills to fill the positions at the highest as well as at intermediate levels. This involves a considerable degree of policy inertia even within those departments in which there are African National Congress (ANC) appointments in ministerial and/or director-general posts. Within ministries and departments, there is limited initiative from below, limited potential for it to pass upward, and, similarly, limited innovation in the opposite direction in response to more progressively minded and reforming chains of command.

Thirdly, the implication is that policy preoccupation is primarily focused on intra-departmental matters and, even where it is not or cannot be, the potential for inter-departmental coordination and coherence is limited by the heterogeneity of intra-ministerial organisation, capacity and goals. It is worth dwelling on how this differs from the situation that prevailed previously, where the promotion of the minerals–energy complex was unambiguously hegemonic in policy-making. The role of the MEC was institutionally formalised with the creation of the Department of Mineral and Energy Affairs (DMEA), initially set up in 1980 by bringing together the previously separated departments covering energy and minerals (DMEA, 1980: 71):

> For the first time in the history of the public administrative system in South Africa all energy related functions are not only housed in one and the same department, but are housed in a department which is responsible for both the energy and the mineral policy of the country.

The concerted exercise of power is explicitly detailed – noting that the Energy Policy Committee (EPC), formed in 1974, had long been responsible for making policy recommendations to the cabinet (p. 71):

> The energy function of the former Department of Environmental Planning and Energy was incorporated into the newly formed Department of Mineral and Energy Affairs on 1st March 1980. This transfer of function included the transfer of the Energy Policy Committee. The Electricity Control Board, the Electricity Supply Commission (Escom), and SA Coal, Oil and Gas Corporation Ltd, (Sasol), were transferred from the former Department of Industries to the Department of Mineral and Energy Affairs on 1 June 1980 as were several other institutions and functions concerned with liquid fuels. Energy functions of the former Department of Commerce and Consumer Affairs relating to coal and liquid fuels were taken over on

7 October 1980 so that all energy functions in the Public Service, with the exception, at present, of the energy-related aspects of coal research, are now vested in the Department of Mineral and Energy Affairs.

The membership of the EPC had itself been made up from the leading public sector figures in energy (including transport, finance, commerce and industry) joined, in 1981 for example, by two private sector representatives (from Gypsum Industries Limited and Sentrachem Limited, both heavy energy users within the MEC and subject to major private corporate affiliate control) (DMEA, 1981: 60). Although there are new institutional developments in the GNU, none of these has the coordinating and executive powers so clearly exercised previously.[22]

Fourthly, in addition, governance under the apartheid system was heavily based on patronage and the capacity of the cabinet to define and coordinate common goals, even if these were to swing with the regime's crisis in the 1980s. This has been lost in the formation, in this context, of the inaptly named Government of National Unity. There is no unity of vision as to what constitutes industrial policy and no unity of purpose in formulating and implementing such policy. Certainly, this role has not and cannot be taken by the Reconstruction and Development Programme.

In short, there is an important institutional background against which progress in industrial policy under the RDP is to be assessed. It does include some dismantling of the previous institutional structures, goals and modes of operation, which exhibited some degree of coherence and coordination. But this has not been replaced by a well-developed alternative.

Not surprisingly, then, there is evidence of substantial policy continuities with the past. This can be highlighted with a number of illustrations. First, for industry lying outside the MEC, industrial policy had been highly dependent on seeking discretionary support in case of difficulties, usually in the form of added protection. As the newly appointed Director-General for Trade and Industry was to observe in his first Annual Report for the Department of Trade and Industry (DTI, 1994: 9):[23]

> My experience thus far as Director-General suggests that, if firms spent only half the resources and time that they are at present giving to lobbying for protective tariffs and the retention of GEIS benefits, and channelled the balance into a critical examination and international benchmarking of their productive processes, a growth rate of 5 per cent could be reached before 1999!

More recently, import protection has been supplemented by export incentives under the general export incentive scheme (GEIS) but has also been subject to the squeezes imposed by commitment to confirm to the newly negotiated GATT agreement.[24] The increasing abandonment, whether appropriate or not, of protected consumer goods industries to the vagaries of the world market, even if cushioned by adjustment programmes in the short run, is evidence of continuity with the past. For it highlights both the lack of broader industrial policy and the relative unimportance of these sectors to the economy and as economic interests. The policies being made may have changed, reflecting the general weakening of the economy and its capacity to offer support, but the way in which the policies are made and their focus have remained substantially unaltered. Indeed, such policy reforms were initiated prior to the formation of the GNU.

A continuity in policy, then, is to be found in the focus on tariffs and protection, even if these are themselves being eroded. Many of the reports, deliberating on what levels of support should continue, note the importance and/or lack of coordination in vertical integration – albeit recognising how pricing along the chain of activities is important to their considerations, as in textiles and clothing (PTG, 1994), where the protection of the one constitutes a cost for the other, and in synfuels (Arthur Andersen, 1995). Similarly, the fragmentation of the car industry into a large number of producers and models is treated as a constraint in setting tariffs rather than as a target of policy itself (BTT, 1995).

A second continuity with the past is the sustained momentum of economic activity organised around the MEC. This is highlighted in the Pre-GNU approval, and continuing ANC-support, of mega-projects, especially Alusaf and Columbus. Together these two investments, for aluminium smelting and stainless steel manufacture, respectively, were projected to absorb almost half of all manufacturing investment between 1993 and 1995 (32% and 15%, respectively) (Moritz, 1994: 36). Both have in common IDC support, dependence on cheap sources of electricity, which is in considerable excess supply, high capital intensity, and the promise of foreign exchange through exports and downstream, more labour-intensive industrial activity. To accrue in practice, these last benefits have to be targeted, in case foreign exchange is transferred abroad and vertically integrated activity does not materialise.

Current prospects for Columbus look bright because of the high price of stainless steel (*Financial Mail*, 17 Feb. 1995; Gleason, 1995). Its R3.5 billion investment is projected to make it the largest single-site stainless steel plant in the world, with an output of 600,000 tonnes at full production by the end of the century, 85% of it to be exported, adding R2.5 billion to GDP per annum and R18 billion in foreign exchange over the next 25 years. Some 6,400 temporary jobs have been created during construction and 8,000–10,000 in engineering and maintenance. However, at the same time, for a fraction of the cost at R100 million investment, Iscor is also expanding its stainless steel capacity by 480,000 tonnes. It has to be doubted whether this dual addition to capacity is justified, and has been examined and coordinated, in the light of uncertainty around export markets and the limited job creation involved for the huge investments in Columbus. Both investments have been supported by the IDC, which stepped in to fill the gap left by Taiwanese withdrawal from participation in the joint venture. This also had the added advantage of tax advantages in early depreciation write-offs.

Alusaf is a R6 billion investment at Richards Bay with the prices paid for electricity and alumina, the main inputs, subject to a sliding scale with the price of aluminium so that profits are guaranteed.[25] It is estimated that R1.5 billion in foreign exchange will be earned out of total sales revenue of between R2.6 and R3 billion. An estimated 1,100 jobs will be created on site, with the potential for a further 30,000 downstream.

The point emphasised here is not so much whether these projects are worthwhile, by whatever criteria, although this is extremely important and could warrant much closer public scrutiny and availability of information. Rather, the capacity to deliver these projects, and the economic and political momentum and public and private institutions pushing to deliver them, are all the product of the past. They are liable to pre-empt the development of other initiatives, let alone the institutions, etc. to deliver them, even when their very rationale depends on them – as in the retention of foreign exchange and employment generation, whether through downstream processing or public or other works based on the financial surplus generated.[26]

Thirdly, the IDC remains a key institution in industrial policy making, with total capital assets of over R7 billion.[27] This figure, large though it is, considerably understates the IDC's importance since much of its investment is in joint ventures with the private or public sector and it can dispose of its shareholdings to finance other projects. Thus, its total funding of industry reached almost R12 billion between 1992 and 1994. Much of this has been financed by the sale of shareholdings in Sasol and Sappi, realising over R4 billion over the same three-year period.[28] Although slackening off in 1994 with the near-completion of the Alusaf and Columbus Steel projects, mega-projects have continued to dominate IDC investment (see Table 5.1). It is claimed that while 112,000 or 7% of

Table 5.1 IDC investments (R million)

Investment type	1994	Past three years
Small and medium	248	777
Large beneficiation	947	8 093
Other industrial	778	1 953
Total industrial	1 973	10 823
Tourism	15	57
Export finance	164	446
Black empowerment	185	345
Total	2 337	11 671

Source: IDC (1994a).

industrial jobs have been lost in the economy as a whole, 26,803 jobs have been created by IDC finance over the past three years (15,147 in SMEs), with 12,545 in 1994 (8,034 in SMEs).[29] Although some concessions have been made to RDP objectives, with support for SMEs,[30] tourism and black empowerment, the financial weight of these activities is limited.

In short, again in conformity with the past, the IDC has always participated to some extent in politically and ideologically motivated activities in response to government imperatives. Previously, for example, it was charged with small business development and decentralisation of industry – that is, token support for black business as part of a totally failed apartheid strategy for separate industrial development. Conveniently narrowing the scope of the meaning of politics, the IDC (1994a: 3) claims:

> We always have been and hopefully will continue to be politically neutral. We have never made a contribution to any form of political fund-raising and our staff members are not allowed to take an active part in politics, on a national or local basis. No politicians are allowed to sit on our Board, which consists entirely of experienced private sector businessman. . . . We have a proven record of objectivity and neutrality and we are trusted to act accordingly by both the private and public sectors.

This is an extraordinarily complacent rewriting of the historical record. Note that the opening pages of the Annual Report for 1994 follow a familiar pattern of displaying photos of the nine Board members (all white males) and the ten senior managers (also all white males).[31] Significantly, the IDC's current activities are apparently in line with the Reconstruction and Development Programme despite having been formulated long before the RDP had itself ever been aired (IDC, 1994b: 6):

> The IDC's latest long range strategic plan covering the period 1991 to 1996 is in harmony with the industrial policy initiatives of the RDP.

A more accurate characterisation of the IDC is as an institution heavily embroiled in the core activities of the MEC but with a reluctant capacity to turn its capabilities to other policy areas if required to do so by government. In such a case, it is, at most, reactive. It would prefer now to be as free as possible from government interference and to present itself as such to potential private investors and partners.[32]

Yet, IDC does continue to have an important influence on policy making, participating with the DTI and BTT in the formation of South Africa's offer to the Uruguay Round of GATT and preparation of the tariff schedule for 1995–99, in revision of GEIS, and in policy research more generally (IDC, 1994b: 17). It also has the capacity to undermine DTI policy, choosing to acquire and finance the South African Foreign Trade Organisation (SAFTO) after the DTI had decided not to continue to fund it for what were reported to be budgetary reasons (*Financial Mail*, 30 June 1995: 68).

Fourthly, the scope for industrial policy making is considerably circumscribed by the globalisation of the operation of South African corporations. SAPPI, for example, in which the IDC has sold a substantial interest, has become the world's largest producer of woodfree coated paper through the acquisition of a US company and generates over 85% of its income (60% of turnover, which totals nearly R8 billion) outside South Africa. Clearly, domestic industrial strategy is liable to be subordinate to its international interests (*Financial Mail*, 14 July 1995: 85). Similarly, Minorco, which was set up by Anglo-American to hold many of its overseas assets outside South Africa, boasts a turnover of almost $5 billion. The issue of how such overseas holdings have an impact on the functioning and efficacy of domestic policy remains unaddressed.

Fifthly, where limited change has been made in the hierarchy within a department, there is a paralysis of initiative and understanding. Consider, for example, the Draft Policy Principles emerging from the Department of Mineral and Energy Affairs (DMEA) in November 1994. The capacity to rewrite history and to draw up the crudest ideology in order to preserve discretion is astonishing (DMEA, 1994: 1):[33]

> South Africa's mineral industry has become a world leader in respect of mineral supply, management and technology. This position was

largely achieved under conditions of free enterprise and subject to the disciplines of the market mechanism, which has provided the stimulus towards increased effort and efficiency. Faced with the rigours of the marketplace, the industry will remain competitive only if is it allowed to operate with minimum intervention from Government. State intervention should be limited to ensuring that the national interest is protected as far as possible.

Of course, this does not and cannot represent policy as such. It is, however, indicative of the paralysis not only in thinking but also in self-presentation. How many could have imagined that a department of a government dominated by the African National Congress (ANC) could have moved so far from the aims of the Freedom Charter in the following proposed principles for ownership of mineral rights (DMEA, 1994: 4):

> The existing mineral laws of South Africa, which make provision for private and State ownership of mineral rights, have stood the country in good stead and were instrumental in making the country a leading mineral producer. Drastic changes in the system, which has evolved over a period of more than a hundred years, cannot be made overnight and would involve substantial practical problems and perceived inequities. Where such changes are indicated, due to the requirements of increased access and optimum utilisation of resources in the national interest, these should be approached with circumspection and taking cognisance of economic conditions and viability.

Apart from continuities in the making of industrial policy, there are breaks with the past but only in the limited sense of the policies themselves in the light of changed circumstances rather than in the way that policy is formulated and implemented. Often, these developments reflect initiatives that pre-date the GNU. The restructuring of the armaments industry provides an example.

The armaments industry was built up through the state-owned industry, Armscor, in order to evade the impact of sanctions while pursuing policies for internal and external 'security'. The industry met with some success, achieving international competitiveness in some products and accounting for a major part of manufacturing exports. Armscor previously incorporated a large number of subsidiaries.[34] These were hived off into a separate company, Denel, in 1992, with Armscor primarily concerned with defence procurement. Subsequently, its net income has dropped from R40 to R5 million; Denel's has risen from R157 to R310 million, although employment in its first two years fell from 25,000 to 13,000.

Conversion to civil production, then, is the major issue facing the South African armaments industry at a time when domestic demand and subsidies are liable to be cut. There is little evidence that the necessary state support to bring about successful conversion is in place; for it requires considerable coordinated and detailed support across a wide range of factors, such as science and technology policy, public procurement, and sectoral intervention. The difficulties faced by the industry in continuing primarily within armaments is illustrated by the failure to win the contract from the UK for 91 Rooivalk (Red Hawk) helicopters. The specifications required US gunsight technology, which was not licensed to South Africa; the United States effectively disbarred its winning the contract in order to promote its own short-run commercial interests in the offer of Apache helicopters through McDonnell-Douglas and to undermine South Africa's long-run armaments capability. Sanctions against South Africa may have been abolished in principle, and it may more readily be able to bid for export orders. But the long-run viability of the sectors depends on diversification through conversion. Market solutions to this problem tend to lead to conversion to unemployment, closure of production facilities, and loss of high and collective skills in research, design and technology.[35]

Further, consider the procurement of four corvettes, which the Ministry of Defence was seeking to order in a R1.6 billion deal with the Spanish Bazan shipyard. In the past, this would have been approved by cabinet command; now, it has been overturned, at least temporarily, with questions over need given changing defence priorities and levels, and a recognition that such orders should be more broadly incorporated into economic policy, engaging with issues of counter-trade and impacts on the balance of payments. The episode indicates that defence priorities have changed and weakened but the capacity to coordinate defence procurement with economic policy remains weak. It is at least as likely that the Defence Department will seek to lobby support for procurement by individual negotiation with other departments than that more permanent mechanisms for coherent policy making will be put in place.

A second example of change with continuity is provided by Sasol. In response to oil sanctions, Sasol has long been manufacturing oil by coal-conversion at costs that exceed international prices, with a subsidy to cover the difference. Necessarily, this would be reconsidered in the light of freely available oil imports, with the added complication that the international oil companies operating refining capacity in South Africa have an interest in seeing the subsidy removed as far and as quickly as possible. The issue, then, has been treated very much as one in these terms. A report by consultants Arthur Andersen (1995) recommended withdrawal of the subsidy by the turn of the century with support of R780 million, R730 million, R520 million, and R320 million in the intervening four years (*Financial Mail*, 14 July 1995). It estimates that this will lead to savings of R5 billion in foreign exchange.

The oil majors have complained that the subsidy gives an unfair advantage to Sasol, which will use it to fund competing investment.[36] Significantly, account is being taken of broader economic implications, as in the balance of payments effects. But, as the *Financial Mail* puts it (p. 24):

> We're not sure that government knows which of its Ministers should intervene. Sasol falls under the energy portfolio but the money is the Treasury's.

Even these are not in principle the only ministries involved. Sasol has spawned a huge petro-chemical complex that will survive irrespective of the fate of coal-to-oil conversion. Industrial and employment policies in these activities will be profoundly affected by the way in which Sasol is subsidised, and is also a matter of competition with other domestic and international producers. Further, energy and employment policies more generally are involved because of the weight of Sasol's energy use. Apart from its own coal mines, which provide more than 30 million tonnes each year for conversion, Sasol is the country's fourth largest corporate purchaser of electricity, accounting for 4.7% of Escom's output and 3.0% of its revenue at over R400 million (Escom, 1994: 21).[37] In short, the Sasol subsidy, reconsidered though it must be, should not necessarily be the central focus of policy-making – which needs to be more broadly cast and coordinated.[38] This is so in view of the importance of the forward and backward linkages involved, particularly for the Eastern Transvaal economy. Arthur Andersen (1995: 45) estimates that 12.1% of the region's GDP and 5.1% of its employment depend upon Sasol's synthetic fuel business.

The Competition Board, which came under the jurisdiction of the DTI in 1994, has been more effectively used in some instances in order to control monopoly pricing. The most important case has been in the supply of cement,[39] which is crucial to the RDP's housing programme, although the impact has yet to be thoroughly tested in this respect given the negligible progress made as yet.[40] On the other hand, the R3.4 billion bread baking industry, despite deregulation in 1991 and the existence of approximately 3,000 in-store bakeries with about 15% of the market and 174 large plant bakeries, continues to exhibit the behaviour of a well-organised cartel (*Financial Mail*, 14 July 1995). In July 1995, there was a simultaneous increase by seven cents in the standard 800-gram loaf. This was despite a 1994 Competition Board investigation to the effect of finding no evidence of collusion, 'especially as there is competition from the new inhouse bakeries'.[41]

Competition policy, even if it were actively pursued, cannot suffice since lowering the price at one point along the chain of bread provision opens up the possibility of the benefits being appropriated elsewhere along the chain (and of eliminating smaller distributors or retailers as large retailers and wholesalers can use bread as a loss-leader). This is particularly so given the diverse holdings of the major South African corporations across the various components of the bread chain, from flour milling to retailing.[42]

The recent Background (to the White) Paper on Competition Policy (Fourie *et al.*, 1995), correctly points to the power of the conglomerate structure to abuse market power and seeks to strengthen the capacity to deal with this. The policy stance, however, has in part been wedded to an unjustified ideology that it is such market power that has been the major factor impeding the desirable growth of SMEs and of corresponding black advancement. In other words, competition policy, which is never going to have more than a limited impact – because economies of scale and scope are important and market power is difficult to identify and rectify – is likely to be used more as a populist symbol of confrontation with big business and its apartheid origins than as one element in a coherent and effective industrial strategy in which the strengths of big business are deployed rather than irritated. After all, the prospects for black advancement and inclusion, including the fortunes of SMEs, rest more upon the prosperity, scale and direction of investment of the conglomerate economy, public and private, than they do on its market structure.

Significantly, the Background Paper does recognise the need for competition policy to be integrated with other components of industrial policy. But, except when dealing with restrictive practices, it tends to see competition policy in terms of horizontal market competition. And, as such, it is much stronger on the way in which policy should be implemented than in defining its content. This is hardly surprising. For unless you believe in the law of large numbers – that competition is more fierce and beneficial the more firms there are, a proposition for which there is neither sound theoretical nor empirical evidence – policy stance towards market competition can only be adequately determined on the basis of industrial policy and strategy more generally. This follows, for example, since a little extra mark-up on lower costs might well be preferable to normal profit on higher costs, irrespective of whether these be achieved through private market forces or state intervention.

There are two areas where industrial/energy policy has made significant breaks with the past. One of these, electrification, represents the capacity to draw on existing institutional capacity, namely the electricity utility Escom, although it has been pushed by developments arising out of the pre-GNU National Electrification Forum, which focused popular pressure for electricity connection as one element of meeting basic needs. Yet, it has to be understood why this element could so readily be met while the others such as housing could not.

The answer rests in part on the capacity to deliver that has developed in Escom, especially as connection to the grid is not expensive and the fixed costs can and have been wrapped up in the charges for electricity use that can be guaranteed by pre-payment meters.[43] Particularly important, however, is the heavy excess capacity that exists within Escom. It is estimated that no new power stations will be needed until towards the end of the next decade even with current expanding demand, and power stations previously under construction have been temporarily moth-balled. Escom has the institutional capacity to deliver electrification, and there are no major obstacles to its doing so.

The programme began in late 1990 and had already realised over 600,000 connections by 1994. But it has accelerated in recent years and peaked at 300,000 connections per annum in 1995, a level to be maintained until the end of the century. It is estimated that electrification brings around one new business for every ten households connected, with tens of thousands of jobs created each year through knock-on effects. Some 12 million tons of firewood will be saved, along with 1.2 million hours of travel time, mainly by women, to collect it, and R8 billion will be spent on appliances over the next decade (*Financial Mail*, 28 April 1995). The electrification programme has also readily made use of foreign assistance with, for example, R1 billion loan from the Export Import Bank of Japan. How great will be the spillover gains from electrification depends on support given to the associated economic activity. Here, institutional capacity has not benefited from a running start equivalent to that provided by Escom itself in the electrification programme.[44]

Yet, even if indirectly, this is where the other break with the past has been most prominent – in the promotion of small business. Here progress has been most impressive in a number of ways, not least because of the lack of significant entrenched institutions and interests and opposition to new ones. First, the weak and ineffective existing framework for support has been essentially sidelined with the marginalisation of the Small Business Development Corporation (SBDC) and the focus of initiatives being centred within a newly created unit around the DTI.[45] A new agency, the Small Business Development Agency (SBDA), is to be formed in 1995/96. Secondly, impressively, a White Paper on small business has already been tabled in Parliament. Drawing on experience throughout the world with bribery, corruption, clientelism and failure to achieve commercial viability, policy is heavily committed to avoiding simply handing out financial support to individual businesses. Rather, the focus is on providing an institutional framework of national and decentralised support in which services will be paid for (p. 19). Attempts will be made to ensure that minimum labour standards are met (p. 36). The programme is detailed, modest in scope, and with provision for monitoring progress to replicate successful ventures and to avoid failed initiatives (pp. 48–51). Overall funding is also modest at R180 million through the DTI, and a further R140 million for agencies such as the SBDA. This is, however, likely to be swamped by other sources of government assistance, whether central, local or parastatal,[46] and foreign donor funds on which small business development will inevitably depend heavily (pp. 52–4).

In short, the progress in breaking with the past in small business development is explained by the weakness of existing institutions, the energy and vision of those promoting the programme, and the political acceptability of the programme across a wide spectrum of opinion, not least because it leaves unchallenged existing power relations embedded in the conglomerates. Although there can be little doubt that the South African SME sector has been underdeveloped because of the restrictions of apartheid and the particular path followed by the economy, the impact of these measures on employment and growth remains unquantified and, almost certainly, unquantifiable. What has also remained primarily unexamined is the dependence of the fortunes of the SME sector on the structure and dynamic of big business.[47] Essentially, the SME strategy is one of providing infrastructure in support of occupying what has previously been underdeveloped territory and, otherwise, to follow the fortunes of the non-SME economy as it permits.

6.   Concluding remarks

The substance of this chapter has been to emphasise how the existing wide and varied institutional structures involved in the formulation and implementation of South Africa's industrial policy exhibit considerable continuities with the past. Not surprisingly, this has had its counterpart in considerable continuity of industrial policy itself, and has been a powerful influence on the alternatives that can and have been adopted where a break has been made with the past. The argument is not, however, one of institutional determinism, calling forth the inertia and resistance of a hierarchical and entrenched white civil service bureaucracy, important though this is. Rather, of more importance are the underlying characteristics of the economy itself, which have been characterised as a minerals–energy complex, based in and around the corresponding core sectors and under the control of highly monopolised, globally organised private corporate capital,[48] with powerful links to state and parastatal corporations and influence over policy and policy-makers themselves.

One of the conclusions of this study, then, is that institutional reform is desperately needed in order that coherent and effective industrial policy can be made, irrespective of the form and direction of the policy. But the nature of the institutional reforms suggested will depend on how the South African economy is understood and what direction it is to take. The following factors require emphasis:

1. The South African economy has developed considerable strength and capacity around its minerals–energy complex, but – in part reflecting a wider weakness of past industrial development and policy – vertical integration between sectors remains undeveloped. The economies of scale and scope in diversifying forward into capital and intermediate goods from the MEC core must be vigorously pursued on a selective basis, as well as the backward integration from the weaker consumer goods industries.

2. South Africa has considerable infrastructural capacity, which must be extended not only as a means of meeting basic needs in public utilities but also as part of a broader strategy to generate industrial employment. In particular, this should be married to the creation of mass consumption industries that meet basic needs and create employment in housing, energy, transport, clothing, schooling, health, etc. In many ways, whatever its history, the unique success of Escom in meeting RDP targets is a testimony to the potential for such a strategy on a much broader front. By accident rather than design, it has had the institutional and productive capacity to deliver. It can be matched in other areas.

3. The South African financial system is often compared with that of Britain, with a highly developed range of financial services and a

corresponding set of financial institutions and regulations. There is some truth to this claim, although the international competitiveness of South Africa in financial services has yet to be tested. Whatever the extent of the parallels, the British financial system is not one to emulate, not least in the context of reconstruction. It has long been recognised that the British financial system has a number of weaknesses as far as domestic industry, as opposed to the fortunes of the City, are concerned. These are:

- An emphasis on international mobility of financial assets at the expense of domestic investment, particularly that in industry.
- Reliance on short-run speculation and borrowing and lending, leading the economy to be particularly vulnerable to economic downturns and short of long-term investment in domestic industry.
- Priority in policy-making to the objectives set by international finance, particularly at the expense of government expenditure and policies more favourable to industrial reorganisation.
- Limited coordination between the provision of industrial finance and the implementation of long-run policies for industrial development.

Not surprisingly, exactly the same characteristics are to be found in the South African financial system. They are all the more inappropriate given that the financial system is attached to a developing rather than a developed economy. There is an urgent need, therefore, to reform the South African financial system with three particular goals at the forefront: to finance expanded government expenditure at the lowest possible cost; to provide for industrial investment, possibly through the state, and forge a closer relationship between industry and finance; and to subordinate financial policy to the goals of economic and industrial policy rather than to those dictated by an elusive business confidence.[49]

4. The political and economic power of large-scale corporate capital has to be confronted directly so that it can be drawn into industrial policy making and the issues both of control and of distributive outcomes can be negotiated. While apparently an aggressive step, it is one more likely to lead to crowding-in of private investment through public investment, and one more conducive to long-term business confidence than rhetorical assaults on big business in the name of black advancement.[50]

5. South African industry has inherited a range of mega-projects. Some of these were prompted more by political than by economic motives, as in

the case of Sasol, Koeberg and what was previously Armscor. Others – like Escom and Iscor – were developed in response to an economic rationale, although their growth and character were and continue to be heavily influenced by their apartheid origins. Moreover, large-scale private capital has persisted in pressing for state subsidies for further mega-projects, such as Alusaf, and these have been granted. This is despite their huge capital requirements, the limited employment they generate, and the failure of their output to meet basic needs directly. Such projects have considerable advantages for capital. They tend to guarantee markets or inputs for existing capacity, which, however, does not necessarily correspond to the direction that should be taken by industrial development. Apart from limiting employment generation, they tend to minimise the extent to which the labour force can actively participate in and influence policy formation. And the huge capital costs involved tend to preempt changes in industrial policy in the immediate future. On the other hand, mega-projects can contribute directly to industrial development through the provision of basic inputs to manufacturing and even in the provision of basic needs through electrification. An indirect contribution can be made through export earnings, as is intended with Alusaf, for example, thereby potentially funding more imports to support more labour-intensive production of basic needs.

There is, however, no guarantee that the costs and benefits of continuing or new mega-projects conform to intended goals in principle nor that they actually accrue in the way that was intended. If, for example, a mega-project is undertaken primarily to generate exports, then the exercise is futile if the foreign exchange is retained abroad by a participating private corporation and used to expand investments overseas. Existing and proposed mega-projects need to be assessed in terms of their ultimate contribution to basic needs and employment generation, and the mechanisms need to be put in place to ensure that anticipated benefits materialise in the way that was intended.

Notably absent from this list are the four issues that have more commonly dominated discussion of South African industrial policy – competition policy, SMEs, trade stance and training. Each of these is important, but none of them can be effectively dealt with, nor make an effective contribution, unless the more fundamental issues are first confronted.

Notes

1. For a discussion of the way in which the World Bank and IMF have set the analytical agenda in development policy, even if not always having their own way, see Fine and Stoneman (1996).
2. See, for example, the contributions edited by Amsden (1994).
3. Paradoxically, Kaplinsky (1995), a leading figure in the ISP approach, rejects distorted factor prices as the explanation for the capital intensity of South African industry, but sees it as due to political factors rather than the direct economic interests of large-scale corporate capital.
4. It is important to recognise, however, that not all sector reports and researchers concur with the overall ISP framework. See the various published sector reports – and the limited reference to them in the overview document! One of the weaknesses of these reports for the purposes of this chapter is that though published in 1995, they rarely extend commentary beyond 1993.
5. For a formal model of how commitment to higher quality products can crowd out those of lower quality serving the needs of the poor, see Atkinson (1995). Fine and Leopold (1993) have made the same argument in the context of the eighteenth century in criticising the notion, due to McKendrick (1982), that Wedgewood's continual innovations in pottery stimulated the industry through a consumer revolution whose benefits trickled down from the elite. In contrast, continual change in products had the effect of impeding the emergence of standardised products for mass consumption.
6. Hence the capacity to become immediate world-wide consultants. Apart from fluidity across countries, the bland analytical content is also reflected in the belief that the approach is readily applicable to the environment, the inner city, the financial system and health – Porter and Vanderlinde (1995), Porter (1995), Porter (1992), and Teisberg, Porter and Brown (1994), respectively. In the last, for example (p. 131):

   > In industry after industry, the underlying dynamic is the same ... competition compels companies to deliver increasing value to customers. The fundamental driver of this continuous quality improvement and cost reduction is innovation.

   Of course, this is not the central issue in health delivery in the United States, let alone South Africa, where it is delivery at all that is at stake for many.
7. There is a semiotic reading to be had of the texts emanating from Monitor, with their fairy tale language and motifs. It is, of course, a neat irony for South Africa that the Diamond should occupy the focus of mystical power.
8. One author, David Green, is reported as having written the Monitor report on South Africa's worldwide competitiveness.
9. See Porter (1995: 55), emphasis added: 'A sustainable economic base can be created in the inner city, *but only as it has been created elsewhere:* through private, for-profit initiatives and investment based on economic self-interest and genuine competitive advantage.'
10. Porter and Vanderlinde (1995) on the environment and Porter (1995) on the inner city both reflect a failure to confront systemic power and how it functions, the former remarkable for seeking solutions in which profit can be made out of environmental improvement, the latter most remarkable for failing to mention race! Nor does Porter's (1992) commissioned report on the

US financial system hold out great hopes for radical improvements in South Africa's capacity to provide finance for industrial investment. Noting the US financial system's short-termism, he reckons that it can be reformed to provide a system superior to that of Japan and Germany but without recommending the creation of financial institutions dedicated to the provision of industrial investment.

11. Now fully reported in Fine and Rustomjee (1997).

12. For a recent contribution along these lines, see Moritz (1994).

13. Note that literature concerned with the crisis of the apartheid economy has now fallen out of favour in the rush to provide constructive advice. This reflects a change in direction and content since it has also meant a substantial decline in consideration of political and economic interests, previously understood around the class-race debate. The literature closed with Gelb's (1991) notion of racist-Fordism, a peculiar imposition of regulation theory in the South African context – it is to be understood as a form of Fordist mass production distorted by racism to limit mass consumption to the whites. Unfortunately, this implies incorrectly that South Africa's industrialisation has been based on the limited growth of consumer goods industries, whereas it is the growth of heavy industry that has been most important. A further irony is that the ISP itself grew out of the COSATU-linked Economic Trends Group (ET) and essentially sees South Africa as racist post-Fordism!

14. See Fine (1995b). It is also particularly disturbing that the Minister of Public Enterprises, Stella Sigcau, as reported in the *Financial Mail*, should believe that privatisation has stimulated growth internationally, when there is absolutely no evidence for this. Significantly, the World Bank has become disillusioned with the impact of privatisation in Africa (Fontaine and Geronimi, 1995: 147). The experience of Latin America suggests that the use of privatisation to improve fiscal stance is a short-run political expedient with long-run costs (Pinheiro and Schneider, 1995).

15. This is not entirely accurate in ideological terms since, as the RDP has been marginalised in scope and content, so paradoxically any economic policy or outcome – particularly if perceived as a success – is captured as presented as part of the RDP.

16. For a comprehensive discussion of this issue, although leading to a different position than the one adopted here, see Chang (1994). Davis (1994), in the South African context, also adopts a wider definition of industrial policy, than as trade policy but protection and export subsidies remain this preoccupation.

17. As previously observed, other 'industrial' policies that have been crucial include the role of state corporations, especially that of Escom.

18. Because of its heterogeneity, its potential as a source of populism and its limited challenge to large-scale capital, the small business sector (itself an ideological construct) is extremely flexible in terms of the range of policies that it can incorporate. Thus, it can be seen as a source of innovation (technology policy), self-employment (employment policy), competition (anti-trust policy), etc.

19. For a recent discussion of this in the context of South Korea – World Bank versus the rest – see the special issue of *World Development*, edited by Amsden (1994).

20. See Nattrass (1995) for a recent account of the gold industry.

21. Although the Department of Transport has charge of airports, it does not have charge of Transnet – which falls under the Department of Public Enterprises – which is weak and primarily concerned with privatisation.

22. It is worth recalling that Pik Botha was appointed as the Minister for Mineral and Energy Affairs, thereby undermining any potential use of the existing institutional structure for coordinating alternative policies.

23. There are remarkable differences between this report and its predecessors, not least in the stance adopted by the Director General's contribution, the omission of a parallel Afrikaans text, and detailed tables on the racial, gender and disabled composition of, and targets for, the workforce (revealing dramatic inequalities). Equally, the bulk of the remainder of the text retains considerable continuity with the past.

24. According to the *Financial Mail* (1 September 1995), R1.7 billion had been extended in various subsidies to industry over the past three years, with a continuing commitment of R839 million. R500 million alone had been granted to Iscor under GEIS. For a detailed discussion of recent trade policy, see Bell (1997).

25. Details from *Financial Mail* (23 June 1995). The guaranteed profits are reminiscent of those accruing to the private coal mines that were dedicated to specific state-owned power stations. See Fine (1992).

26. Account must also be taken of the import bill of such investments. In 1994, imports rose by R16 billion, a 28.1% increase over 1993, with almost half of this for machinery (which usually amounts to about one-third of imports). The main part of this increase was for computing equipment, the mega-projects, the electrification programme and the cellular telephone network – with implications for the corresponding programmes' impact on balance of payments. An interesting feature of the (corrected) official figures is an import bill from the US of R3.9 billion for brake linings. I estimate this would have sufficed to provide every member of the population with a full set – providing a warning over the accuracy of official data. See *Financial Mail* (14 July 1995).

27. The following account is drawn from IDC (1994b) unless otherwise stated.

28. IDC proudly presents itself as not having drawn on government funds since 1954. This sets aside the way in which state support and pricing in parastatals have more or less guaranteed its capacity to generate a financial surplus and access to finance.

29. All job creation claims must be treated with considerable caution, for two different reasons. First, other agencies may be involved, in which case the same jobs can be claimed to have been created many times over. Secondly, gross job creation can be accompanied by job displacement, especially where subsidy is concerned. Thus, support for a highly capital-intensive project may create some jobs at the expense, through productivity increase, of the loss of even more jobs in competing enterprises. Only a full and proper economic analysis, including these considerations and counterfactual assumptions, can ascertain the extent of net job creation. Not surprisingly, IDC (1994a: 2) claims to have created 301,000 of 1,125,000 jobs, 25%, in industry since 1940.

30. It is appropriate that the M(icro) should be dropped from SMMEs. For the IDC, SMEs are defined as manufacturing enterprises with total assets not exceeding R100 million! Half of the enterprises supported by the IDC over the past three years (32% in 1994) had assets exceeding R10 million, and one suspects that

most of its finance has been absorbed by these. The IDC also reports that over the past three years, 505 enterprises have been supported with an average approval of R1.5 million assistance, the creation of 15,147 jobs at an average cost of R141,000 per job, and increased exports of R1.2 billion or 3.2% of manufactured exports.

31. The Board is open to change by the new Minister for Trade and Industry.

32. This view follows from the perusal of a number of documents about the IDC and a number of informal interviews with those who have had dealings with it. It is a moot point whether the IDC is changing in its orientation or is becoming more sophisticated in presenting a more acceptable image of itself.

33. This text is ripe for semiotic analysis in terms of its real meanings and messages.

34. See *Financial Mail* (9 June 1995), and also Branscomb (1994).

35. It has long been recognised that the problems of conversion are not of the tanks to kidney machines type but of the economic and social policies to provide alternative markets and employment.

36. Controversy also surrounds major differences between the draft and final reports, and undue Sasol influence and lack of broader consultation. Between the two reports, Sasol has been favoured by approximately an extra two-thirds. There is also debate over whether the support is a subsidy or a tariff.

37. This is total Sasol electricity use, including activities other than coal-to-oil conversion but the latter is very heavily dependent on electricity as well as coal.

38. This is recognised by the DTI (1994: 13): 'Chemical and fuel production are integrated and, consequently, the fuel price and the price of other intermediate inputs to downstream (relatively labour intensive) manufacturing, becomes an issue of industrial policy. There is close cooperation and coordination the DTI and the Department of Mineral and Energy Affairs in moving towards a resolution of this volatile matter.'

39. DTI (1994: 12) also refers to the cinema industry where apartheid has left white-dominated control over much film distribution.

40. *Financial Mail* (7 April 1995), in its first year review of the RDP, reports provision of 878 low-income houses by the end of February!

41. The situation particularly disturbs the major retailers such as Pick 'n Pay. Their oligopoly is another story.

42. The Chair and Chief Executive of Premier Foods, leading flour miller, reveals honesty and knowledge of the laws of competition in equal measure in responding to the charge of a cartel. Admitting that regular cost meetings take place, he argues (*Financial Mail*, 14 July 1995, p. 66): 'Due to the tight level of competition, when one group increases its price, the news travels fast and all the major groups tend to move in sync.'

43. The background to the electrification programme and its potential impact are discussed in MERG (1993).

44. In this context, the DTI (1994) Annual Report admits (p. 11): 'Due to the weight of activities in other areas, the DTI did not do much work in linking industrial expansion with RDP infrastructure projects in 1994, but expects to develop clearer policy options in this regard in 1995.'

45. Other institutions with interests in SMEs include the IDC, which will be more than happy to be relieved of responsibility, and the Development Bank of

Southern Africa (DBSA), whose future and role remain uncertain. Is it an accident that SBDA is an anagram of DBSA? While proud of its 'commitment to enterprise' through buying policies, management advice and technical support, Escom only reckons to create 2,400 jobs (only 435 realised by the year ending in May) in 800 small black businesses in 1995 *Escom Newsbrief*, no. 14, July 1995).

46. Currently estimated at R700 million.

47. The main exceptions are in stressing the oligopolistic exclusion of SMEs from market access and the unsuitable character of financial institutions in providing loans for investment.

48. It is arguable that the most pressing issue in industrial policy is direct foreign investment – not, however, that of attracting inward flows. These are liable to be futile when set against the outward foreign direct investment of South Africa's own private corporations. The ending of apartheid has unleashed a flood of international acquisitions, mergers and overseas investments, complementing an earlier illegal flow of as much as 7% per annum. This, of course, raises the issue of how effective industrial policy can be made in these circumstances, when the most important decisions about the levels and locations of investment are not known let alone under any control.

49. See Fine (1995a).

50. In this instance, I am in serious danger of agreeing with the *Financial Mail* (22 September 1995), in its insistence that the issue of antitrust/competition policy be disassociated from that of black exclusion/advancement. The logic of its position is, however, to back off on both issues rather than to pursue each vigorously.

References

Amsden, A., ed. 1994. 'The World Bank's The East Asian Miracle: economic growth and public policy'. Special section, *World Development,* vol. 22, no. 4.

Arndt, D. 1991. 'Review of Porter (1989)'. *Millennium*, vol. 20, no. 2: 335–7.

Arthur Andersen. 1995. 'Sasol Synfuel Protection Study'. A Report to the Liquid Fuels Industry Taskforce. Mimeo.

Atkinson, A. 1995. 'Capabilities, exclusion and the supply of goods'. In Basu *et al.* eds (1995).

Basu, K., P. Pattanaik and K. Suzumura, eds. 1995. *Choice, Welfare, and Development: A Festschrift in Honour of Amartya K. Sen.* Oxford: Clarendon Press.

Bell, T. 1997. 'Trade policy'. In J. Michie and V. Padayachee, eds, *The Political Economy of South Africa's Transition.* London: Dryden Press.

Branscomb, L. 1994. 'An analysis of South African science and technology policy', Science and Technology Policy Series, no. 1. Pretoria: FRD.

BTT. 1995. 'Proposal for a Revised Phase VI Motor Industry Development Programme'. Board of Trade and Tariffs. Mimeo.

Chang, H. 1994. *The Political Economy of Industrial Policy.* London: Macmillan.

Davis, G. 1994. *South African Managed Trade Policy: The Wasting of a Mineral Endowment.* London: Praeger.

DMEA. *Annual Report,* various years. Braamfontein: Department of Mineral and Energy Affairs.

DMEA. 1994. 'Draft principles on which a mineral and mining policy for South Africa should be based'. Mimeo. November.

DTI. *Annual Report of the Director-General of Trade and Industry*, various years. Pretoria: Government Printer.

Escom. 1994. *Annual Report*, Sandton.

Escom. *Newsbrief.* Various issues.

Fine, B. 1992. 'Total factor productivity versus realism: the South African coal mining industry'. *South African Journal of Economics*, vol. 60, no. 3 (Sept) : 277–92.

Fine, B. 1995a. 'Politics and economics in ANC economic policy: An alternative assessment'. *Transformation*, no. 25: 19–33.

Fine, B. 1995b. 'Privatisation and the RDP: a critical assessment'. *Transformation*, forthcoming.

Fine, B. 1995c. 'Flexible production and flexible theory: the case of South Africa'. *Geoforum.*

Fine, B. and E. Leopold. 1993. *The World of Consumption.* London: Routledge.

Fine, B. and Z. Rustomjee. 1997. *South Africa's Political Economy: From Minerals – Energy Complex to Industrialisation.* London: Hurst.

Fine, B. and C. Stoneman. 1996. 'The state and development: an introduction'. *Journal of Southern African Studies*, vol. 22, no. 1 (Mar.).

Fontaine, J-M. and V. Geronimi. 1995. 'Private investment and privatisation in sub-Saharan Africa'. In Cook and Kirkpatrick (1995).

Fourie, F. *et al.* 1995. 'Towards competition policy reform in South Africa'. Background Working Paper, Feb.

Gelb, S. ed. 1991. *South Africa's Economic Crisis.* London: Zed Press.

Gleason, D. 1995. 'The commissioning of Columbus Stainless'. *Optima*, vol. 41, no. 2 (Sept.) : 2–7.

IDC. 1990. *Modification of the Application of Protection Policy: Policy Document.* Industrial Development Corporation, Sandton.

IDC. 1994a. *Annual Report.* Sandton: IDC.

IDC. 1994b. 'Presentation on IDC's activities before the Standing Committee on Trade and Industry'. 7 Sept. Mimeo.

ISP. 1995. *Improving Manufacturing Performance: Report of the Industrial Strategy Project.* Cape Town: UCT Press.

Jones, G. 1991. 'Review of Porter (1989)'. *Business History*, vol. 33, no. 2: 352–4.

Kaplinsky, R. 1995. 'Capital-intensity in South African manufacturing and unemployment, 1972–90'. *World Development*, vol. 23, no. 2, 179–92.

McKendrick, N. 1982. 'Commercialization and the Economy'. In N. McKendrick, J. Brewer and J. Plumb, eds, *The Birth of a Consumer Society: The Commercialization of Eighteenth Century England.* London: Europa Publications.

Macroeconomic Research Group (MERG). 1993. *Making Democracy Work: A Framework for Macroeconomic Policy in South Africa.* Cape Town: CDS.

Miller, M. 1990. 'Of pushcart vendors and management consultants'. *Public Interest*, no. 101: 103–6.

Monitor. 1995. *Global Advantage of South Africa Project.* Presentation to the Parliamentary Standing Committee on Trade and Industry and to the media, 5 Apr.

Moritz, L. 1994. *Trade and Industrial Policies in the New South Africa.* Research Report no. 97, Nordiska Afrikainstitutet, Uppsala.

Nattrass, N. 1995. 'The crisis in South African gold mining'. *World Development*, vol. 23, no. 5: 857–68.

Pinheiro, A. and B. Schneider. 1995. 'The fiscal impact of privatisation in Latin America'. *Journal of Development Studies*, vol. 31, no. 5 (June): 751–76.

Porter, M. 1989. *The Competitive Advantage of Nations.* New York: Macmillan.

Porter, M. 1992. 'Capital disadvantage – America failing capital-investment system'. *Harvard Business Review,* vol. 70, no. 5: 65–82.

Porter, M. 1995. 'The competitive advantage of the inner-city'. *Harvard Business Review,* vol. 73, no. 3: 55–71.

Porter, M. and C. Vanderlinde. 1995. 'Green and competitive – ending the stalemate'. *Harvard Business Review,* vol. 73, no. 5: 120–34.

PTG. 1994. 'Long-term strategic plan for the textile and clothing industries in South Africa'. Panel and Task Group for the Textile and Clothing Industries. Mimeo.

RDP. 1994. *The Reconstruction and Development Programme.* Johannesburg: Umanyano Publications.

Roberts, R. and D. Green. 1995. 'Privatising the private sector'. *Financial Mail,* 7 July, p. 38.

Rogerson, C. 1994. 'Flexible production in the developing world: the case of South Africa'. *Geoforum,* vol. 25, no. 1 (Feb.) : 1–17.

Teisberg, E., M. Porter and G. Brown. 1994. 'Making competition in health-care work'. *Harvard Business Review,* vol. 72, no. 4: 131–41.

Thurow, L. 1990. 'Review of Porter (1989)'. *Sloan Management Review,* vol. 32, no. 1: 95–7.

White Paper. 1995. *National Strategy for the Development and Promotion of Small Business in South Africa.* Government Gazette, vol. 357, no. 16317, 20 Mar.

World Bank. 1993. *An Economic Perspective on South Africa.* Washington, DC: The World Bank.

6

Land Reform as a Strategy for Development: The Relevance of the Zimbabwe Experience for South Africa

Abdallah Hamdok and Lala Steyn

1. Introduction

Land reforms were initiated in Zimbabwe in the 1980s and are on the political agenda in South Africa in the 1990s. In both countries demands are being made, land conflicts mediated, proposals discussed and policies debated. The role that land reform can play within a development context is critical in South Africa, where a new democracy has adopted an ambitious Reconstruction and Development Programme (RDP). South Africa needs to take on board the international lessons concerning land reform. Zimbabwe, as a Southern African neighbour, has many interesting lessons for South Africa.

Both countries were subject to a colonial history of conquest through which indigenous people were dispossessed of their land. This history also ensured that an alien concept of land and property rights achieved dominance over an indigenous system based on the notion of communal ownership and use. Southern Africa is also experiencing enormously high unemployment and underemployment, particularly in the rural areas. At the same time, rural economies are stagnating and the countryside is in decline.

This chapter examines perspectives on land reform through an analysis and comparison of the Zimbabwean historical experience and the development of the debate in South Africa. An attempt will be made to place on the agenda elements of an overall development strategy within which a land reform programme should be located. The second section provides an international context and conceptual framework for land reform in South Africa. The third section of the chapter reviews the Zimbabwe experience with land reform. It explores achievements and constraints and provides an overview of prospects for policy options. This is followed by an examination of the South African situation, with a description of the proposed government programmes and criticisms of government policies, and then by a look at the relevance of the Zimbabwean experience for South Africa by examining possible lessons. Finally, the conclusion summarises the findings and provides an outline of the elements of a suggested strategy for land reform as a component of development.

2. Conceptual framework

The debate on land reform is influenced by regional debates on agricultural development in general and land reforms and resettlement programmes in particular. It is also influenced by the international debate on the role of the market *vis-à-vis* the state in land reforms. The international development debate during the last two decades contained significant differences, particularly the clash of conceptions about modes of production and their articulation in the world capitalist system. In this debate, some emphasised the existence of a unitary mode of production, resulting from the global homogenisation process involving world markets and technology, while others argued for the existence of multiple modes of production disarticulated in the world capitalist system (Moyo, 1995).

The historical context

The broad problems of land and agricultural development in the rural history of Southern Africa (mainly South Africa and Zimbabwe) are peculiar because of the colonial history and the apparent robustness of their economies unlike the economies of most other African countries. A key aspect of this history has been continued land grievances and the associated disarticulation of rural society, the rural economy and institutions.

The low income quasi-stable equilibrium trap of Leibeinstein clearly demonstrates and accurately conceptualises the current situation of these economies. Characteristics of such a trap can be observed in the vicious circle of low productivity, low incomes and poverty in the rural economies and the absence of an interaction between the modern industrial sector and the predominantly subsistence rural sector.

The most fundamental aspect of this marginalisation is the residual role played by smallholder agriculture, where both allocative and microeconomic inefficiencies in land and labour markets coincide. The micro-economic inefficiency arises from limited access to resources, poor quality of resources, population pressure, prevalence of external constraints in supportive services, poor access to necessary inputs and credit, and vulnerability to natural disasters. The macroeconomic inefficiency is represented by the fact that both labour and land could be reallocated in a manner that could raise labour productivity per person and total output and incomes as a whole. The deadweight status of the smallholder peasant agriculture is reflected in structural and institutionalised entitlement failures with respect to land and labour (Mhone, 1994).

Land entitlement failure arises as a consequence of the unequal access to productive resources – including land – between large commercial farms and peasant agriculture. This situation is partly a consequence of the differential incidence of public support measures and partly due to the manner in which land has been used. The result is a dichotomised agricultural sector with imperfect land markets, reflected in the fact that at one end, in the commercial subsector, land commands high market value, but tends to be underused, while at the other extreme, in rural areas, land is over used and its market value is non-existent or indeterminate.

The dichotomous land-use pattern and associated failure in land entitlements is also closely linked to the devaluation of labour power to the point where its value in the market is unable to rise significantly above an institutionally determined subsistence income. On the commercial farms, labour exists as a captive resource operating under paternalistic semi-feudal relations. In smallholder agriculture, on the other hand, due to overpopulation and the slow rate of growth in formal sector employment opportunities, underemployment is the norm for the majority there (Mhone, 1994).

The South African context

Despite all the debates and activities around land reform in South Africa today, there are different conceptualisations of land reform. This in itself is not strange, as different interest groups have different positions on land reform. Definitions of land reform vary according to what the proponents of each definition want to achieve and are based on different arguments for land reform, which can be divided into three main groupings:

- *Ideological positions*: For example, to achieve national liberation or as part of a programme on collectivisation or socialisation of agricultural production.

- *The social equity/justice argument*: exploitation of the landless by landowners is unacceptable. Underlying this is an assumption that land reform will alleviate the impoverishment of the dispossessed.
- *Economic grounds*: to increase efficiency of agricultural production.

There are, however, two points of concern. First, discussing the equity and efficiency argument as an either or, has been found to be unsatisfactory. In recent policy documents the Department of Land Affairs (DLA) has adopted a position that combines equity and efficiency arguments. The National Land Committee (NLC), an NGO representing the interests of the land hungry in South Africa, has adopted a broad view, stating that 'comprehensive land reform is necessary for social, economic and political development' that should contribute to 'redressing historical injustices, restructuring power relations, alleviating rural poverty, stimulating economic growth and creating long term security'.

Secondly, despite a clearer conceptualisation that has combined the equity and efficiency arguments, there are presently three critical areas that are not satisfactorily addressed. In the international debate it has emerged that the questions of restitution and redistribution must be more closely tied with those of tenant rights, rural labour, customary land rights and urban land issues. In South Africa the questions of restitution, redistribution and tenant rights have been closely linked. Nevertheless, the issues of labour rights, customary land rights and urban land issues require further conceptual clarification.

Rural labour rights

As a result of the commercialisation of agriculture the demands of farm workers/tenants have come to focus increasingly on labour rights, improved conditions of employment, security of housing and access to a subsistence plot. Tenancy and rural labour laws are needed to redistribute rights to and over the land rather than the physical land itself. This involves rural labour legislation, tenancy protection and limiting the nature of private land rights. As these issues are dealt with by different government departments, they often fall between the cracks. It is important that they be clearly incorporated into a conceptual under-standing of land reform that is appropriate for South Africa today.

Customary and indigenous land rights

The question of customary land rights is raised in a variety of forms in South Africa. It is partially addressed in terms of tenure reform and rural local government/traditional authorities. This is, however, highly contested terrain. Internationally, there has been a resurgence throughout the world of indigenous and tribal peoples' land claims, mostly small minorities in Westernised countries. In 1989 the ILO adopted an Indigenous and Tribal Peoples convention that, among other things, recognises the collective aspects of indigenous peoples' relationship with their land and indigenous peoples' rights of ownership and possession over traditional lands.

Many indigenous peoples' organisations are demanding territorial rights that are linked to land, cultural elements, language and tradition. 'Territorial rights' mean different things to different groups. The more radical groups claim all territories that belong to a specific ethnic group. On the other side of the spectrum, organisations demand more heterogenous occupation of space and the recognition of indigenous authorities. For all groups, territorial rights, as opposed to land rights – which are more limited – include the right to exploit all natural resources on and under the land. In South Africa communities are also talking about the right to exploit natural resources for mining, fishing or other activities.

Land reform in an urban context

Land policy and land reform in an urban context need to be clarified. In the past land was treated as part of an urbanisation process and housing policy. Internationally, it appears as if the trend is towards a focus on land delivery as a land issue specifically, distinct from the other components of housing delivery. It is also clear that land in an urban context needs to be an integral part of an urban development/housing programme and overall urbanisation strategy. Urban land policies need to provide criteria and procedures for the identification, speedy release and development of urban land to the benefit of the landless. The problem of land reform in an urban context needs to be conceptualised, drawing on the international debate and spelling out the relationship between land policies, urban policies, land reform and housing programmes.

It should be emphasised that over the past year a conceptualisation of land policy and land reform has emerged in South Africa that combines different aspects of previously opposing arguments. This conceptualisation argues that both equity and efficiency can be complementarily promoted if a comprehensive strategy for the economy as a whole, which places land reform as a central force in the agro-industrial complex, is adopted. This requires strategic interventions in the policy environment as well as targeting of land reform projects. Land reform is also conceptualised as a central part of the reconstruction and development of South African society. Land reform, and specifically the restitution programme, aims to address the historical injustice of the past.

The emerging vision of land reform in South Africa is one in which such reform contributes to economic development both by giving households the opportunity to engage in productive land use and by increasing the number of employment opportunities available through productive land use. It is one of land reform that contributes to greater investment in and returns from productive land use. It is one where there is a more even distribution of agricultural land, including small holdings, medium-sized farms and large farms. It is a vision where both equity and efficiency are complementarily promoted through a combined agrarian and industrial strategy in which land reform sparks the engine of growth and development.

3.   Agricultural reforms in South Africa: The relevance of the Zimbabwean experience

The Government of Zimbabwe's major policy instrument to reduce inequalities in land distribution was the resettlement programme. Initiated in 1980 at the Lancaster House negotiations that culminated in Zimbabwe's independence, the plan was to resettle 18,000 families over three years on about 1.2 million hectares of land previously owned by white settlers. The Transitional Development Plan of 1982 raised the target number to 162,000 families to be resettled on 10 million hectares of land (Cusworth, 1990).

Land reform models

The land reform programme and other related issues is analysed here and discussed in detail according to five development models:

- Model A (Normal)
- Model A (Accelerated)
- Model B
- Model C
- Model D

Model A (normal)

This scheme allocates land on an individual family basis. A family is allocated a residential plot within a planned village and arable land of 5 hectares, in addition to a grazing allocation based on the number of livestock units (usually 5–15 units) and the agro-ecological zone. A typical scheme includes approximately 245–593 settler families on 21,700–25,500 hectares of land (Cusworth, 1980). The schemes are provided with other infrastructural features, such as rural services centres, health centres and primary schools. This is the predominant model and represents over 75% of the resettlement schemes.

Model A (accelerated)

Perhaps the only difference between the two model A schemes is that settlers in the accelerated scheme are provided with only limited infrastructural support, whereas in the normal model A scheme substantial support is provided prior to the settlement. In addition, the average scheme is smaller than the normal model A. Nearly 6% of the resettlement programme area has been settled under this model.

Model B

This model is based on cooperative farming and communal living. All properties including land and equipment are cooperatively owned. About 6% of land has been resettled using this model, though it was intended to be the centrepiece of the government's policy for the transformation of agriculture.

Model C

In this model an estate provides production and marketing services and settlers are out-growers. In a similar way to model A, individuals are allocated a plot of arable land and grazing is communal. The estate management is responsible for the organisation and coordination of production and marketing activities. This model is of relatively minor importance, representing about 1% of the resettlement area.

Model D

This model involves improving grazing management in areas adjacent to communal lands mainly in natural regions IV and V. It has been tried on only a few acquired commercial farms, yet it represents a large area of land compared with models C and B – about 12% of the total resettlement area.

Land reform and agrarian change in Zimbabwe: Achievements and constraints

Given the long-term neglect and the confinement of the majority of the population to the low resource potential 'reserves', it is not surprising that the peasant sector as a whole came to be noted for the acute problems of overcrowding (of people and livestock) and the over-use of the available land resources. This has resulted in land degradation in areas of poor quality with low agricultural potential, a situation that fuelled among other things calls for land redistribution. Further justification for the distribution of land came from the perceived need to provide new economic opportunities for the landless and the war-displaced people as well as to reverse the historical trend whereby a large proportion of the country's high-potential land had over time come to be allocated to the white settlers.

The Transitional Development Plan's main objective was to achieve a more egalitarian land distribution, of course without adversely affecting aggregate production (Government of Zimbabwe, 1982). In articulating the objective 'Growth with Equity', the plan envisaged the land resettlement programme as part of a wider agrarian reform that sought to redress imbalances in the provision of agricultural services between the peasant and commercial subsectors. A review of developments in the land resettlement programme since 1980 is provided here, though it is not possible to present a comprehensive account of the programme. Nevertheless, progress and problems will be highlighted and particular attention will be given to issues related to the effects of the land resettlement programme on the communal areas residents and its contribution towards relieving resource pressures in these areas.

The criteria for choosing settlers focused, among others, on land-lessness, returning Zimbabwean refugees, and unemployed and poor households willing to give up their right to land in the communal areas. In 1985 experienced farmers (master farmers) were added to the list. Former communal farmers make up to 85% of those who have received land; about 5% to 10% are farm workers and the rest are returning refugees and ex-combatants (Durevall, 1991). Each settler received three permits – for residence, cultivation and livestock keeping. These permits are for no specific duration and there is currently no prospect of their being upgraded to leasehold or freehold status. The land thus continues to belong to the state and the permits can be recalled.

The implementation of the programme turned out to be slower than planned, and there seems to be a feeling that only a small part of it has been carried out so far. Nevertheless, when assessing the achievements of the programme some other aspects of central importance ought to be considered too. There has been a significant redistribution of land, with as many as 845,398 people resettled on about 3.4 million hectares that formerly belonged to large-scale commercial farms (LSCFs). These people make about 8% of the total population. The LSCF subsector declined from about 6,113 to 4,660 farms, which in terms of land area is about 30% (Roth, 1990; SAMAT, 1995).

Furthermore, Zimbabwe's land reform has an important distinguishing feature. That is that settlers usually live in communal areas and have to move to former LSCFs, which are divided into smaller plots or, in some cases, turned into cooperatives. Hence, there is widespread lack of infrastructure, such as roads, schools, clinics, village water supplies, cattle dips, staff housing and fencing, all of which have to be constructed. This has made the programme expensive and complicated to implement.

To better appreciate the advance of land reform in Zimbabwe, it should be compared with other experiences in the African continent. A relevant comparison is the case of Kenya, which in the 1960s had a structure that resembled Zimbabwe's. Bearing in mind the lack of experience of the new government, Zimbabwe has done quite well, when judged by the number of people moved and transferred together with the other social services and programmes. Kinsey (1983: 102), comparing the magnitude of Zimbabwe's land reform programme with that of Kenya, noted, 'In only eighteen months Zimbabwe transferred from white to black control only ten percent less land than Kenya had transferred under its smallholder resettlement schemes dating from independence to the middle of 1976 – a period of more than fifteen years.' A factor that is quite often cited as one of the obstacles to speedy land reform is the Lancaster House Agreement of 1979, which stated that the government could, until 1990, only acquire cultivated land on a 'willing seller, willing buyer' basis and at the prevailing market prices. The agreement has probably resulted in less access to land and higher prices than otherwise would have been the case. However, the short- to medium-term indirect costs of resettling more households on new farms could have been very high in the form of lost government revenue, lower economic growth and less food security. Perhaps one of the major arguments here is that the current programme involves the transfer of land between producers with a fundamentally different approach to land use, very different resource bases and, above all, differences in the contribution they make to the national economy.

The LSCFs consist of a relatively small number of very large holdings, using relatively capital intensive, technically modernised farming techniques. The sector is vital for the Zimbabwe economy; it produces 85% of all marketed beef, 100% of milk, 99% of sugar, 99% of Virginia tobacco, 97% of all coffee and tea, 99% of wheat, 99% of soya, 48% of all cotton, and 45% of maize. Besides, 40% of the raw material inputs in manufacturing are from agriculture, and over 30% of all exports are agricultural products (Durevall, 1991). On the other hand, the prospective settlers from the peasant agriculture of the communal areas, come from an area where traditional agriculture dominates and modern production technology is hardly used. These peasant farmers mainly produce for home consumption and subsistence is their primary concern. This sector therefore produces mainly food crops, with a relatively insignificant contribution to the national economy.

This issue relates to a central concern in the land reform debate, namely how resettled farmers compare with LSCFs in levels of output and productivity. It has been generally acknowledged that many of the settlers are those least likely among the communal areas peasant farmers to be able to make full use of the productive potential of the resources being allocated to them. These ideas were echoed in the work of Kinsey (1983), who stands as a representative of early critics of land reform. In his opinion, resettling a total number of 162,000 households would require the acquisition of the greater part of the LSCFs. A resettlement programme on this scale would lead to a very high level of unemployment as a great number of jobs would be lost from LSCFs, probably resulting in no net gains in terms of relieving land pressure in the communal areas. The losses in terms of production and export earnings were assumed to be proportional to the land area acquired for resettlement. He also emphasised the budgetary implications of buying the land and of the provision of accompanying infrastructure and services.

Many of Kinsey's assumptions have been criticised, as in the work of Munslow (1985), Weiner *et al.* (1985), Mhone (1991, 1994) and Moyo (1990, 1995). However, Kinsey also made a number of pertinent criticisms of the implementation of the programme, pointing, for example, to the lack of financing for draught animals, the insecurity of tenure on resettlement schemes, and problems created by the policy of requiring that settlers be landless and hold no jobs outside the resettlement schemes. This last requirement meant that sometimes the least experienced farmers were selected and that they were barred from sources of income that could be tapped for productive investment on the land.

There are other areas of dissatisfaction with the programme that deserve to be mentioned. These include the skewed land distribution, which continues with over 11 million hectares of land remaining in the hands of the predominantly white commercial farmers. The problem of over-population in communal areas was not ameliorated, as population continued to grow with far higher rates than the pace of the programme implementation and finally the issue of land use within the resettlement schemes. Although the number of resettled communal farmers is quite small compared with the total number of inhabitants, even those resettled still keep some ties with their former communal areas. Perhaps among other factors contributing to this phenomenon is the security or otherwise of the tenure in the resettlements schemes as reported by Cusworth (1992):

> Whilst there is no substantial evidence that settlers feel particularly insecure under resettlement, there is evidence that settler households are reluctant to cut their ties completely with the CAs from which they came and in particular to release their right to cultivate land there. This feature of settler attitudes frustrates one of the objectives of resettlement which is to release land in overcrowded CAs and may also act as a disincentive for settlers to invest in the medium and long term future of their holdings.

An important factor remains the extent of land use and the intensity of arable cultivation under the resettlement programme. This issue is closely linked to the livestock stocking rates, as the overall intensity of land use will to a large extent be determined by the level of use for grazing. As mentioned by Cusworth (1992), more than half of settler households own no cattle, with a further 21% having fewer than the planned number. At the same time, 28% of the settler households own herds larger than the planned number, amounting to 78% of the cattle. Considerable underutilisation of grazing resources in some resettlement schemes has resulted from this highly skewed pattern of cattle ownership. This pattern of land use ultimately leads to the situation where resources are both overutilised and underutilised. Rich farmers will overstock by keeping more cattle than required and in most cases poor farmers will keep fewer cattle, which will underutilise the available resource. This points to a central dynamic feature and characteristic of land reforms where, in most cases, inequalities increase as programmes reach their maturity.

The most significant structural change in the large farm sector since 1980 has been in the way factors of production are used in agriculture, especially land. There has been considerable shift away from maize production to industrial or horticulture crops and the substitution of capital (in the form of machinery) for labour following the introduction of minimum wage legislation. Conversely, the communal areas have filled the gap by increasing their share of marketed maize and cotton, using the improved accessibility of commercial marketing channels and the greater availability of hybrid maize varieties. In total, there has been no significant reduction in crop production in the country as a whole.

Yields in resettlement areas are higher than those in communal areas, partly due to the better endowment of the lands. Incomes to the households have surpassed target incomes in average years. However, some households have failed to meet the targets, especially in the drier regions, because, being poor, they did not arrive with sufficient cattle, and there was no credit programme to help make up this deficiency, unlike the credit available for crop production.

Prospects for policy options

The discussion now focuses on issues of land reforms in the 1990s and beyond, and the likely direction of change of the programme. With the expiration of the Lancaster House Agreement in 1990, the legal protection of the large-scale commercial farmers' property rights disappeared, thereby nullifying the excuse of high cost. At the same time, among the public the expectation that the agrarian problem would be solved was rapidly growing. However, these events coincided with the launch of an economic structural adjustment programme (ESAP) in the very same year. This was viewed by many as a large step away from the earlier goals of equity and socialism. To calm its black constituency, the government decided to revitalise the land reform programme by announcing that another 110,000 households would be resettled on approximately 5 million hectares of land.

The new programme is still very sketchy and has not yet taken its final form. There is no information on how fast the programme will advance or which farms will be acquired. Indeed, so far, the figures given appear to have been taken out of thin air, as was the case with the 162,000 settler programme of 1982.

The Zimbabwe Framework for Economic Reform (ZFER) (GOZ, 1991) did not suggest any specific time horizon for the completion of the reform. However, in the 1991/92 budget a total of only Z$37 million was allocated for the land reform and the figure is not different in subsequent budgets. Given the size of these figures, it is likely that the expected time for the completion of the programme will be considerably longer than five years.

Many factors are contributing towards making the land reform of the 1990s somewhat different from that of the previous decade. One of the important factors is that only those with a proven experience in farming will be eligible for resettlement. In practice, these will be the so-called master farmers who hold relatively large plots of land, and comprise the wealthiest 15–20% of the communal farmers. Farm workers and landless, communal farmers with small plots will no longer be resettled. It is hoped that in this way land will be used more efficiently (Mangwende, 1991).

As mentioned earlier, the resettlement in the 1980s did not reduce the overcrowding in the communal areas since the population growth rate was well above the number that was given land. The new policy seems to have abandoned the idea that land reform could solve the problems of overcrowding in the communal areas. However, if all those 110,000 who are to be offered new land were master farmers, a great deal of land could be redistributed within the communal areas to the poor and landless.

Another important aspect of the programme of the 1990s is that many more farm workers will lose their jobs and homes, compared with the 1980s experience. The main reason is that a great deal of the land acquired in 1980s had in fact been abandoned or was only lightly utilised. With the reduction of the area and number of LSCFs, the level of use has increased, and, in relative terms, many more farms are hosting large numbers of farm workers with their families – an estimated 1.3 million to 1.8 million people (Durevall, 1991). Nonetheless, the attitude seems to be that since farm labourers received low wages and live under such poor conditions it is a good thing that their numbers decline. What they should instead do for a living is not at all clear.

Finally, the way in which the programme is implemented is vital for its success and can have great impact on the issues discussed above. However, continuing the strategy of buying blocks of several farms as was done in the 1980s would inevitably lead to the closing down of a number of very efficient LSCFs and the eviction of many farm workers. This ultimately means that the large-scale approach to resettlement has to be complemented or replaced with a more flexible scheme.

4. Land reform in South Africa

The colonial history of conquest in South Africa is one of dispossession of indigenous people from their land and the introduction of an alien concept of land and property rights that ultimately achieved dominance over the indigenous system based on communal forms of tenure. After 1652, which heralded the arrival of the colonialist, most indigenous communities lost formal control over land through a long process of purchase, negotiation, force, legal decree and fraud. In the twentieth century state intervention entrenched black people's alienation from the land and limited their access to less than 13% of the land in reserves. After 1948, the nationalist government implemented its apartheid policies, reinforcing its homeland policy and undertaking forced removals of over 3.5 million people.

About 40 million people live in South Africa, 76% of whom are black. According to the latest statistics, 49% of the entire South African population is classified as poor, with a high concentration being in rural areas. Of the total rural population 68% live in poverty. Rural households engage in a wide range of activities to make a livelihood. The most common source of income (38% of all families) is the wages of workers who are employed in other areas. After this come employment in the secondary labour market (37%); agricultural production (36%); and pension and social welfare support (20%).

Although agricultural production makes up only 10% of the income of rural African households, it is the third most common source of livelihood and one of the most viable. The main reason income from agriculture is limited is because black South Africans have limited access to land. Agriculture continues to play a dual role – as a safety net for the poor and as a source of income accumulation for the commercial farmer. A land reform programme that changes this can make a significant impact on poverty.

The share of agriculture in the gross domestic product has fallen over the past decades to only 5.1% in 1994. However, it provides much more in spillover and multiplier benefits through secondary and value added industries. It creates greater opportunities for cost effective social investment by providing higher employment returns on investment. Presently there is an underutilised potential in agriculture, in both labour and land. An area of farmland normally produces considerably more livelihoods if divided into small family-operated farms. This also applies to off-farm employment through the multiplier effect on the local economy. These economic factors, as well as the need to redress the historical injustices of the past, make land reform a necessity in South Africa today.

The aim of land reform in South Africa is to redistribute rights in land to the landless, farm workers, tenants, women and the historically disadvantaged for homes, subsistence and production to improve their livelihoods. To be successful, it must include the required support services and infrastructure that enable people to make productive use of land. Land reform should be implemented in a manner that strengthens democratic processes, local control and local government. It should be part of the effort to create just and fair land distribution, and to build national reconciliation and stability.

Land reform in South Africa takes place within the context of a negotiated settlement and a Government of National Unity. In this context the government has chosen to adopt a willing seller/willing buyer approach where possible, using expropriation as a last resort. The Interim Constitution includes a property clause and the requirement that just and equitable compensation be paid. This property clause limits the scope and scale of land reform, entrenching the property rights of existing land owners and undermining the rights lost by landless people. It also places constraints on the ability of the state to expropriate land when necessary. This is exacerbated by macroeconomic and fiscal constraints where there are limited resources for development.

South Africa, as a young democracy, does not yet have a culture of coordinated and integrated governance. It also has severe capacity constraints that limit its ability to deliver quickly on ever-increasing expectations. In the debate about land reform it should not be forgotten that there are also natural resources constraints – in South Africa only 11% of the land is arable and water is a scarce and valuable resource. South Africa is also subject to such an unpredictable climate that irate farmers are forced into berating the erratic nature of the heavens!

The government's land reform programme

The government's land reform policy is underlined by the following principles:

- *Demand driven*: Previous land policies operated from the basis of government-initiated plans and a supply driven approach. This resulted in inappropriate and unpopular programmes. To avoid this it is necessary that demand be a driving force in the programme, and that mechanisms and structures be established to respond appropriately.
- *Government as facilitator*: Due to the marginalisation of rural people and the weakness of rural organisation, the government is concerned that the demands of the most needy will not be articulated in an organised way. The government is therefore committed to facilitate the expression of demand, to educate and inform people about options, and to initiate programmes based on broad demand aimed at specific beneficiary groups.
- *Flexibility*: Regional variations across the country require flexible application of policy within the framework of national norms and standards. Land reform policies need to be able to adapt in the light of experience.
- *Poverty focus*: Priority is to be given to the poor who are in need of land to contribute to income and food security. State assistance in land acquisition must be given primarily to communities and groups unable to enter the land market. The financing arrangements for the programme must be structured to ensure access for people with little or no equity.

- *Participation, accessibility and democratic decision-making*: The participation of the communities and individuals as equal partners with government and other agencies is necessary. Decisions must be made democratically at local level. The extent to which this is achieved depends on organisation and capacity building, the establishment of sound and simple administrative processes to support land reform, the development of local government, and widespread dissemination of information.
- *Gender equality*: The land reform programme must bring about opportunities for equal access to and equal rights to land for women and men. It is necessary to ensure that the programme gives priority to facilitating the participation of women.
- *Coordination of departments and levels of government*: Fundamental to the success of land reform is a sound working partnership between national, provincial and local level administrations. In particular, cooperation between government departments concerned with livelihoods and the provision of services must be promoted and strengthened.
- *Partnership between the private and NGO sectors, and government*: As government is not the only actor in land reform the establishment of cooperative relationships with the private sector and NGOs is vital. Implementation mechanisms and procedures must facilitate this cooperation.
- *Monitoring and evaluation*: A key element of land reform is an information system that can track the progress of different measures. Through this, it is hoped to provide feedback to land reform managers and to the public.
- *Economic viability and environmental sustainability*: Planning of land reform projects developed at the local level must ensure that projects are economically viable and environmentally sustainable.
- *Leverage of resources*: Due to limitations of financial and other resources, leverage is essential. Government grants must be used to leverage other financial resources, both credit and own contributions.

The government's land reform programme involves a three-pronged strategy: land restitution, land redistribution, and land tenure and administration reform. The Department of Land Affairs, the government department responsible for these programmes, offers a number of grants and services in support of these programmes. The design of these grants and services recognises that the provision of land and tenure security alone is not sufficient to guarantee an improvement of life for land reform beneficiaries. To ensure the productive use of land, the programme includes settlement support for land development and capacity building to enable beneficiaries to maximise the benefits gained out of securing access to land. Experience has shown that the grants and services in support of land reform should be capable of responding to a highly segmented land market, where land is needed for a variety of purposes, including residential, the provision of community facilities, agriculture, mining and other productive purposes.

Grants and services

A wide range of grants and services can be itemised, from settlement grants to dispute resolution to information.

- *Settlement grant*: This grant is set at a maximum of R15,000 per beneficiary household, to be used for land acquisition, enhancement of tenure rights, and investment in infrastructure, home improvements and fencing, according to beneficiary plans.
- *Settlement planning grant*: The purpose of this grant is make the services of planners and other professionals accessible in order to assist the beneficiaries in preparing project proposals and settlement plans.
- *District planning*: This offers an integrated framework for decision-making for the allocation of resources for land reform and settlement on a district level. DLA will financially assist provincially supported district planning exercises.
- *Facilitation services*: This service is to ensure that eligible land reform beneficiaries have access to necessary information and are empowered to seek access to appropriate services and assistance.
- *Training and capacity building services*: Training will be offered at a community level so as to better support people for the land reform process and to equip them and service deliveries with the means to manage development.
- *Dispute resolution service*: As land reform is highly contested and conflictual by its very nature, it is essential that disputes be prevented where possible and resolved when they arise. DLA is currently in the process of investigating and planning the establishment of a dispute resolution system that will have the capacity to prevent and resolve land conflicts.
- *Cadastral and information service*: The cadastral services of surveying and registration are essential for land reform. An information system that retains a state land register is critical.

Restitution

Forced removals to serve racial discrimination and segregation have caused enormous suffering and hardship in South Africa. No settlement of land issues can be reached without addressing such historical injustices. The aim of restitution is to restore land and provide other remedies to people dispossessed by racially discriminatory legislation and practice, as an integral part of a broader land reform programme. The restitution programme will benefit individuals, communities or their descendants who lost their land rights because of racially discriminatory laws passed by previous governments on or after 19 June 1913. This will be done in such a way as to provide support to the vital process of reconciliation, reconstruction and development, particularly in underdeveloped rural areas.

The Interim Constitution sets a framework for the restitution of land rights, instructing the legislature to put in place a law to provide redress for the victims of acts of dispossession that took place after 1913. Parliament, in turn, enacted the Restitution of Land Rights Act, 1994, creating the Commission on the Restitution of Land Rights and the Land Claims Court. The Act stipulates the following time frames: All claims must be lodged within three years, ending 30 April 1998. The Commission and Court must finalise all claims within five years and all court orders must be implemented within 10 years. Restitution can take different forms. It may involve restoring the land itself, or alternative land, or monetary compensation or other relief. The form restitution takes depends on the circumstances of each claim. If it is no longer feasible to restore the actual land, then alternative forms of compensation apply. In each case the claimant will be involved in negotiating the settlement.

Resolving urban claims of the approximately 130,000 families who were forcibly removed under the Group Areas Act, 1950, the Community Development Act, 1966, and the Resettlement of Blacks Act, 1954, is particularly difficult. The reason for this is that the land has often been developed and changed to a great extent since dispossession and the demands on remaining undeveloped land are great. Another problem is that the overwhelming number of urban claims could create a budgetary and administrative crisis. The investigation alone of each claim on an individual basis could bankrupt the restitution programme before any remedial compensation is granted.

Given the importance of the RDP and pressing need for housing and renewal projects to move forward quickly, it is imperative that the urban restitution programme be directed towards development solutions driven by local needs and concerns. Urban claimants are therefore encouraged to form groups and committees for each affected town, suburb or former group area. These groups should enter negotiations with the relevant authorities assisted by the Commission, the Department of Land Affairs and NGOs. Where actual restoration is not feasible, claimants will be encouraged to work together to plan and develop what land is available.

To date a total of 4,902 claims – 1,943 rural and 2,930 urban (with 29 unidentified) – have been received by the Commission on the Restitution of Land Rights. The judges to the Land Claims Court have been appointed and it will be operative shortly.

Redistribution

The government presently has the following two programmes:

- Land redistribution under Provision of Certain Land for Settlement Act 126 of 1993, which provides for the designation of land for rural settlements and for financial support to communities to acquire land for residential and productive purposes. While a number of projects are being addressed in terms of the provisions of the Act, it is under review in the light of emerging policy.
- The Land Reform Pilot Programme (LRPP), which aims to develop efficient, equitable and sustainable mechanisms of land redistribution in rural areas, as a kick-start to a wide-reaching national land reform programme. The LRPP represents a first step: addressing land needs in areas where poverty and the pressure for land are most acute, while developing institutional mechanisms for land redistribution and rural development. It is a pilot programme in-so-far as it is an experimental undertaking. The wider programme need not wait until the end of the pilot, however, but will build on the structures and mechanisms developed through the pilot and adopt lessons learned through implementation.

Programmes still to be implemented will have a dual focus: to provide state assistance for land transfers to the poorer sections of population, and to create an environment enabling disadvantaged entrepreneurs to gain access to land financing through market mechanisms. State assistance will take the form of the grants and services mentioned above. There will be a single, yet flexible, programme that embraces the very poor, labour tenants, individuals as well as emergent farmers. The programme is based on a willing seller/willing buyer basis with state intervention taking different forms in different circumstances. If a situation should arise where no land is available on the market to satisfy such urgent land need, the state will consider expropriation.

The programme is targeted at:

- Landless people who wish to gain access to settlement opportunities in rural areas.
- Women who wish to have access to land.
- Farm workers and their families who wish to improve their settlement and tenure conditions.
- Labour tenants and their families who wish to acquire and improve the land they hold or alternative land, in accordance with the proposed Land Reform (Labour Tenants) Bill.
- Rural residents who wish to secure and upgrade the conditions of tenure under which they live.
- The historically disadvantaged who wish to acquire rural property for productive purposes.
- Victims of forced removals who fall outside the ambit of the Restitution of Land Rights Act, 1994.

Civil society – organised agriculture, the private sector, non-government organisations, community groups – can play a major role in meeting the need for land. The private sector has taken various initiatives and discussions are under way with representatives of the sector, including agricultural input suppliers, agri-business concerns, non-agricultural corporations holding private land, private banks and individual commercial farmers. Potential options include sales of corporate land, farm worker equity schemes, contract farming and strategically located input depots for small farmers. In some cases, private sector involvement will require direct government assistance, such as modest start-up financing for emergent farmers.

The non-government sector has also been active in proposing and entering partnerships with government to fill the existing capacity gaps and speed up delivery. Community groups have organised themselves, coming forward with plans for land acquisition and development. These initiatives create the impetus for the government to respond to, rather than land reform being a top-down activity driven by the state.

Rural financial services

As mentioned before, one of the most disturbing features of South Africa's economy is the under-utilisation of human and natural resources despite widespread poverty, particularly in the rural areas. The provision of financial services in these areas is one of the most important means for unlocking this potential. For reform to be successful, in view of the state's limited resources and ability to deliver, it is essential that access to financial services be broadened. Presently this is not possible, as mortgage-based lending does not, in most instances, appear feasible or attractive to private lenders because the prospects of repossessing land in the event of default are not good. A mortgage indemnity scheme (underwritten by government) would allay these concerns, but merely by transferring the problem back to government. Experience has shown that the state is rarely successful when it tries to engage directly in financial markets.

In the light of these difficulties a Presidential Commission of Inquiry into the Provision of Rural Financial Services (the Strauss Commission) was established to investigate objectives of the RDP and to make recommendations for the improvement of these services for rural households, farmers and other entrepreneurs. Although it is not possible at this stage to preempt the recommendations of the Commission, it is possible to highlight a few matters. The Commission has found that rural financial markets are best understood as markets for liquidity, rather than markets for credits or savings. Rural people save, borrow and repay loans but do not have access to financial institutions that can service their liquidity needs. This points to the importance of transmission instruments and therefore to sustainable, accessible and flexible rural financial institutions.

The establishment of a Wholesaler Trust that would provide wholesale credit on soft terms to private 'retailers' (but not indemnify them against bad debts) would make a significant difference. These retailers would on-lend to land redistribution participants at whatever higher interest rate would be necessary to cover risk and administration (e.g. a margin of 6–7%). It is possible that this might require the establishment of a rural bank to fulfill this and other functions in the long term. As there is a lack of coordination of existing services, a national coordinating function will be necessary to overcome this difficulty.

Land tenure and administrative reform

Tenure relations are complex and proposed tenure reforms need to be carefully assessed for possible undesirable impact on various groups, local economies and the national economy. To succeed, tenure reforms must involve the participation of all affected parties and communities. The programme has two main components, a consultative policy review, involving public consultation and research on tenure issues, and a legislative reform programme flowing from this. It estimated that a two-year period, from August 1995, will be needed to finalise new tenure reform policies and legislation.

Major aims of the tenure reform are:

- To ensure equal status in law and adequate administrative support for different forms of tenure.
- To extend secure tenure rights to all rural and urban South Africans.
- To create a framework for diverse tenure forms, including communal, group and individual tenure, on the basis of local preference.
- To ensure that communal and group tenure rights are protected and effectively administered.
- To improve tenancy laws to ensure fair terms and conditions of tenancy.
- To ensure gender equity in all aspects of land holding systems.
- To provide for interim administrative and legislative measures to reduce tenure insecurity and administrative chaos where these currently exist.
- To develop a land tenure information system for policy, rules, different tenure forms and the specific rights of communities and individuals.
- To develop registration systems for recording diverse rights.

In the interim, three bills have been proposed to parliament to protect holders of informal rights from hasty or unfair removal or loss of rights. A fourth bill aims to enable communities and groups to acquire, hold and manage property under a written constitution. It provides for communities or groups who want to hold land jointly to do so as long as they conform to basic standards of fair process, democratic accountability and equality.

Criticisms of government policy

Government policy has been criticized on a number of fronts that can be summarised as follows:

- The market based, demand driven approach is inadequate as it eludes the marginalised and destitute, placing them at the mercy of the landowner.
- The restitution programme is too limited – it excludes those who were dispossessed prior to 1913 and it excludes certain categories of dispossessed people.
- The grants and services proposed by the government are too limited – R15,000 will not enable people to enter the market as farmers.
- The emphasis on participation by beneficiaries in planning their land use should be more strongly limited by land use controls.

- Land is not important to rural communities and the state should place its limited resources in other areas, e.g. infrastructural investment, urban development.
- The government has no right to be prescriptive about the poor and women being beneficiaries; this should be left to traditional/community leaders to decide.
- Delivery is very slow and an appropriate delivery system is not in place.

5.   The relevance of the Zimbabwe experience for South Africa

Zimbabwean land reform started in the early 1980s and underwent a policy shift to a focus on master farmers as potential beneficiaries. South Africa is in the fortunate position to be able to learn from the experiences of other countries such as Zimbabwe. One of the major lessons it has incorporated into its policies is to avoid a static model and adopt a flexible approach. It has thus not excluded those who can be defined as 'master farmers'. But the government does not have the resources to finance this group exclusively with huge grants, and is attempting to reorient financial services so that this group can gain access to credit and other necessary services. For the poor, who could be tomorrow's 'master farmers', the government is looking at creative ways to offer them a toehold in agriculture such as through leasehold arrangements, so as to enable them to enter the market fully at a later stage if appropriate.

In South Africa, where land reform is only beginning to be implemented in the mid-1990s, the question of who the beneficiaries should be is contested terrain. Although the Department of Land Affairs has taken a strong position in favour of the poor, it is proposing a flexible programme that will embrace the very poor, labour tenants and individuals, as well as emergent (master) farmers. This approach is criticised by a number of role players who say that it is impossible for a farmer to get established with a grant of R15,000. Grants or subsidised interest rates amounting to R1,000 have been suggested as an alternative approach. This has been resisted by the Department of Land Affairs, which argues that in equity terms this is unjustifiable.

The international environment in which Zimbabwe started its programme was different from that which faces South Africa at present. Despite this, it is interesting that there are a number of similarities in the constraints to the land reform programmes in the two countries. Often cited as an obstacle to Zimbabwean land reform was the Lancaster House Agreement, with its 'willing seller/willing buyer' provision. This agreement probably resulted in less access to land and higher prices than otherwise would have been the case. South Africa's new democracy is also part of a negotiated settlement in which a property clause, including provisions for compensation, is entrenched in the constitution. Interpretations of this clause vary, but there is no doubt that it places constraints on pricing. The South African government has chosen to base its land reform programme on the market with varying degrees of state intervention. It has opted for the 'willing seller/willing buyer' provision with the caveat that, where need be, it will expropriate land. However, the international climate does not allow for an alternative approach, as nationalisation and expropriation without compensation would lead to an international outcry and the withdrawal of much needed investment.

One of the critical comparisons that needs to be made is that concerning the approach adopted. Zimbabwe adopted a fairly top-down uniform bureaucratic approach to its programmes. South Africa has chosen a flexible approach that takes account of the local circumstances responding to different natural and human conditions and is trying to develop institutions for delivery that are appropriate to these circumstances. It is attempting to decentralise administration and devolve decision-making to potential beneficiaries, moving away from a technocratic and bureaucratic approach to planning. One of the critical factors for this to be successful is to broaden access to financial services so that beneficiaries are not reliant on state grants and services. Another is for the state to enter into partnerships or agency agreement, which is fast track delivery.

Underlying this flexible approach is an active civil society, which through grassroots, organisations and the non-government sector, is actively agitating for land reform. The existence of this sector, albeit their focus in small parts of the country with the areas where poverty is concentrated often being unorganised and weak, is the critical reason why land reform is firmly on the South African agenda. In Zimbabwe the land reform debate often took place at more rhetorical political party level. The strengthening of civil institutions through capacity building and access to resources is critical for land reform.

6.   Conclusion

This chapter has provided a discussion of one of the central issues in the development process in Southern Africa, particularly Zimbabwe and South Africa. The Zimbabwe experience of land reform and resettlement provides clear lessons for South Africa: the need for a flexible approach to land reform, the necessity of conducting land reform within a balanced strategy that addresses all the other sectors, and the importance of popular participation in programme design and implementation. In South Africa land reform is now a firm item on the development agenda as there is broad consensus on the need for it. A land reform programme should, however, be framed and implemented within a sustainable development strategy that balances agrarian and industrialisation policies.

References

Amin, N. and J. T. Chipika, 1990. 'The differentiation of the peasantry in Zimbabwe: some implications for land redistribution'. Economics Department, University of Zimbabwe, Harare.

ANC. 1992. 'Ready to govern'. ANC Policy Guidelines for a Democratic South Africa.

Barrow, R. and M. Roth. 1989. 'Land tenure and investment in African agriculture: theory and evidence'. Land Tenure Centre Paper No. 136, Madison, Wisconsin.

Blackie, M. J. 1984. 'Research design and implementation in the Sebungwe region of Zimbabwe'. In P. Malton, R. Cantrell, D., King and M. Benoit-Cattin, eds, *Farmers Participation in the Development of Technology: Coming Full Circle*. Ottawa: IDRC.

Bruce, J. W. 1986. 'Land tenure issues in project design and strategies for agricultural development in sub-Saharan Africa', LTC, Paper No. 128, University of Wisconsin, Madison.

Central Statistical Office. 1988a. 'The Economy of households in Zimbabwe: main preliminary results from the income, consumption and expenditure survey 1984/85'. Harare, Zimbabwe.

Central Statistical Office. 1988b. *Statistical Yearbook*. Harare, Zimbabwe.

Central Statistical Office. 1989. *Statistical Yearbook*. Harare, Zimbabwe.

Central Statistical Office. 1990a. *Statistical Yearbook*. Harare, Zimbabwe.

Central Statistical Office. 1990b. 'Sample design for the second round of the income, consumption and expenditure survey 1990/91'. Memo. Harare, Zimbabwe.

Central Statistical Office. 'Crop production of large scale commercial farms'. Various issues. Harare, Zimbabwe.

Central Statistical Office. *Quarterly Digest of Statistics*. Various issues. Harare, Zimbabwe.

Central Statistical Service. 1995. 'October household survey'. South Africa.

Chavunduka, G. L. 1982. 'Report of the Commission of Inquiry into the Agricultural Industry'. Government of Zimbabwe, Harare.

Cliffe, L. 1986. 'Policy options for agrarian reform in Zimbabwe: a technical appraisal'. FAO, Rome.

Cliffe, L. 1988a. 'The conservation issue in Zimbabwe'. *Review of African Political Economy*. no. 42: 48–58.

Cliffe, L. 1988b. 'Zimbabwe's agricultural success and food security'. *Review of African Political Economy*, no. 43: 4–25.

Cousins, B. 1987. 'A survey of current grazing schemes in the communal lands of Zimbabwe'. Centre for Applied Social Science, University of Zimbabwe, Harare.

Cousins, B. 1990. 'Livestock production and grazing rights in Communal lands and resettlement schemes in Zimbabwe'. Background paper. Zimbabwe Agricultural Sector Memorandum, The World Bank.

Cusworth, J. 1990. 'Land resettlement issues'. Background paper. Zimbabwe Agriculture Sector Memorandum, The World Bank.

Cusworth, John. 1992. 'The dynamic nature of land reform: issues arising from the land resettlement programme in Zimbabwe'. *International Agricultural Development*, vol. 12, no. 2: 9–10.

Data Research Africa. 1995. 'The composition and persistence of poverty in South Africa'. Second draft report.

Davies, R. 1989. 'Trade, trade management and development in Zimbabwe'. Department of Economics, University of Zimbabwe, Working Paper no. 23.

Durevall, D. 1991. 'The Zimbabwe economy in the 1990s: trade liberalization and land reform'. Report prepared for the Swedish International Development Cooperation Agency (SIDA).

Government of South Africa. 1994. 'RDP base document'.

Government of South Africa. 1995a. 'Draft land policy principles', Department of Land Affairs.

Government of South Africa. 1995b. 'Grants and services of the land reform programme'. Department of Land Affairs.

Government of Zimbabwe (GOZ). 1982. 'The transitional national development plan 1982/83 – 1984/85'. Harare, Zimbabwe.

Government of Zimbabwe (GOZ). 1985. 'Communal lands development plan'. Harare, Zimbabwe.

Government of Zimbabwe (GOZ). 1988. 'First five-year national development plan 1986–1990'. Harare, Zimbabwe.

Government of Zimbabwe (GOZ). 1989. 'The national land policy'. Ministry of Lands Agriculture and Rural Resettlement'. Harare, Zimbabwe.

Government of Zimbabwe (GOZ). 1991. 'Zimbabwe: a framework for economic reform (ZFER) 1991–95'. Harare, Zimbabwe.

Kinsey, B. H. 1983. 'Forever gained: resettlement and land policy in the context of national development in Zimbabwe'. In J. D. Y. Peel and T. Ranger, eds, *Past and Present in Zimbabwe*. Manchester, UK: Manchester University Press.

Levin, R. (1994). 'The politics of agrarian reform in South Africa'. Paper delivered at the Institute for African Alternative Workshop.

Mangwende, W. 1991. *The Land Question in Zimbabwe: 10 Years After*. Harare, Zimbabwe: SAPEM.

Mhone, G. C. T. 1991. 'The environmental issue in Zimbabwe in a macroeconomic context'. ZERO, Harare, Zimbabwe.

Mhone, G. C. T. 1994. 'Macroeconomic implications of land reform and resettlement'. SAFER, Harare, Zimbabwe.

Ministry of Lands, Agriculture and Rural Resettlement. 1986. 'Conceptual framework for the communal lands development plan'. Harare, Zimbabwe.

Moyo, S. 1990. 'Agricultural employment expansion: smallholder land and labour capacity growth'. ZIDS, Monograph Series no. 2.

Moyo, S. 1995. 'The land question in Zimbabwe'. SAPES, Harare, Zimbabwe.

Moyo, S. and T. Skalnes. 1990. 'Zimbabwe land reform and development strategy: state autonomy class bias and economic rationality'. ZIDS, Research Paper no. 3.

Moyo, S., P. Robinson, Y. Katerere, S. Stevenson and O. Gumbo. 1991. *Zimbabwe's Environmental Dilemma: Balancing Resource Inequalities*. ZERO, Harare, Zimbabwe.

Munslow, B. 1985. 'Prospects for socialist transformation of agriculture in Zimbabwe'. *World Development*, vol. 13, no. 1:41–58.

Plant, R. 1993. 'Non-market approaches to land reform: a review of the international experience'. Paper delivered to LAPC Land Redistribution Options Conference.

Roth, M. 1990. 'Analysis of agrarian structure and land use pattern'. Background paper. Zimbabwe Agriculture Sector Memorandum, The World Bank.

Rukuni, M. 1990. 'The development of Zimbabwe agriculture 1890–1990'. Department of Agriculture Economics and Extension University of Zimbabwe Working Paper no. AEE 7/90.

Sender, J. 1993. 'Rural poverty and land distribution: some macro-economic issues'. Paper delivered at LAPC Land Redistribution Options Conference.

Southern African Multi-disciplinary Advisory Team (SAMAT). 1995. 'Design of policies and programmes for growth and employment promotion in the non-formal sector in Zimbabwe'. SAMAT, Harare, Zimbabwe.

Southern African Team for Employment Promotion. 1991. 'The promotion of economic development employment and equity in Zimbabwe'. SATEP, Harare, Zimbabwe.

Weiner, D., S. Moyo, B. Munslow and P. O'Keefe. 1985. 'Land use and agricultural productivity in Zimbabwe'. *The Journal of Modern African Studies*, vol. 23, no. 2: 251–285.

World Bank. 1993. 'Options for land reform and rural restructuring in South Africa'.

7

Regional Economic Integration: Reflections on South Africa and the Southern African Region

Rashad Cassim and Harry Zarenda

1. Introduction

The question of economic growth in South Africa has never been as urgent as now. At a time when overriding political conflict has largely dissipated, policy-makers are seeking strategies to encourage economic growth. An important question is where economic integration features in the larger debate on growth and development in South Africa. Is there an underlying consensus that South Africa's future economic prospects are inextricably tied to the economic prospects of the region as a whole?

Empirical evidence on the general relationship between regional integration and output growth is inconclusive: the implication is that the major impetus to economic growth comes from national economic policies. Another question remains, however, as to whether economic integration can play a very important role in *sustaining* growth in the Southern African region.

Regional integration, therefore, ought not to be considered a substitute for dealing with pressing national development imperatives. The approach to such integration ought to be to seek out those elements that would conform to and enhance narrower development prerogatives, rather than prove antithetical to these. At the same time, narrow political and vested interests must not be allowed to adversely affect broader development. Given the enormous dominance of South Africa within the region, a situation of a rapidly growing 'core' with little or no positive growth-enhancing spillover effects into neighbouring countries is equally untenable.

2. International trends in economic integration

The chapter begins with a look at some of the recent world-wide trends in regionalism. As De Melo and Panagariya (1993) emphasise, 'Today regionalism is back with a vengeance. In its current incarnation, regionalism has engulfed all major players in the world economy'. Their sentiments are echoed by many, and there is, moreover, consensus in the literature that European economic integration played an important role in encouraging intra-European trade. While economists may disagree about the impact of European economic integration on, for example, macroeconomic indicators, its differential effects on economies in the union and the pattern of income distribution in the various member countries, there seems to be consensus that the integration experience was successful because it succeeded in increasing trade among these countries, albeit at the cost of liberalisation specifically incorporating the Common Agricultural Policy (CAP) and non-tariff barriers (NTBs). This is not to suggest that Europe was a fortress. Intra-regional trade in the European Union (EU) increased from 35% in 1960 to an estimated 70% of total EU trade currently. In contrast, one of the startling facts of regional integration arrangements in developing countries is that they have not led to a sustained rise in intra-regional trade. Part of the problem is that intra-developing country trade is not as high as intra-developed country trade. Moreover, trade between developing countries is even less developed than trade between developing and developed countries.

The North American Free Trade Agreement (NAFTA), on the other hand, provides some interesting contrasts to the European Community experience. First, it is the first North–South regional integration arrangement to be concluded with very high per capita income differences between the United States and Canada, on the one hand, and Mexico on the other. The disparities between the United States and Mexico far exceed, for example, those of Southern European countries such as Spain and Portugal, which joined the European Community in the 1980s. Secondly, there is no existing precedent or theoretical model suited to explain the NAFTA. It represents more than a free-trade agreement in the traditional sense where capital mobility, or the free movement of capital, is integral to the agreement. Labour mobility is restricted, however, which means that it cannot be likened to a common market. It is not a customs union in the sense that there is no common external tariff between the United States, Canada and Mexico. NAFTA could more appropriately be described as an investment agreement in the sense that the free movement of capital, specifically allowing US firms to move freely to Mexico, is the most significant aspect of the agreement (Cassim, 1994).

The process and time frame of NAFTA differ from the EU experience. No major institutions have been set up to facilitate the NAFTA integration process, primarily because of the strong anti-institutional bias in the United States. The process is administered from the trade missions and trade ministries of the respective countries. In sharp contrast to NAFTA, the EU established a complex institutional arrangement to deal with issues such as labour mobility and workers' rights, compensatory arrangements, social clauses regarding labour and environmental standards. Economic integration in the EU was also more gradual than the NAFTA process.

East Asia, on the other hand, is different from both Western Europe and North America in that it has not had significant regional integration agreements during the past four decades, yet the share of its intra-regional trade is growing. Intra-regional trade is at present approximately 40% of all East Asian trade. This is high by developing country standards, but modest by comparison with the EU, and is considerably higher than intra-regional trade in North America. The most systematic attempts, by Asian standards, at regional economic cooperation in Asia are among the Southeast Asian countries as expressed in the Association of South-East Asian Nations (ASEAN), which itself is a very loose cooperation agreement. Thus East Asia provided an important case study in open regionalism – a market-induced phenomenon, rather than one introduced by preferential trade policies. In terms of economic relationships East Asia is substantially less institutionalised than other economic regions. It has no common market, customs union or free-trade area (FTA). It be may precisely this lack of institutionalisation that led to the great success of the East Asian economies in taking advantage of the GATT multilateral trading system (Cassim and Setai, 1994).

The critical lesson from the East Asian experience is that growing intra-regional trade is a by-product of growing extra-regional trade. This means that these economies became increasingly competitive with each other rather than complementary. Their export success was largely a result of extra-regional trade with the industrialised countries of North America and Western Europe.

A central question is how the East Asian experience of market-led integration contributed to an increase in intra-regional trade from 20% in 1970 to 30% in 1990. Cable and Henderson (1994) provide three reasons for this: first, that it is driven primarily by cross-border private capital flows searching out profitable opportunities; second, that integration is most intense in cross-border zones where firms can best take advantage of low transport costs and other cost differentials to outweigh the continuing penalties of trade barriers with the region. A third feature is that while liberalisation was taking place, it was unilateral rather than regionally negotiated.

A quick glance at certain international experiences shows that there are various ways in which economic integration in specific regions evolves. The importance of policy-induced integration is encapsulated in the EU and the NAFTA experiences, which contrast with the more market-driven approach of the East Asian experience. The literature points conclusively to the fact that factors such as high economic growth in the region, particularly in China and the ASEAN, and foreign direct investment (FDI) from Japan and the newly industrialised economies (NIEs) in the region, have been the major driving forces for regional economic integration in East Asia. This FDI has taken advantage of the benefits offered by host countries and has facilitated intra-regional trade. The 12 East Asian countries now take in 37% of the total trade, far ahead of either North America (31%) or Europe (17%) (Thomsen, 1994: 118). These experiences raise a number of critical questions for Southern Africa, where economic growth is lagging and the economies remain, by and large, fragile. What may be necessary is a new paradigm for approaching economic integration. An important question is whether the new literature on economic integration provides a more useful framework for economic integration.

3. A review of selected theoretical perspectives

A historical perspective on integration trends suggests that the first wave of regionalism (during the 1960s) was heavily concentrated in and affected by the European experiences. Other attempts, at that stage, to embrace universally an active set of regional integration projects were thwarted by the lack of support from the United States – interested more in general multilateral free trade – as well as by the relatively protectionist, inward-looking, import-substituting industrial policies that many developing countries tended to follow.

With the second wave of regionalism, many of these factors had changed profoundly. The United States has supported regional integration in North America. Wider and deeper integration in Europe has become a reality and the successful completion of the Uruguay Round, as well as developing countries being forced to liberalise their protectionist regimes as part of their adjustment programmes, all provided impetus. This environment, which is radically different from that of three or four decades previously, is engendered an optimism that regionalism is here to stay.

In line with these developments, theoretical analyses of the effects of regional economic integration abound. As Robson (1994) points out, the central thrust of much of the analysis has had two main focus areas. The first of these involves an evaluation of regionalism in terms of the interests of the respective blocs themselves. The second stream (and closely related to the first) attempts to theorise about the effects of increased economic regionalisation on the world trading system and on world welfare in general.

Robson (1994: 171) makes the point that much of the analysis in the modern approach tends to rest on less restrictive assumptions than was the case with preceding analyses and that it tends to identify a range of non-orthodox sources of benefit. Expanding on these, he argues that potential benefit in the newer approaches arises from at least two sources. The first is the gains from overcoming the costs associated with some of the market distortions and barriers that result from government policies. These, he emphasises, are not limited to the traditional static allocative costs of tariffs (which represented the core of earlier trade creation and diversion analyses) and equivalent quantitative restrictions. Rather, the present emphasis focuses on the impact of integration on investment creation and diversion as well as on administrative efficiency and transaction costs. Another source of potential gain arises from economies of scale in the operation of public sector policy coordination. Robson (1994: 172) concludes by incorporating two additional considerations – that a *sine qua non* for successful integration is that the potential benefits of such schemes be acceptably distributed and that particular attention must be devoted to the issue of credibility. If these factors are absent, the whole arrangement could falter and investment, as well as other potential gains, could be severely jeopardised.

Despite the proliferation of regional integration agreements, the share of global trade taking place within regions has hardly changed since the postwar years, with the exception of the EU. This suggests that agreements themselves hardly affect trade patterns on an *ex post* basis and that possibly successful agreements are more likely to occur between countries that *ex ante* exhibit high levels of trade complementarity. On this particular issue one should bear in mind the point made by the World Trade Organisation Report on Integration – that the number of agreements applied for under GATT regulations *per se*, is a deceptive measure, as some of these have never operated or been implemented, and others have ceased to operate (WTO, 1995).

Srinivasan *et al.* (1993) are quite persuasive in arguing that the new regionalism will be unlikely further to change regional trade patterns in the global economy. Despite the current climate of liberalisation and outward orientation, the authors maintain that the new regional integration (RI) agreements are 'more defensive than integrationist in nature, with small countries seeking "safe-haven" trade agreements with larger countries'. The authors make the points that the newer agreements tend to focus on smaller trade linkages than the older regional schemes and that there is considerable doubt as to whether there is genuine new liberalisation in such agreements. Along similar lines to Robson, the authors argue that the classic Vinerian trade creation/trade diversion framework is not well suited to the study and quantification of more recent regional integration.

The queries posed in this selected literature review indicate that any assessment of the impact of the new regional revolution must, of necessity, be more thoroughgoing than a simple application of the partial static tools of international trade. Both the motives behind the new shift to regionalism and the effects are highly complex. These motives could be founded on a belief that regional integration is indeed conducive to economic growth. Yet they may also reflect a defensive reaction, within less developed countries, to the pace of multilateral or global economic liberalisation and/or the world-wide formation of dominant trading blocs. Assessing the potential impact of the process on some of the more recent integration arrangements (comprising parties quite desperate to overcome their economic stagnation) using criteria that are too narrowly defined and incorrectly applied might be extremely harmful and lead to erroneous conclusions. Falsely defined hopes can lead to disillusionment.

De Melo and Panagiriya (1993: 184) emphasise the requirements for successful regional integration schemes for developing countries under the present international dispensation in the following way: such schemes 'tend to benefit from a convergence in objectives, from having few partners, and from the willingness of countries to surrender some national autonomy and commit to supranational rules. If these institutional considerations are met, it is likely that dynamic gains reflected in higher growth will be reaped'. These 'dynamic' effects are not peculiar to RI arrangements, however. In a large number of past RI schemes, the benefits of coordination to supranational bodies were absent in the integration arrangements and, given the vastly divergent objectives from participating countries, failure was inevitable. De Melo and Panagiriya

(1993) also emphasise the potential dynamic benefit emerging from economic cooperation in those areas where significant externalities and public goods (education, research and development, infrastructure, environment) exist. They regard this as lacking in the earlier regionalism and if implemented properly in the present milieu could enhance the potential gains of new co-operative agreements.

4.   Is regional integration viable in Southern Africa?

Most analysts acknowledge that it is premature to talk of economic integration in Southern Africa, and that the preferred term 'economic cooperation' more aptly captures the regional programme for the area. However, despite consensus among South African policy makers, there are various initiatives that seem to go beyond simple cooperation. Calls for a common market by the Common Market for East and Southern Africa (COMESA), and a FTA by the Southern African Development Community (SADC), are testimony to the fact that policy-makers are more ambitious about the pace of economic integration in Southern Africa than a limited programme of cooperation.

There is indeed very little disagreement on the need for economic cooperation among countries in Southern Africa. Where disagreement emerges is on the pace of economic integration, the kind of institutional backup and the sequencing of the integration process. Moreover, the significance of integration for development is not clear-cut. It is unclear to what extent integration may positively affect developing countries' terms of trade, create dynamism in industry of the region, and so on.

What is clear is that the new literature has far greater relevance for developing countries than the traditional approaches in that it explains, in a more accurate and comprehensive way, both the motivation and benefits to integration, as well as presenting a more dynamic analysis of the impact of integration. Yet, although the new literature on economic integration provides an assessment of the prospects for economic integration that is more congenial to developing countries, the Linder hypothesis – which maintains that countries at similar levels of development tend to trade more than countries at disparate levels of development – still provides a major challenge to the region. In other words, 'countries with similar living standards will share a broader range of tradeable goods and hence particularly inter-industry trade will be higher. On the other hand, GDP per capita differences are highly correlated with differences in factor endowments and hence smaller differences could reduce trade, especially comparative advantage driven intra-industry trade' (Foroutan, 1993). This problem is compounded by the fact that small markets and low per capita incomes – characteristics of most countries in the SADC region – have not been conducive to significant trade based on scale economies and product differentiation (de la Torre and Kelly, 1992: 36). Moreover, they have very similar export structures with very little scope for exchange, unlike developed country intra-industry trade. A sober assessment of these issues requires an appraisal of the essential characteristics of the Southern African economy.

5. The Southern African economy

Countries in the Southern African region differ considerably in both size and level of development.[1] For example, South Africa recorded a GNP per capita of $2,902 for 1993 while Mozambique's was $80. Mozambique has the lowest GNP per capita in the region and Lesotho is the smallest economy in the region. Zimbabwe has the fourth highest GNP per capita, but is the second largest economy in the region. South Africa, on the other hand, is without exception the largest both in terms of the GNP per capita and in terms of the size of the economy.

The asymmetry between South Africa and the rest of the region is startling. South Africa accounted for 82% of the total GDP of the region in 1993; and South Africa and Zimbabwe together contributed close to 90% of the GDP of the region. Industrial capabilities in the region differ considerably, with South Africa at the one extreme with a very diversified industrial sector and countries such as Angola and Namibia with very small industrial capabilities. This restrictive industrial structure will strongly influence the way policy-makers approach strategies for economic integration in Southern Africa.

6. The prospects for increasing trade

This section focuses on what may be considered the bedrock of economic integration: the ability of regions to integrate through trade. Foroutan (1993) formulates an interesting modification of the usual classic taxonomy of regional integration arrangements (free trade area, customs unions, common markets). She identifies five types of integration: goods market or trade integration; labour market integration; capital market integration; monetary integration; and integration of government activity and regulation, alternatively known as cooperation. The advantage of this taxonomy, when applied in the context of Southern Africa, is that it allows each of these possible cases of integration to occur in conjunction with or separately from the others. Foroutan's conclusion is that trade integration in combination with regulation, for example, has more chance of success in the sub-Saharan African (SSA) region if it is approached as providing 'an enabling environment to those producers that begin competing in world markets' (Foroutan, 1993: 239). Complete trade and labour integration ought to remain a longer-term objective. There is a general feeling among policy-makers that this is the route Southern Africa ought to follow. In fact, as Foroutan (1993) explains for sub-Saharan African countries, the appeal of some form of RI is 'almost intuitive'.

Intra-regional trade in sub-Saharan Africa

Until recently, debates about the potential impacts of integration arrangements have frequently excluded Africa or treated the continent only superficially. Various surveys on the state of integration have focused on the EU and North America. Whether this reflects the general feeling that African regional arrangements do not merit serious analysis because so many have failed, or because of an implicit recognition of Africa representing a 'basket case' not worthy of consideration, can be debated. Given the small size of countries in the region (approximating Belgium in terms of GNP) and the fact that these are the poorest in the world, with poor endowments of human and physical capital as well as infrastructure, the perpetual failure of various agreements has led many to be sceptical about RI as a model of development.

Pessimism has also been reflected in some of the recent ex ante empirical work conducted by Michaely (1994) and reproduced in the World Bank's Global Economic Prospects (1995). Using a trade complementarity index to provide some indication of the likelihood of successful integration in new trade arrangements, the index suggests that trade potential for sub-Saharan Africa is extremely limited – a figure of 0.09 on the index compared with 0.53 for the EEC and 0.56 for NAFTA. The low complementarity reflects the similarity in respective countries' production structures, with exports matching the imports of trading countries only poorly. 'In such a setting, countries have little to gain from regional arrangements and should focus mainly on unilateral or multilateral trade liberalisation' (World Bank, 1995b: 20). As the range of the index is between zero (when no good exported by one country is imported by the other) and one (when the shares of one country's import correspond exactly to the other's exports), a value closer to one would indicate a higher probability of successful integration.

It must be emphasised that there are problems with the use of the Michaely index as the definitive guide to the viability of regional integration initiatives. First, the index makes the assumption that the structure of trade is not heavily distorted by trade barriers between the two partners, an assumption that is not accurate in heavily protectionist SSA countries. Secondly, the construction of the index does not account for a small country trading with a larger one, the latter importing from a variety of other countries. Thirdly, the lack of successful integration and free trade arrangements could also account for the low value of the index. Different institutional configurations could profoundly affect the pattern of trade. In addition, it must be realised that the construction of the index is based on official trade flows. Given the large volume of unrecorded trade in SSA, a substantial volume of such trade may be missed. Furthermore, if a set of regional arrangements proves successful and yields dynamic benefits in the form of investment in the region, growth, and a massive improvement in transportation, physical and human capital as well as financial infrastructure, a radical readjustment in trade patterns may be forthcoming.

A final point about regional trade scepticism in sub-Saharan Africa ought to be made. As discussed above, such pessimism is derived from historical failures of various arrangements, as well as Michaely type trade complementarity analyses suggesting that trade with the rest of the world ought to be the overriding priority, through a process of general liberalisation. These arguments can be criticised for the underlying assumption that all important national obstacles to foreign trade apply equally in all countries; this argument is most coherently dealt with by Weeks and Subasat (1995). In their analysis of the potential for agricultural trade integration within the COMESA agreement, they establish a substantial case for such regional trade. They emphasise that, for a wide range of COMESA members, trade-facilitating factors such as transport, insurance, marketing channels and market information, and intra-regional trade mechanisms, are much less developed than extra-regional mechanisms (p. 4). They identify a duality in the agricultural trade of COMESA countries; traditional exports such as coffee and cotton go to developed countries rather than to other countries in the region, basic foodstuffs on the other hand generally do not leave the region.

Large capital intensive firms produce for the developed country market and small-scale firms for the local, national and regional markets. Substantial investment in trade facilitating factors could greatly enhance the potential for regional trade and reduce such dualities. 'A policy framework that treats intra-regional trade as a derivative aspect of general trade promotion is likely to reinforce duality' (Weeks and Subasat,

1995: 5). Further research has shown that in the case of agriculture, for example, the agro-climatic suitability for growing food crops among countries such as Malawi, Tanzania, Zambia and Zimbabwe makes for differences in their natural advantage for producing the main staples (maize, cassava, beans, sorghum and millet). This reflects the scope for complementarity, not only in the growing and harvesting of certain crops but in further downstream agro-processing activities.

As far as manufactured goods are concerned, the argument is that, historically, import substitution policies induced similar patterns of industrial structure, thus negating the possibility of trade in manufactured goods. However, intra-SADC trade in similar labour intensive products such as textiles, clothing and shoes may be an important source of competition for member countries and could encourage more aggressive extra-regional exports. Moreover, the potential for increasing intra-industry trade in this sector is large. However, the trade potential differs among different countries and sub-sets of countries in the region partly because of the diverse levels of industrialisation among the respective economies. Hence the scope for trade for countries with small industrial bases, such as Malawi, Lesotho, Botswana or Mozambique, is more limited than is the scope for trade with larger economies such as Zimbabwe and South Africa, specifically intra-industry trade.

There are various grounds for optimism about increasing intra-regional trade. One is redirecting trade flows. The policy proposal to redirect trade flows is based on trade data (ADB, 1993) showing that certain countries in the SADC region import a similar range of products from outside the region that certain countries within the region export. It is estimated that goods worth about US$1.8 billion that are exported by COMESA countries to non-COMESA countries are imported by other COMESA countries from non-PTA countries. Moreover, most economists now accept that official trade statistics grossly underestimate the true potential of intra-regional trade in Southern Africa since a great deal of trade among neighbouring countries goes unrecorded. This growing informal or unofficial trade proves that there is far greater scope for complementarity.

South Africa's trade with the region

The nature and extent of intra-regional trade in Southern Africa is fairly predictable. Most economies in the region conduct over 90% of their trade with the rest of the world. Southern Africa represents the familiar story of being heavily reliant on the international market for the imports of capital and technology intensive goods for which there are generally, with the exception of South Africa, no competing intra-regional substitutes.

Table 7.1   Primary commodity exports as percentage of total exports

Country	Primary exports as % of total exports
Angola	95
Botswana	98
Lesotho	n.a.
Malawi	76
Namibia	95
South Africa	70
Swaziland	n.a.
Tanzania	79
Zambia	90
Zimbabwe	56
Average	82

Sources: *SADC Review* (1993); *African Development Indicators* (World Bank, 1995a).

Table 7.1 shows that primary commodity exports dominate the exports of all countries in SADC with an average of 82% of total SADC exports.

Not surprisingly, South Africa's total exports and imports dwarf the SADC total. According to 1993 data South Africa accounted for 70% of total SADC exports and 62% of total imports. The second largest exporter after South Africa was Angola, which accounted for an estimated 8% of total SADC exports.

Table 7.2 shows the measure of openness of the respective SADC countries including South Africa. Most of the SADC economies are well integrated into the world economy with the values of imports and exports to total GDP being very high – averaging 80% from 1980 to 1993. The import to GDP ratio has also remained fairly constant, although exports have dropped marginally. What this represents is that trade as a percentage of GDP in these countries has not grown in any significant way. Moreover, the high trade intensity is a reflection of extra-regional trade with minimal growth in intra-regional trade.

According to South African customs and excise data (1994), Africa accounts for 9.5% of the Southern African Customs Union's (SACU) total world exports. However, 70% of total SACU exports go to the rest of SADC, with a large proportion going to two or three countries. Figures for South Africa's, as opposed to total SACU, exports in the African market differ considerably since the BLNS countries (Botswana, Lesotho, Namibia and Swaziland) rely heavily on South African imports. Rough estimates for 1992 suggest that just over 16% of South Africa's total exports are destined for the BLNS countries and the rest of SADC. South Africa's exports to

Table 7.2   SADC total imports and exports

Country	1980 X + M/GDP (%)	1990 X + M/GDP (%)	1993 X + M/GDP (%)
Angola	47.6	53	60.4
Botswana	118.2	105.8	83.5
Lesotho	131.0	121.2	126.7
Malawi	47.6	38.5	30.5
Mozambique	49.4	63.5	68.5
South Africa	56.8	39.6	37.49
Swaziland	155.5	130.7	156.0
Tanzania	32.5	61.5	47.3
Zambia	66.2	84.1	52.6
Zimbabwe	52.0	47.7	52.8

Notes
X = exports; M = imports.
Source: *African Development Indicators* (World Bank, 1995a).

SACU alone are around 12% of South Africa's total world exports and just under 5% for the rest of the region. The proportional share of the region in South Africa's total imports is considerably less than it is for exports. South Africa absorbs an estimated 7% of total imports from the rest of SADC, with 5% from the BLNS countries and close to 2% from the rest of SADC (ADB, 1993).

The nature of South Africa's export potential in the international and regional markets has been well documented. Data for 1994 show that South Africa's largest exports (excluding unclassified goods such as gold and arms) in decreasing order (based on rand value) are: precious and semi-precious stones, base metals, mineral products, chemical products, machinery and appliances, motor vehicles and parts, and vegetable products. It is surprising that South Africa exports a sizeable proportion of chemical products and machinery and appliances to the African market when in fact it is considered not to be competitive in these products internationally. The country's seven largest imports (in decreasing order) are the following: machinery and appliances, vehicles and components, chemical products, plastics, textiles, optical and photographic, and base metals.

South Africa presents a typical developing country export profile with a preponderance of primary exports as a percentage of total exports. A geographical disaggregation indicates that approximately 40% of South Africa's[2] manufacturing exports are destined for the African market.

SACU's trade with Africa has expanded rapidly in the last few years – by 40% in 1989, 22% in 1990 and 25% in 1991, slowing to 9.48% from 1992 to 1993 but picking up to 23.4% from 1993 to 1994 (calculations are in nominal rand value terms). From the perspective of SADC countries exporting to South Africa, the percentage growth of exports increased in 1993 to 1994 by 22.61% from a low growth of 2.87% the previous year, implying greater two-way trade flows.

The extreme disparity between South Africa's production pattern and its trade pattern indicates that the economic powerhouse of the region is not competitive in international terms. Despite this, SACU enjoyed a 3.4 billion trade surplus in 1992 with SADC. This increased to 4.5 billion and is likely to grow in the future. However, for South Africa–SADC trade, for which figures are less readily available, South Africa's trade surplus is likely to increase because of its high levels of trade with the BLNS countries.

This raises the question of growing trade deficits with South Africa for the SADC countries. Why should South Africa be interested in forming a more far-reaching integration agreement when in fact its trade in the African market is increasing anyway? Various studies show that there is considerable potential for the non-SACU countries to switch supply from third countries to South Africa. While the Southern African market may provide an important outlet for South African manufactured exports, a major challenge is to prevent a kind of 'hub and spoke bilateralism' where South Africa becomes the hub and the surrounding countries, the spokes. South Africa could dominate the region further by encouraging bilateral trade with individual Southern African countries and, in doing so, discourage trade among the spoke economies (see Cassim, 1994).

A critical issue for South Africa is the extent to which it can compete with third country suppliers in the SADC market when in most of its manufacturing sector it is not internationally competitive. Preliminary evidence suggests that South Africa's close geographical proximity to the regional market may be an important factor in explaining the country's ability to compete in certain products with third country suppliers. In particular, the cost, insurance and freight (cif) levels are lower for South Africa than for third country suppliers. Another factor considered important in explaining South African manufactured exports to the region is licensing agreements that forbid South Africa from exporting to the international market, but allow exports to the regional market.

It should be emphasised that although increasing intra-regional trade is a major objective of economic integration, it should not be seen as a substitute for extra-regional trade. Instead, it should complement extra-regional trade. Hence, competition among firms in the region could act as an important impetus towards expanding extra-regional exports. There is a general view that world markets have a much greater capacity to absorb exports than regional markets. This point is particularly relevant for a country such as South Africa that wants to expand into the African market. The prospects for South African exports on the regional market are severely limited – the regional GDP of the SADC region alone is just 25% of the total GDP of Hong Kong, for example.

Labour standards and unequal development

Often overlooked issues relate to what has been referred to as free and fair trade, and the inequality of partners in an integration arrangement. These have come to the fore as a result of the NAFTA. They have also gained much prominence in the Southern African region, specifically in the context of a recently renewed bilateral agreement between South Africa and Zimbabwe.

The issue of 'free and fair trade' emerges when partners in a regional trade agreement have different labour and environmental standards. Unfair advantages are bestowed on those countries with lower wage costs and employment standards, as well as on those countries prepared to sacrifice environmental safety procedures. A paradox arises in that comparative labour costs may represent a country's trading advantage, but cheaper goods within the region offer consumers an increase in real incomes. However, if regional trade agreements involve massive job losses either through direct trade or massive migrations of cheap labour, the sustainability of such agreements is jeopardised as employment standards are a crucial element of a nation's level of development.

Most nations establish minimum wage and maximum work-hour laws, child labour and compulsory schooling laws, occupational safety and health laws, equal opportunity or anti-discrimination laws, and laws governing dismissal. The level of unionisation in a country would obviously affect the extent of compliance with such standards. Similar arguments pertain to environmental legislation. Countries that have managed to achieve a certain decency in labour and environmental practices may face cost disadvantages when compared with undercutting partners in a regional trade agreements. The incorporation of a 'social clause' would in theory remedy this asymmetry. The establishment and enforcement of such a clause is problematic, however. There is no denying the necessity for some institutional monitoring arrangement for determining and enforcing such a clause as a precondition for a free trade regional arrangement. Harmonisation of such labour and environmental issues as far as is possible could go a long way to determining the success of the arrangement.

The issue of labour market interaction in a region of 'integration' such as Southern Africa is ambivalent to say the least. The analysis can be conducted on at least two fronts. First, there is the rather obvious inference that as other countries integrate more with South Africa – the dominant economy with the largest labour market – the major issue that will no doubt influence much of the debate is the unrestricted movement of labour from the small neighbouring countries to South Africa. Such movement of labour is taking place already and the xenophobic reaction of the South African labour movement represents a predictable response to such events. Comparative estimates of wage levels in non-primary sectors of industry show that, for South Africa, the real wage growth was 127% for the decade of the 1980s, while for Malawi it was 63%, Mozambique 53%, Swaziland 64%, Zambia 59% and Zimbabwe 104%.

The African Development Bank (1993) estimates (probably a serious underestimate) that migrants to South Africa in 1991 were approximately 600,000, with the principal areas of outmigration being Lesotho, Mozambique, Swaziland and Zimbabwe. One of the concerns of trade unions in South Africa is the possibility of depressing wage levels in the country. The issue of minimum wages and strong union organisation in South Africa has other ramifications as it could encourage local South African companies to relocate to neighbouring countries to take advantage of lower wages and relatively unorganised labour. Another aspect relates to the employment of secondary workers, female and child labour at substantially lower wage rates, as well as to the lack of minimum standards in both sets of countries. It is in this connection that the issues of the social clause and claims of unfair labour have emerged. However humanitarian these concerns are, they may be countered by arguments that liberalisation could induce a lowering in costs of living and, as such, serve to increase real wages. The arguments have to be carefully balanced, so as not to aggravate the potential social costs arising from an unregulated haphazard approach to integration, which could have important and complex consequences for labour markets in the region.

As far as the issue of unequal geographic development is concerned, debates on this aspect have a long history, from the theory of cumulative causation through the 'core-periphery' relationship to the more recent 'hub and spoke' framework, to the location of economic activity in an arrangement that may have been the outcome of 'serendipity' (Fine and Yeo, 1994: 15). Fine and Yeo (1994) discuss further how South Africa could provide the logical geographic centre of leadership in an SSA-type arrangement by virtue of its size and power in terms of population, income and infrastructure.

An earlier and most insightful contribution to this analysis is provided by Vaistos (1978) in a comprehensive survey of the prevailing difficulties of regional integration. Vaistos argues in a most persuasive fashion that the effects of trade liberalisation within regional groupings are most unlikely to lead to cumulative and comprehensive processes of growth and development. In fact, he suggests that this could lead to regional disintegration as it would accentuate inter-country polarisation effects with new investments and activities gravitating towards the zones of countries that already enjoy the larger markets and more adequately developed physical and human infrastructure. Furthermore, a concentration on the commitment to trade liberalisation could constitute a retrogressive step as regards other elements in the regional integration process, by relegating these to a low order of priority. Thus elements such as regional programming, infrastructure development, human investment, financial facilitation, etc. could be neglected in the environment of complacency accompanying the notion that trade liberalisation is sufficient to stimulate regional integration (Vaistos, 1978: 746). Vaistos also suggests that the reduction of regional tariffs could evoke a defensive response in weaker countries that could significantly increase the importance of non-tariff barriers. He argues that tariff liberalisation could conflict with other important national objectives of economic policy such as employment growth and income distribution.

A synthesis of the foregoing analyses suggests that in the process of regional integration, free trade tends to accentuate inequalities among countries, with the resulting polarisation increasing distributional differences rather than levelling them in both the short and long run. As a remedy Vaistos suggests direct interventions, particularly in the location of productive activities. These should be effected on an intra-industry/inter-sectoral basis rather than a holistic harmonisation strategy, until such inequalities are remedied. Joint and programmed production deepening and qualitative changes in local capabilities require a co-ordinating institution among the respective partners to prevent simple market integration becoming a strongly disintegrative force.

A key question is to what extent the integration of the market will exacerbate regional disparities within the region and thereby jeopardise the objective of convergence. This is of critical importance for Southern Africa in view of much speculation surrounding the impact of economic integration in individual countries. A cursory analysis by the Industrial Development Corporation (IDC) shows that South Africa has most to gain from a free trade agreement and some of the least developed countries will derive very little benefit. It is generally accepted that differential benefits to countries in terms of the relative impact on their gross domestic product are probably unavoidable in any economic union. IDC calculations from a static partial equilibrium model show that a FTA in the region would on average lead to an overall increase in GDP, although some countries would be worse off. In terms of industry, South African products that are likely to benefit are processed foods, chemicals and machinery.

While South Africa, as the regional giant, has to carry the responsibility of economic development in the region, the high level of unemployment in the country constrains its ability to transfer wealth to the region (Cassim, 1994). This opens an important debate about the role of donor funding and economic integration. If the facility to distribute the losses and gains from economic integration is critical to a programme of market integration, donors need to re-establish the priorities for their funding.

Foreign direct investment and trade

While the importance of encouraging FDI to the region can never be emphasised enough, very little consideration has been given to the relationship between regional integration and FDI. FDI can act both as an agent for and as a consequence of regional integration. Fine and Yeo (1994) advance the hypothesis that economic integration in SSA is more important in securing the accumulation of physical and human capital, by, for example, luring FDI, than it is in increasing intra-regional trade, at least in the short to medium term.

At one level, regional integration could potentially play an important role in encouraging investment in the Southern African region. Many multinationals are showing considerably more interest in, and support for, the lowering of intra-regional trade barriers. Access to a regional Southern African market may be an important attraction for multinationals. Investors, both foreign and domestic, will view the region as offering a range of advantages where firms would be able to invest in a range of different activities across countries – from investing for extraction of resources, to processing, sub- and final assembly, sale and distribution, technology development or overhead function (Cassim, 1995). This is important since in most SADC countries very little investment has been forthcoming because of, among other factors, small markets, poor economic growth and political instability.

At another level, direct investment could play a critical role in encouraging integration. Both domestic and foreign cross-border investment could encourage forward and backward linkages among firms and industries in the region. Cross-border investment is important in view of the fact that intra-regional trade in Southern Africa is very low. To a large extent it is investment flows that could be the driving force for growing intra-regional trade in the region.

Although seeking foreign investment itself, South Africa is a potential investor in the region. Some South African companies have already invested in the region. At this stage investment is concentrated in services, particularly retail, finance and insurance and, more recently, tourism. However, there is strong evidence of South African firms investing in processing and manufacturing activities, too. South African investors, particularly light labour-intensive footloose industries, may invest part of the operations in other SADC countries as a cost-saving mechanism in response to international competition.

There is a strong likelihood of increasing intra-regional trade, with South African companies investing in the region's various joint venture schemes between South African firms and firms in neighbouring countries that were formed immediately after South African's first democratic national elections. For example, a large South African beverage company, South African Breweries (SAB), has formed joint venture schemes in various countries, starting in Tanzania and followed by Zambia, Swaziland and Mozambique. These kinds of schemes are taking place in the tourism sector, too. Indeed, such cross-border investment is likely to engender increasing amounts of intra-firm trade in goods and services in the region. There is also a great deal of evidence that South Africa is becoming a launchpad among foreign investors to serve not only the Southern African market but the entire sub-Saharan Africa region. Various international firms in telecommunications and the motor industry, for example, are exploring joint venture schemes with South African companies to serve the sub-Saharan African market.

An interesting question is whether South African foreign direct investment in the region will be trade-enhancing or trade-substituting. In other words, will South African firms invest in the region to serve those markets or use these investments as a launch pad to increase potential exports? Initial signs suggest that South African investment in the region is likely to lead to an increasing proportion of intra-regional trade to be accounted for by intra-firm trade, albeit from a small base.

7.   Economic policy harmonisation

This section attempts to put the conditions for economic integration in Southern Africa into perspective. It shows that although conditions may not be ripe for a full-blown common market, readiness indicators prove that conditions are far more conducive to integration than they were a decade ago. The reasons behind low levels of intra-regional trade in SSA have been well documented and this paper will not dwell on these issues. However, it does attempt to assess whether some of the reasons given at least in the 1980s are still valid in the changing economic environment in the mid-1990s. In particular, the international institutions such as the World Bank, through structural adjustment programmes, and the WTO, through trade liberalisation, have played an important role in the process of harmonising the economies in the region.

Trade policy harmonisation

The traditional literature points out that the trade regimes as well as other practical trade problems in developing countries acted as an important impediment to the success of any regional integration programme. Apart from inward-looking trade regimes, the inability of countries to liberalise stems from their high dependence on trade revenue as well as very dispersed tariff structures that make harmonisation difficult.

It is important to note that countries in the region have to liberalise not only among themselves but also with third countries. The central issue is whether there is any logic in following a two-track approach to liberalisation. In other words, what benefits would there be for countries to liberalise at a faster rate at a regional level than at a multilateral level.

Countries in Southern Africa were typically characterised by highly dispersed effective protection, with little intra-regional trade occurring prior to integration. This stemmed from the inward-oriented development strategies by most member countries (de la Torre and Kelly, 1992: 36). The average mean tariff (nominal) of individual countries is lowest for Angola, with an average *ad valorem* tariff of 14%, and highest for Zimbabwe, with an average of 40%. The average is 23% for the region as a whole. This excludes non-tariff barriers, which still exist in some countries. The high level of tariff dispersion has also been mooted as one of the major reasons why an extension of SACU in the near to medium term is not a workable option.

A major obstacle to liberalisation is the tariff-revenue constraint, directly as a result of the import-substitution strategies. A preference-induced tariff revenue loss may actually necessitate a further increase in tariffs against the outside world to raise their trade barriers *vis-à-vis* the rest of the world after integration (Foroutan, 1993: 254). An important question is whether countries have reduced their dependence on trade taxes in the last decade. The preliminary evidence is mixed, with some becoming more dependent and some less than others. Despite this, however, most economies are less dependent today than they were a few years ago on revenue from import duties, but such duties are still an important source of revenue.

Macroeconomic harmonisation

The lack of macroeconomic harmonisation in the region has been identified as a major obstacle to economic integration in developing countries. The notion of macroeconomic convergence has gained much prominence in recent years in the European Union. Macroeconomic harmonisation is more common in countries at a fairly advanced level of development, as exemplified in the EU. One of the main reasons macro harmonisation becomes important stems from the fact that as countries trade more deeply with each other, they become more vulnerable to each others' macroeconomic behaviour.

Nadal De Simone and Genberg (1993) make two important points about macroeconomic policies and economic integration. First, they argue that it is important to establish the degree of macroeconomic policy coordination and discipline that is necessary for economic integration agreements to have their desired affects. Secondly, they say it should be determined whether increased market integration affects the incentives of policy-makers to surrender part of their policy autonomy and to submit to a degree of discipline that they otherwise would not have observed.

The greater the degree of economic integration that is sought, the more the need for coordination of fiscal and monetary policy among the integrating economies. Greater coordination is necessary to avoid situations in which external imbalances jeopardise the process of liberalisation within the regional integration agreements. In RI agreements involving economies of different size, the dominant economy has no choice but to assume the main responsibility for macroeconomic discipline, and in so doing RI may help the governments of smaller economies to become more disciplined in their monetary and fiscal policies. Insofar as discipline contributes to economic growth, this becomes an additional contribution of RI to boosting global welfare.

The critical issue is whether there is any merit in looking at the harmonisation of fiscal and monetary policies when more practical issues such as border controls, transport and so on, seem to be more urgent stumbling blocks to regional integration in Southern Africa. It is perhaps only in the SACU area that countries are most directly affected by South Africa's macroeconomic behaviour. How important is macroeconomic policy for the success or failure of regional integration arrangements, and is it possible to make an inventory of macroeconomic preconditions that facilitate such integration? In other words, economic integration requires participating countries to achieve a minimum degree of discipline over their macroeconomic policies (Hufbauer and Schott, 1994, p. 72).

It is important to understand that macroeconomic harmonisation in the context of Southern Africa has a very different meaning from that in the EU, for example. In the latter, close integration as manifested in a high level of intra-EU trade means that convergence has become a necessity. In the context of Southern Africa, however, it is merely to act as an important impetus to trade. The question really is whether it is possible to have harmonized policy in the context of highly variable growth rates, etc. Growth rates in GDP per capita for Southern African countries from 1985 to 1993 varied from an average annual growth rate (based on nominal US dollar values) of 13% for Botswana at one end to a –13% for Tanzania at the other end. Variations among countries are even greater when one looks at inflation rates and interest rates.

The question that arises is whether macroeconomic convergence will be the cause or consequence of regional economic integration. Consolidation of macroeconomic policy reform resulting from regional economic integration could be very beneficial to countries in the region. This suggests that countries in a regional grouping with poor macroeconomic records would be subject to the macroeconomic discipline of countries with a more favourable history. As the most powerful economy in the region, South Africa should be able to provide a monetary anchor or macroeconomic discipline for the smaller economies. However, this view hinges on the assumption that South Africa has a stable macroeconomic environment.

Fine and Yeo (1994) envisage an external guarantor such as the European Union as an underwriter for sound regional domestic policies that would enhance the mobilisation of private investment, initially from foreign sources. Credible commitments by respective governments to sensible and stable macroeconomic and trade policies could, if managed by a neutral institution, stimulate sustained investment and growth, which could be 'equitably' managed by such an institution.

8.   Conclusions

The benefits of economic integration should not be exaggerated. Although regional integration agreements could bring potentially large benefits to the Southern African economy, the asymmetry between South Africa and the rest of the region, the diverse macroeconomic behaviour of

SADC countries, and the limited and uneven industrial capabilities could readily abort a fully-fledged market driven regional programme. In the final analysis, integration cannot be a substitute for good domestic policies and does not render them any less necessary. But the arguments that favour its pragmatic retention as a policy tool in developing countries, in part as a means of reinforcing good policies, appear to be more compelling than those that simply argue for its blanket rejection on orthodox trade-based considerations. Foroutan (1993) suggests a combination of regulation and government activity in the integration process. This would imply similar tax and investment codes, harmonisation of administrative and bureaucratic rules, the creation of joint administration (e.g. customs administration), joint development of infrastructure and common services, such as air services, multinational universities, and the like, as a pathway to integration.

Despite the fact that the conditions in Southern Africa now are more conducive to economic integration than a decade ago, poor economic growth in most of the countries, continued dependence on primary exports, balance of payments problems and other macroeconomic constraints continue to dampen the prospects for economic integration. Moreover, the asymmetry between South Africa and the rest of the region puts an undue burden on an economy that itself is fragile by international standards.

Notes

1. This section is based on data from the South African Reserve Bank, World Development Reports and SADC data.
2. Although the data are presented as SACU exports to Africa, one could comfortably estimate that more than 98% of exports in these three categories emanate from South Africa, rather than the BLNS countries.

References

African Development Bank (ADB). 1993. *Economic Integration in Southern Africa*, vols I & II. Oxford: Biddles Ltd.

Anderson, K. and R. Blackhurst. 1993. *Regional Integration and the Global Trading System*. Harvester Wheatsheaf.

Balassa, B. and L. Bauwens. 1988. 'The determinants of intra–European trade in manufactured goods'. *European Economic Review*, 32: 1421–37.

Baldwin, R. 1994. *Towards and Integrated Europe*. London: Centre for Economic Policy Research.

Cable, V. and D. Henderson. 1994. *Trade Blocs? The Future of Regional Integration*. Royal Institute of International Affairs. London: Redwood Books, distributed by Brookings Institution.

Cassim, R. 1994. 'The single European market and Eastern Europe, lessons and implications for Southern Africa'. African Regional Conference, University of Botswana, 20–4 June.

Cassim, R. 1995. 'Rethinking economic integration in Southern Africa'. *Trade Monitor*, no. 8 (September), UCT.

Cassim, R. and A. Hirsch. 1995. 'A free trade agreement between the EU and SA: Policy options'. TPMP brief paper.

Cassim, R. and M. Setai. 1994. 'Economic integration and Asia: lessons and implications for South Africa'. *Trade Monitor*, no. 8 (December).

Chowdury, A. and I. Iyanatul. 1993. *The Newly Industrialising Economies of East Asia.* London and New York: Routledge.

Collier, P. and J. W. Gunning. 1993. *Linkages Between Trade Policy and Regional Integration*, Paper presented for the African Economic Research Consortium launch workshop on Regional Integration and Trade Liberalisation, Nairobi, 1–3 December.

Davies, R. 1995. Presentation to SADC National Workshop, Helderfontein, 1/2 June.

de la Torre, Augusto and M. R. Kelly. 1992. *Regional Trade Arrangements.* Occasional Paper 93, IMF.

De Melo, J. and A. Panagariya. 1993. *New Dimensions in Regional Integration.* Cambridge, Centre Economic Policy Research.

Ehrenberg, R. 1994. *Labour Markets and Integrating National Economies*, The Brookings Institute, Washington, DC.

Fine, B. and S. Yeo. 1994. 'Regional integration in sub-Saharan Africa: dead end or a fresh start?'. AERC, Nairobi.

Foroutan, F. 1993. 'Regional integration in sub-Saharan Africa: past experience and future prospects'. In De Melo and Panagariya (1993).

Hufbauer, G. C. and J. Schott. 1994. *Western Hemisphere Economic Integration.* Washington, DC: Institute of International Economics.

Michaely, Michael. 1994. *Trade Preferential Agreements in Latin America: An Ex Ante Assessment.* Latin America and the Caribbean Region, Washington, DC: The World Bank. A summary of the Michaely findings is contained in World Bank (1995).

Nadal De Simone, F. and Genberg, H. 1993. 'Regional Integration agreements and macroeconomic discipline. In Anderson and Blackhurst (1993).

Robson, P. 1994. 'The new regionalism and developing countries in economic and political integration in Africa'. In S. Bulmer and A. Scott, eds. Oxford: Basil Blackwell.

Saasa, O. S., ed. 1991. *Joining the Future: Economic Integration and Cooperation in Africa.* African Centre for Technology Studies, Kenya.

SADC. *SADC Review.* Various issues. Southern Africa Development Community.

Shiells, C. 1995. 'Regional trade blocs: trade creating or diverting. *Finance and Development*, March.

Srinivasan, T. N., J. Whalley and I. Wooton. 1993. 'Measuring the effects of regionalism on trade and welfare'. In K. Anderson and R. Blackhurst, eds, *Regional Integration and the Global Trading System.* Geneva: Harvester Press.

Stewart, F. 1991. 'A note on "strategic trade" theory and the south.' *Journal of International Development*, vol. 3, no. 5.

Thomsen, S. 1994. 'Regional integration and multinational production'. In Cable and Henderson (1994).

Vaistos, C. 1978. 'Crisis in regional economic cooperation (integration) among developing countries: a survey'. *World Development*, vol. 6.

Weeks, J. and T. Subasat. 1995. *Agricultural Trade Integration for Eastern and Southern Africa*. ODA.

World Bank. 1993. *World Development Report 1993*. London and New York: Oxford University Press.

World Bank. 1995a. *African Development Indicators*. Washington, DC: The World Bank.

World Bank. 1995b. *Global Economic Prospects and the Developing Countries*. Washington, DC: IBRD/The World Bank.

World Trade Organisation (WTO). 1995. *Regionalism and the World Trading System*. Geneva: WTO.

8
Real and Monetary Determinants of the Real Exchange Rate in South Africa[1]

Janine Aron, Ibrahim A. Elbadawi and Brian Kahn

1. Introduction

Issues related to exchange rate management are among the most important concerns of the current debate on economic reform in South Africa. The real exchange rate[2] is an important relative price signalling intersectoral growth in the long run. The level of the real exchange rate (relative to an equilibrium real exchange rate level) and its stability have been shown to be an important influence on exports and private investment (e.g. Caballero and Corbo, 1981; Serven and Solimano, 1991). Policy issues that stand out in this regard for South Africa include judging an appropriate level of the real exchange rate that is consistent with 'sustainable' long-term capital flows, or the equilibrium real exchange rate. Another concern is the level of real exchange rate that will be consistent with a more open and hopefully more export-oriented economy in the future, with diminished dependence on the non-renewable resource base. The mining sector has not only been the mainstay of an otherwise relatively well-diversified economy, but has also influenced macroeconomic policy, especially exchange rate policy (Kahn, 1992).

The evolution of the real exchange rate is characterised by considerable volatility. Influences on the real exchange rate that need to be made explicit include the role of fiscal, monetary, exchange rate and trade policies; the effect of terms of trade shocks (especially in the gold sector); and the massive shifts in capital flows that closely reflect South Africa's volatile political cycle over the last 25 years. When dealing with large capital flows the authorities face a trade-off between allowing the exchange rate to appreciate, thus having a negative impact on the competitiveness of exports, and sterilising these effects, thus inducing losses to the reserve bank. Recent events have shown that the management of capital flows in a more internationalised economy presents a formidable challenge for South Africa's policy-makers.

To the best of our knowledge, this chapter presents the first formal definition and estimation of the fundamental (long-run) and short-run influences in a model for the real exchange rate in South Africa. (See Table 8.1, which outlines the detailed parity changes in South Africa's foreign exchange market from 1961 to 1995.) The model aims to focus

Table 8.1 Detailed parity changes in the South African foreign exchange market

Date	Parity change
14 Feb. 1961	The currency is decimalised, and continues to be linked to the £ sterling at R2.00 = £1.00.
Nov. 1967	The rand does not follow the sterling devaluation of 14.3%.
23 Aug. 1971	The £ sterling link is changed to a US$ link with the float of the US$ on 15 Aug. 1971, at R1.00 = $1.40.
21 Dec. 1971	The rand is relinked to the £ sterling at R1.9543 = £1.00.
30 Jun. 1972	The sterling link is maintained after the £ sterling's float on 23 June 1972, and the dismantling of the sterling area.
24 Oct. 1972	The rand is relinked to the US$ at R1.00 = $1.22732.
14 Feb. 1973	Devaluation of the US$ in Feb. implies a revaluation: R1.00 = $1.4193.
5 Jun. 1973	The rand is revalued by 4.98%: R1.00 = $1.49.
24 Jun. 1974	Move to 'controlled float' with an effective rand rate.
27 Jun. 1975	Return to a fixed US$ peg at the rate of R1.00 = $1.40.
22 Sept. 1975	The rand is devalued 17.85%: the new rate is R1.00 = $1.15.
24 Jan. 1979	A two-tier exchange rate system is established. An official rate of R1.00 = $1.15 is renamed the commercial rand and put on a controlled float, applicable to foreign trade, authorised capital transfers and current payments including remittance of dividend and interest payments. A free-floating financial rand replaces the market-determined securities rand, applicable to non-residents' financial transactions, including direct foreign investment, repatriation of capital and profits, and outward capital transfers by residents and emigrants.
7 Feb. 1983	The dual exchange rates are unified to a controlled float of an effective rand.
2 Sept. 1985	The two-tier system is re-established, with commercial and financial rands.
Mar. 1995	The dual rates are unified

Note From the 1960s, a securities (or 'switch') rand was operative for the purchase of South African securities by non-residents, which were not transferable between non-residents. This was then replaced by the financial rand in 1979.
Source: SARB *Quarterly Bulletin*.

only on the period of South Africa's dual exchange rate regime, and estimation is quarterly from 1970:1 to 1995:1, in which quarter the two exchange rates were unified.[3]

Cointegration methodology and single equation error correction models[4] are used to investigate simultaneously both the short-run and long-run equilibrium determinants of the real exchange rate in South Africa. The cointegrated equilibrium is obtained from a theoretical model of the real exchange rate that uses the macroeconomic balance approach, focusing on the requirements for achieving internal and external balance simultaneously (e.g. Williamson, 1985, 1994; Polak, 1995). Equilibrium is thus characterised as 'the relative price of non-tradeable to tradeable goods which, for given sustainable values of other relevant variables such as taxes, international terms of trade, commercial policy, capital and aid flows and technology, results in the simultaneous attainment of internal and external equilibrium' (Edwards, 1989). This notion of equilibrium is intertemporal, as the path of the equilibrium real exchange rate is affected not only by current values of the fundamentals but also by expectations about the future path of these variables. Given unit root non-stationarity of the exchange rate and its long-run fundamentals, a cointegration/ equilibrium-correction model of the type used in this chapter will be shown to account for the empirical conditions of the definition above.

For the remainder of this section we provide an overview of exchange rate policy and external balance since the 1970s. Section 2 outlines the theoretical model of the real exchange rate, and derives a reduced form empirical model. Motivating the estimation of an empirical model is a discussion in Section 3 of the evolution of the real exchange rate in South Africa and the fundamental variables that influence the real exchange rate. In Section 4 the model is applied to South Africa to estimate a dynamic equilibrium-correction specification for the real exchange rate. Conclusions and some policy implications are collected in Section 5.

Overview of exchange rate policy and external balance in South Africa, 1970–95

During the period under review, major shocks in the form of significant gold price changes and political crises, resulting in capital outflows and intensified trade sanctions, have complicated the management of the exchange rate and blurred the objectives of macroeconomic policies. At the same time, the period was marked by rising inflation, with inflation rates well in excess of 10% being a characteristic of the 1980s. Macroeconomic policies, particularly monetary and exchange rate policies, were aimed at different objectives at different times: in some periods the balance of payments was the main focus, while in others, an anti-inflation stance became the primary objective. Moreover, at various points, monetary, fiscal and exchange rate policies were in conflict with one other (De Kock Commission, 1984). Fiscal policy was not closely coordinated with the other policies for most of the period, and only since the early 1990s have questions been raised about the sustainability of fiscal deficits.

Overview of exchange rate policy

The movements of the real effective exchange rate can be seen in Figure 8.1. During the 1970s, South Africa's exchange rate policy mirrored volatile developments on the international front, and during the period under review there were a number of significant regime shifts (see also Kahn, 1992). These regime changes were not only of a technical nature (see Table 8.1) but also related to changes in policy objectives. Until 1979, the exchange rate was essentially fixed, being pegged to one currency or another. Alterations in the rate were determined by policy makers, and took the form of discrete step-changes. In August 1971 the rand, which for the previous decade had been linked to the pound sterling, was pegged to the US dollar. The peg reverted to sterling the following December, devaluing by 12.3%, and the link was maintained in June of the following

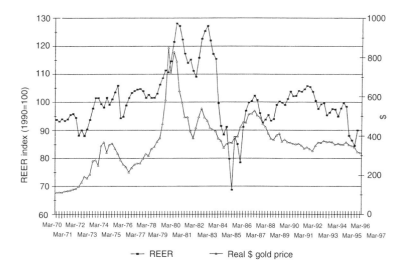

Figure 8.1   REER and the gold price

year when sterling floated. The peg changed back to the dollar in October 1972, appreciating the rand by 3% against other currencies. Nevertheless, the 10% devaluation of the dollar in February 1973 was not followed by the rand and in June 1973 the rand revalued by 5% against the dollar. In June 1974, a system of independent managed floating was adopted that involved a number of small but frequent adjustments to the middle market rand/dollar exchange rate; 11 adjustments were made between June 1974 and June 1975, Following speculative pressures on the rand, the Reserve Bank pegged the rate to the dollar in June 1975. But with continued pressure on the balance of payments, the rand was devalued against the dollar by 17.9% in September 1975. The link with the dollar was thereafter maintained until 1979.

An integral part of the exchange rate regime was the control on capital movements or exchange controls. Existing controls were intensified in 1961 following the capital outflows that came about in the aftermath of the Sharpeville shootings and the consequent political upheavals. Essentially the controls restricted resident flows, and the proceeds of the sale of assets by non-residents were placed in blocked rand accounts, which made repatriation of capital a difficult process (Garner, 1994). In 1976, the system was modified to allow for the transfer of assets between non-residents.

Greater flexibility was introduced into the foreign exchange market in 1979 with a dual currency exchange rate system, following the recommendations of the Interim Report of the De Kock Commission (1984). The reserve bank announced an official or commercial exchange rate on a daily basis in line with market forces. This practice ceased from 1983 with the commercial rate determined in the market subject to direct intervention by the reserve bank. A second exchange rate, the financial rand, applied to most nonresident portfolio and direct investment. All other transactions, including all current account transaction (as well as repatriation of profits, interest and dividends) were channelled through the commercial rand market. Foreign loans, including trade credits, were also transacted at commercial rand rates. Apart from limited intervention in the early 1990s, the reserve bank did not intervene in the financial rand market, resulting in a freely floating exchange rate. However, the thinness of the market made it a highly volatile rate. The intended impact of the financial rand was to break the direct link between domestic and foreign interest rates, as well as to insulate the capital account from certain categories of capital flows. Any outflow of non-resident capital had to be matched by an inflow, and was achieved through movements in the financial rand rate.

In 1983, the financial rand was abolished in line with the liberalisation moves recommended by the de Kock Commission (1984). There were no longer any controls on non-resident capital movements. Controls on residents remained but a more lenient attitude was taken to applications from residents for direct investment abroad, particularly from 1980. The unified currency remained stable for a few months but, following the gold price decline in 1983, the rand began a sharp descent, which was arguably exacerbated by the lack of the financial rand cushion. In 1985, following the debt crisis, which was precipitated by the refusal of American banks to roll over South Africa's short-term foreign debt, the rand fell even further. The ensuing financial sanctions resulted in a foreign debt standstill, and a subsequent series of rescheduling agreements between 1985 and 1994. The financial rand was reintroduced and controls on residents were tightened. The dual currency system then remained in existence until the unification of the rand a decade later in March 1995.

Following the moves towards more market determined exchange rates in 1979, the reserve bank maintained a direct influence on the exchange rate through active intervention in both the spot and the forward markets, although the low levels of reserves at certain times limited the extent of intervention. Various objectives have influenced intervention in the foreign exchange market.

There is some evidence to suggest that from 1979 to 1988 exchange rate intervention was directed at maintaining profitability and stability in the gold mining industry by smoothing the real rand price of gold,[5] despite large fluctuations in the dollar price of gold (see also Kahn, 1992). Any divergence from a stable real rand gold price can be explained by real shocks in the form of the excessive rise in the dollar price of gold, and the debt crisis shock of 1985, when lack of reserves constrained the authorities from intervening to prevent a real depreciation. The reserve bank's intervention is reflected in the changes in foreign exchange reserves shown in Figure 8.2. Whether the stable real rand gold price was by design or not, the outcome was a highly variable real exchange rate that cushioned the gold mining industry from terms of trade fluctuations, but had a negative impact on the manufacturing export sector. Since 1988, the real rand price of gold has been allowed to fall with a concomitant decline in the importance of gold as a proportion of foreign exchange earnings.

Since 1988, however, the reserve bank has appeared to be more active in stabilising the real effective exchange rate, partly out of concern for the international competitiveness of South Africa's manufacturing exports and, in particular, to prevent excessive appreciation of the real exchange

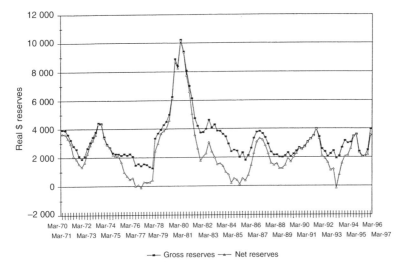

Figure 8.2 Central bank reserves

rate at times when the nominal exchange rate was tending to appreciate. The result has been a far more stable real exchange rate measured on a trade-weighted basis. The real effective exchange rate index (on a 1990 base year) appreciated gradually from 96.00 at the end of 1988, to 104.02, by the end of 1992, whereafter it depreciated to 97.18 by the end of 1994. The nominal exchange rate index depreciated from 109.39 to 72.70 over the same period. Thus, the nominal exchange rate movements did not always fully offset inflation differentials. Political uncertainty after 1992 began to put increased pressure on the exchange rate. From the end of 1992 to mid-1994, the nominal effective exchange rate depreciated by 18.7%, and as this exceeded the inflation differential between South Africa and her major trading partners, it implied a real effective depreciation of about 10% over the period, thus offsetting the real appreciation from 1988.

The reserve bank's concern about excessive depreciation has derived from its strong anti-inflation stance since the late 1980s. This concern poses a dilemma for the bank in that to the extent that there is a persistent inflation differential between South Africa and its major trading partners, maintaining a stable real exchange rate could conflict with the objective of a stable nominal exchange rate providing a nominal anchor for inflation. This dilemma has decreased somewhat with the decline in the inflation rate over the past few years. Nevertheless, since unification in 1995, there has been greater variability of the real and nominal exchange rates.

It should be noted that there was never any explicit policy to stabilise the real exchange rate, and during the period 1988–94, exchange rate and monetary policies were fundamentally aimed at ensuring a current account surplus to finance the capital outflows resulting from the debt rescheduling agreements. The reserve bank's current position is that the exchange rate is market-determined and they only intervene to iron out what are deemed to be excessive fluctuations in order to maintain financial stability. Although a stable real exchange rate is seen as a desirable outcome, the intervention of the reserve bank to achieve this object will be through acting on the real exchange rate fundamentals, rather than following some form of real rule that requires continuous direct intervention.

External balance

Both political shocks and gold price fluctuations have played an important part in the evolution of South Africa's balance of payments since 1960. South Africa has experienced a pattern of current account deficits financed by capital inflows, followed by periods of capital outflows and current account surpluses. These trends are in large part a reflection of political developments that have had their impact on the capital account and therefore on the adjustment process. Capital account deficits were experienced in the wake of the Sharpeville massacre in 1960 and the subsequent political unrest, the Soweto riots of 1976, and the prolonged period of political unrest beginning in mid-1984 that ultimately culminated in financial sanctions and the debt crisis of 1985.

From the late 1960s, the emerging euro currency markets had become an important source of capital for the South African economy, whereas previously direct investment flows had played an important role. Until 1976, South Africa was a major borrower in the long-term syndicated markets. However, following the political unrest in 1976, South Africa was cut off from this source of capital. Given the prevailing fixed exchange rates, standard expenditure reduction policies were put in place to finance the capital account deficit, with the brunt of the burden being borne by declining domestic investment. By 1979/80 a rise in the gold price to record highs took the pressure off the current account and also brought about a reassessment of South Africa in the international markets. Although new loans were forthcoming, these were at much shorter maturities than before (in fact this was a general phenomenon at the time, in the wake of the international debt crisis).

In 1985, following a prolonged period of political upheavals in the country, American banks began recalling their loans. The result was a debt crisis followed by a debt standstill, and subsequently a series of four debt rescheduling agreements whereby the South African authorities agreed to repay foreign debt at a specified rate. No new bank loans were forthcoming apart from trade credits; coupled with the requirement to repay capital and interest, this implied that the capital account remained in deficit until 1994.[6] The 1985 crisis was more severe than previous crises in that not only were new loans not being granted but also previous debt had to be repaid in terms of the debt rescheduling agreements. The situation was aggravated by the fact that at the time of the debt crisis, approximately 72% of South Africa's debt (which then stood at 42% of GDP) was short term (i.e. of a maturity of less than one year.).

The capital account surplus had averaged over 4% of GDP between 1980 and 1985 (Figure 8.3). For the five years after the debt crisis the capital account deficit averaged 2.25% of GDP and was financed by a current account surplus of 2.7% of GDP. In 1993, capital outflows increased significantly, partly as a result of the increased uncertainty associated with the first democratic elections in April 1994. Total net capital outflows exceeded R16 billion (over 4% of GDP) and the current account surplus was insufficient to cover this. The reserve bank's gross foreign exchange reserves declined to 5.9 weeks of imports, despite the reserve bank increasing its short-term foreign borrowing from R1.6 billion to R5.8 billion during the

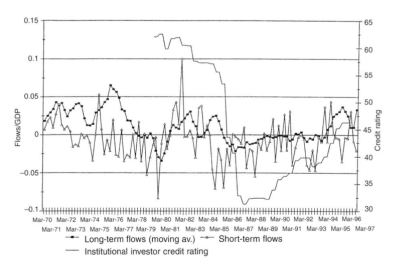

Figure 8.3 Capital flows

second half of 1993. In addition, R2.8 billion was borrowed by the government from the IMF (South Africa's first borrowing from this source since 1982) to help meet balance of payments commitments. With continued capital outflows before the elections, reserve bank foreign borrowing had risen to R8.5 billion by May 1994. However, the peaceful transition to a new government resulted in a reversal of capital outflows, and the bank was able to reduce these liabilities to R5.7 billion by the end of July.

At the end of 1993 gross reserves amounted to US$ 2.68 billion. By the end of June 1994, following the large outflows, reserves had fallen to US$ 1.94 billion, equivalent to 25 days import cover, while gross reserves of the monetary system as a whole amounted to 35 days coverage. Net reserves of the reserve bank (i.e. gross reserves less estimated liabilities against reserves) became negative from March 1994 and reached a low of minus US$ 909 million in May. Following a turnaround in capital flows after that, the situation improved somewhat and by the end of 1994 the bank's gross reserves amounted to 5.4 weeks of import cover.

The impact of the debt crisis and the continuing pressure on the capital account required an adjustment in the economy to maintain current account surpluses around 2% of GDP and trade account surpluses of approximately 5% of GDP (see Leape, 1991). The adjustment to the capital account deficit came about partly through a depreciation of the rand, and partly through a collapse of domestic investment, due to a decline in private investor confidence. (At the same time there was also a decline in parastatal investment.) The impact of the adjustment to the debt crisis is well illustrated by the events of 1988, when for the first time since 1985 domestic investment and growth began to increase. This resulted in a current account deficit in the second quarter of 1988, given the strong procyclical nature of imports as a result of the country's dependence on intermediate and capital goods imports. The response of the monetary authorities was to raise interest rates substantially – between May 1988 and November 1989, the bank rate was successively increased from 9.5% to 18%, which had the effect of reversing the positive growth trends. In addition, import surcharges were periodically increased (see Section 3 on these surcharges). Thus, until mid-1994, monetary policy was dictated to a significant degree by balance of payments considerations.[7]

2.   Theoretical framework for a real exchange rate model

We first present a version of the basic traded–non-traded model of Dornbusch (1973), which further disaggregates tradeables into exportables and importables, and gives the equilibrium exchange rate that solves the equilibrium condition in the home goods market under static expectations, assuming a given level of capital flows. We begin with an identity for nominal domestic absorption, A:

$$A = EXP_G + EXP_P \tag{1}$$

where EXP_P is private domestic expenditure, and EXP_G, is government expenditure, and is given as a fixed ratio to GDP:

$$EXP_G = g \cdot Y \tag{2}$$

Furthermore, government expenditure on non-tradeables, EXP_{GN}, is given as a fixed ratio to total government expenditure, EXP_G:

$$EXP_{GN} = g_N \cdot g \cdot Y \tag{3}$$

On the other hand, the ratio of private-sector expenditure on non-tradeables relative to total private-sector expenditure, EXP_{PN}/EXP_P, is endogenously determined as a function of the domestic prices of exports (P_X), imports (P_M), and non-tradeables (P_N):

$$EXP_{PN} = d_{P_N}(P_X^l P_M^l P_N) \cdot EXP_P = d_{P_N}(P_X^l P_M^l P_N) \cdot [A - g \cdot Y] \tag{4}$$

Now equations 3 and 4 allow stating the demand for non-traded goods as follows:

$$EXP_N = EXP_{PN} + EXP_{GN} = d_{PN}(P_X^l P_M^l P_N) \cdot [A - g \cdot Y] + g_N \cdot g \cdot Y \tag{5}$$

The supply of non-traded goods relative to GDP is also specified as a function of the three aggregate prices:

$$S_N = S_N(P_X^l P_M P_N) \cdot Y \tag{6}$$

and Equation 7 sets the equilibrium condition in the non-traded goods market ($S_N = EXP_N$):

$$S_N(P_X^l P_M P_N) = d_{PN}(P_X^l P_M P_N) \cdot \left[\frac{A}{Y} - g\right] + g_N \cdot g \tag{7}$$

Let the (dollar-denominated) international prices of exportables and importables be given by P_X^* and P_M^*, respectively. By invoking the small-country assumption, $_X^*P$ and $_M^*P$ can be considered as exogenous variables. Therefore, for a given set of exchange rate and commercial policies, the corresponding domestic prices P_X and P_X are determined by P_X^* and P_M^*, respectively. Let E be the nominal exchange rate units of domestic currency per US dollar, and let t_X and t_M be, respectively, the net export and import tax rates. The domestic price of exports and imports can be defined as follows:

$$P_X = E(1 - t_X)P^*x \tag{8}$$

$$P_M = E(1 + t_M)P_M^* \tag{9}$$

Then, for $0 < \alpha < 1$, the real exchange rate e is defined as:

$$e = P_N/E \cdot P_X^{*\alpha} \cdot P_M^{*(1-\alpha)} \tag{10}$$

Equations 1 through 10 can be solved for the level of the real exchange rate that ensures instantaneous equilibrium in the non-traded goods market for given levels of some exogenous and policy fundamentals:

$$e = e\left(\frac{A}{Y}, \frac{P_X^*}{P_M^*}, t_{X'} \, t_{M'} \, \frac{EXP_{GN}}{EXP_G}, \frac{EXP_G}{Y}\right)$$

$$(+) \, (?) \, (+)(+) \quad (+) \qquad (?)$$

This solution suggests that higher and 'sustainable' levels of the domestic absorption ratio, foreign trade taxes and public expenditure on non-tradeables (indicated by the plus signs under the variables) are consistent with equilibrium real exchange rate appreciation; on the other hand, the effects due to changes in the terms of trade (i.e. price of exports over price of imports) and the total government expenditure ratio could not be assigned *a priori*. However, consistent empirical regularity shows that improved terms of trade and higher government expenditure tend to lead to real exchange rate appreciation, because the income effect of terms of trade improvement usually dominates its substitution effect, and government tends to have a higher propensity to spend on non-traded goods than does the private sector (e.g. Edwards, 1989).

The solution above does not account for supply side effects. In particular, it does not account for the Balassa–Samuelson productivity effect (Balassa, 1964; Samuelson, 1964), which in its extreme form states that with intersectoral factor mobility, non-traded goods supply and, eventually, relative prices, are set exclusively by the level of productivity in the two sectors. In Equation 6, increasing productivity will have a negative effect on the supply of non-traded goods. We modify our equation to include a productivity measure, *TECHPRO*, where higher productivity operates through shifting the relative schedules of traded and non-traded goods, allowing a higher level of the real exchange rate to be consistent with equilibrium (holding other variables fixed):

$$e = e\left(\frac{A}{Y^I}\frac{P_x^*}{P_M^*}, t_x^I t_M^I, \frac{EXP_{GN}}{EXP_G}, \frac{EXP_G}{Y}, TECHPRO\right) \qquad (11)$$

$$(+)\,(?)\ (+)(+)\ (+)\quad\ (?)\qquad\ (+)$$

where *TECHPRO* is measured as the ratio of total factor productivity in traded goods to non-traded goods, relative to trading partners.

A forward-looking equilibrium real exchange rate model

The equilibrium solution above does not satisfy the identification conditions set by Edwards' definition, since it ensures only non-traded goods equilibrium at a given point in time and does not account for the effect due to the anticipated evolution of the fundamentals. Nor does it offer any guidance as to how to internalise the concept of 'sustainability' of the fundamentals, or the dynamic behaviour of the actual real exchange rate around its equilibrium. This section provides an extension of the model along these lines. The linearised empirical version of Equation 11, which will be the one used for further analysis, is:

$$\log e_t = \alpha_0 + \alpha_1 \log(TOT)_t + \alpha_2 \log(TARIFF)_t + \alpha_3 \log\left(\frac{A}{GDP}\right)_t$$

$$+ \alpha_4 \log\left(\frac{EXP_G}{GDP}\right)_t + \alpha_5 \log\left(\frac{EXP_{GN}}{EXP_G}\right)_t + \alpha_6 TECHPRO_t \qquad (12)$$

where *TOT* is the terms of trade and *TARIFF* is measured as trade taxes over GDP. Note also that empirical regularity regarding the terms of trade and EXP_G/GDP effects is assumed.[8]

Equation 12 is assumed to hold at present and in the future for sustainable values of its arguments. The equation by itself is not adequate for real exchange rate determination, since *A* is endogenous (as potentially are *GDP* and G_N as well). To complete the model, we endogenise *A* by specifying an equation linking private absorption to sustainable levels of net long-run capital inflows *NLRCAP* (i.e. to the sustainable current account deficit), to the expected depreciation and to the level of foreign exchange reserves:

$$\frac{A}{GDP} = a\left(\frac{NLRCAP}{IMP}, \frac{RES}{IMP}, \sigma \cdot [\log(e_t) - {}_t\log(e_{t+1})]\right) \qquad (13)$$

$$(+)\qquad (+)\qquad\quad (-)$$

where *NLRCAP* is a measure of 'sustainable' net capital inflows; σ is the share of non-traded goods in consumption, and the notation ${}_tX_{t+j}$ means the expectation of X_{t+j} at time *t*; and *RES* is a measure of reserve bank reserves relative to imports.

Expected real depreciation relative to the current rate (i.e. $\log e_t - {}_t\log e_{t+1} > 0$), increases the demand for saving and thus reduces absorption relative to income.[9] The reserve ratio represents the liquid end of wealth, and an increase in reserves should promote absorption. Inclusion of the stock of official reserves in the set of the fundamentals is consistent with models in the literature that link the asset market to the stock of official reserves relative to the stock of foreign assets held by the private sector (e.g. Edwards, 1985; Elbadawi, 1992). If equilibrium in the asset market is not assumed, the ultimate reduced form solution of the equilibrium real exchange rate in this case leads to the inclusion of the ratio of the stock of official reserves to the stock of foreign assets held by the private sector in the equilibrium real exchange rate fundamentals. Such an extension could be interesting when asset market disequilibrium is likely to have significant effects on official reserves (as was the case in many SSA countries during the 1980s; see Kiguel *et al.*, 1997), or when exchange rate unification is considered.

We rewrite Equation 13 in the following linearised form:

$$\log\left(\frac{A}{Y}\right)_t = \beta_0 + \beta_1\left(\frac{NLRCAP}{GDP}\right)_t + \beta_2\left(\frac{RES}{IMP}\right)_t + \beta_3(\log e_t - {}_t\log e_{t+1}) \quad (14)$$

Solving equations 12 and 14 together yields the following reduced form dynamic equation for the real exchange rate:

$$\log e_t - \lambda_t \log e_{t+1} = \delta_0 + \delta_1 \log(TOT)_t + \delta_2 \log(TARIFF)_t + \delta_3\left(\frac{NLRCAP}{GDP}\right)_t$$
$$+ \delta_4\left(\frac{RES}{IMP}\right)_t + \delta_5 \log\left(\frac{EXP_G}{GDP}\right)_t + \delta_6 \log\left(\frac{EXP_{GN}}{EXP_G}\right)_t + \delta_7 TECHPRO_t \quad (15)$$

where $\lambda = \alpha_3 \beta_3/(1 + \alpha_3\beta_3) < 1$, and where the δ's are corresponding coefficients on the right hand side.

The equilibrium real exchange rate $\tilde{e}$, is that value of the real exchange rate that satisfies Equation 15 for sustainable values of the right-hand side variables. Equation 15 can be solved forward for $\log(\tilde{e})$ by recursive substitution. By defining the parameter vector $\delta = (\delta_0, \delta_1, \delta_2, \delta_3, \delta_4, \delta_5, \delta_6, \delta_7)'$ and the vector of fundamentals:

$$F = [1, \log(TOT), \log(TARIFF), \frac{NLRCAP}{GDP}, \frac{RES}{IMP}, \log\frac{EXP_G}{GDP},$$
$$\log\frac{EXP_{GN}}{EXP_G}, TECHPRO] \quad (16)$$

we get the following forward-looking expression for $\tilde{e}$ for given sustainable values of the fundamentals vector (we denote sustainable component of $\mathbf{F}$ by $\tilde{\mathbf{F}}$):[10]

$$\log e_t = \sum_{j=0}^{\infty} \lambda^j \delta_t' \tilde{F}_{t+j} \qquad (17)$$

It can be shown that if $\tilde{\mathbf{F}}$ are stationary in first differences (i.e. are I(1) variables)[11] then the following cointegration relationship exists (e.g. Kaminsky, 1988):

$$\log \tilde{e}_t = \frac{1}{1-\lambda} \delta' \tilde{F}_t + \eta_t \qquad (18)$$

where $\delta'/(1 - \lambda)$ is the cointegration vector, and η is a stationary disturbance term.

Abstracting from the 'sustainability' issue, Equation 17 is identical to the equilibrium solution given by the basic model. A fundamental advantage of the cointegration assumption is thus that it allows the derivation of a simple empirical framework from a much more complicated theoretical model.[12]

An equilibrium correction equation for the real exchange rate

If the cointegration relationship in Equation 17 is valid, then that equation not only can be interpreted as long-run equilibrium but is also consistent with a dynamic equilibrium correction specification (Engle and Granger, 1987). The equilibrium correction equation consistent with the (assumed) cointegration equation is as follows:[13]

$$\Delta \log e_{t+1} = b_0 \left(\frac{1}{1-\lambda} \delta' F_t - \log e_t \right) + b_1 \Delta F_{t+1}$$
$$- b_2 \Delta \log E_{t+1} + b_3 \Delta \log \left(\frac{DomCred}{GDP} \right)_{t+1} + b_4 \Delta \left(\frac{NSRCAP}{GDP} \right)_{t+1} + \varepsilon_{t+1} \qquad (19)$$

where E as previously defined is the nominal exchange rate in terms of domestic currency per unit of the foreign currency, *DomCred* is total domestic credit extended by the monetary sector, *NSRCAP* is a measure of net short-run capital inflows, and the disturbance $\varepsilon_t{+}1$ is a stationary random variable composed of the one-step-ahead forecast error in the real exchange rate (i.e. $\Delta \log e_{t+1} - t\Delta \log e_{t+1}$).

The equilibrium correction term $[1/(1 - \lambda)\,\delta' F_t - \log e_t]$ in Equation 19 clearly incorporates the forward-looking sources of real exchange rate dynamics. Starting from an initial condition of real over-valuation (i.e. the equilibrium correction term is negative), the self-correcting mechanism that calls for future depreciation in the actual real exchange rate will be set in motion. This effect is captured by the negative equilibrium correction term and its positive coefficient in the $\Delta \log e_{t+1}$ specification. The speed with which this automatic adjustment operates depends on the parameter b_0 which falls in the interval [0,1]. The value of b_0 equal to one signifies prompt adjustment over just one period; smaller values signify slower rates of adjustment.

In addition to the equilibrium long-run impact of the fundamentals, which is captured by the cointegration, vector $\delta'/(1 - \lambda)$, temporary changes in the fundamentals may also have short-run effects, which are captured by the vector b_1. Short-run effects due to expansive macroeconomic policy are given by the coefficient of $\Delta \log(DomCred/GDP)$. Finally, the short-run impact of nominal depreciation is given by the coefficient $(-b_2)$. As pointed out by Edwards (1989), a nominal devaluation will help the adjustment process only to the extent that the initial situation is one of over-valuation, and only if the nominal exchange rate adjustment is accompanied by supporting macroeconomic policy – in other words, in terms of our equation, if the equilibrium correction term is negative and the rate of domestic credit expansion net of real GDP growth is not positive.

3.   Background on the real exchange rate fundamentals

Following the theoretical model of Section 2 setting out the determinants of the real exchange rate, this section examines the evidence on the quarterly evolution of the following fundamental variables expected to influence the real exchange rate in South Africa over the last two decades and a half: trade policy; the terms of trade, including the real gold price; long-run (and short-run) capital flows; foreign exchange reserves; government expenditure; and productivity growth differentials. The empirical proxies for these variables used in the regressions are defined in Table 8.2.

Trade policy

Increasing trade liberalisation is expected to depreciate the real exchange rate (Section 2). There have been significant changes in South Africa's trade regime since the 1960s that have a bearing on the real exchange rate (measures of trade policy are given in Figure 8.4). South Africa adopted a policy of import substitution from the late 1960s, involving various instruments of protection including quantitative restrictions (QRs),

Table 8.2 Definitions of variables used in the regressions

log (*REER*)	Real effective exchange rate from the South African Reserve Bank: a multilateral trade-weighted index for the real exchange rates of four trading partners (defined as the ratio of the wholesale price index to the nominal effective exchange rate index multiplied by the trading partners' wholesale price indexes): weights redefined in August 1995.
log (*TOTXG*)	Log (terms of trade excluding gold)
log (*PGOLD*)	Log (real dollar gold price)
log (*TARIFF*)	Log ([customs receipts + surcharge]/imports)
log (*OPEN*)	Log ([exports + imports]/GDP). The variable is constructed using the residual of a parsimonious equation for log (*OPEN*) on lags of the dependent variable, the terms of trade and real gold price, in order to purge the effects of trade shocks.
LRCAPFLO	Long-run capital flows/GDP, using a four-quarter moving average
TCAPFLO	Total capital flows/GDP
RESERVES	Rand gross reserves of the reserve bank/GDP
log (*GOVEXP*)	Log (total government expenditure/GDP), using a four-quarter moving average
log (*GCUREXP*)	Log (government consumption/*GOVEXP*), using a four-quarter moving average
NOMDEV	Nominal depreciation was instrumented with two different parsimonious equations for the fixed and floating exchange rate periods: the fixed period uses some of the dummies for discrete devaluations or revaluations as tabulated in Table 8.3; the floating period uses lagged *NOMDEV* terms, a dummy for the debt crisis D(83:3–85:4), and the fourth change in the gold price.
DOMCRED	Δ log (total domestic credit extended/GDP)
SRCAPFLO	Short-run capital flows/GDP
DTECHPRO	The annual rate of change of per capita real GDP (South Africa) averaged over the previous three years, minus the equivalent for per capita real GDP (OECD countries). The variable is constructed using the residual of a parsimonious equation for real per capita GDP (*SA*) on lags of the dependent variable, the terms of trade and real gold price, in order to purge the effects of trade shocks.

customs duties and import surcharges. Until 1982, QRs remained an important component of the protection regime, but thereafter tariffs rapidly began to replace QRs. According to Bell (1992), the proportion of the value of imports subject to QRs was reduced from 77% in 1983 to 55% in 1984 and 23% in 1985, while the proportion of tariff items subject to QRs was reduced to 28%. By 1994 the proportion of tariff items subject to

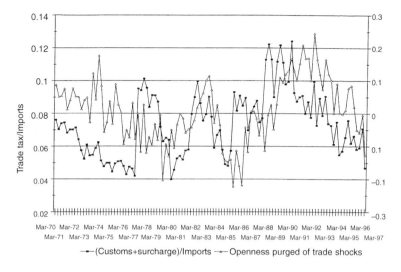

Figure 8.4   Trade policy

QRs was around 20%, representing mainly agricultural goods and textiles, and since 1994 there have been further reductions in the tariff levels. The substitution of tariffs for QRs has involved some liberalisation with the new tariff levels lower than the tariffs implicit in the QRs.

While trade liberalisation has progressed gradually during the last decade, customs duty and surcharge as percentage of total government revenue has only declined from 8.7% in 1982 to 6.0% in 1992. In terms of international comparisons the overall level of protection in the South African economy is not high, but the system has been found to be excessively complex and unstable, and it has an extremely high degree of tariff dispersion – partly explained by special interest group pressure (Fallon and Pereira de Silva, 1994).[14] The average statutory tariff weighted by the value of imports was 27.5% in 1989–91, which puts South Africa below most developing countries, though it is nevertheless a highly protected economy relative to developed countries.[15]

Tariffs have been the main instrument of protection, but other instruments such as export incentives and import surcharges have also been used. The periodic use of import surcharges over and above the tariff regime has *de facto* induced a considerable tightening of the trade regime. The main motivation for their use was to protect the balance of payments. They were first used in April 1977 following the cessation of capital inflows after the Soweto riots in 1976, and remained in force until March 1980 when the high gold prices took the pressure off the current account. They were put in place from February 1982 until November 1983, only to be reintroduced in September 1985 following the debt crisis. The surcharges were increased in 1988 following the increased pressure on the current account, and at times in the subsequent years generated more revenue than customs duties. The surcharges were eventually abolished towards the end of 1995.

Ad hoc export promotion has included customs duties drawbacks and exemptions from customs duties, exporters' allowances and sector-specific export incentives.[16] As with most trade policy over the period, however, there was no clear export promotion policy, and very often export incentives were introduced and withdrawn soon thereafter. The policies of the 1980s were an *ad hoc* response to the balance of payments crisis. Today, export growth, notably of manufacturers, forms part of the government's long-term growth strategy. Policies do not yet bear out this change of priorities, however, and export policy remains complex, fragmented and expensive.

Terms of trade

Our next consideration is the terms of trade. While the effects of trade shocks as remarked in Section 2 are theoretically ambiguous, we expect dominance of income over substitution effects for the real price of gold, reflecting the dominant role of gold in the South African economy as well as its relative enclave status *vis-à-vis* the rest of the economy. Although the real gold price is presented as a separate determinant of the real exchange rate in our model, it is worth noting that when gold is included in the terms of trade, gold price movements tend to outweigh the non-gold terms of trade, resulting in an upward trend of the overall terms of trade during most of the period 1970–81, whereafter the two measures move very closely together (see two overall measures in Figure 8.5). With a decline in the relative importance of gold since the mid-1980s, the impact of gold price changes on the real exchange rate is expected to diminish. The ratio of gold exports to non-gold merchandise exports (excluding services) averaged 0.61 from 1970–79. Between 1980 and 1985, the average ratio increased to 0.93; it began to decline thereafter, largely because of the decline in the dollar gold price but partly because of the increase in the volume of non-traditional exports. Between 1986 and 1990 the ratio was 0.59 and declined further to 0.39 for the period 1991–95 reaching a low of 0.27 in 1995.

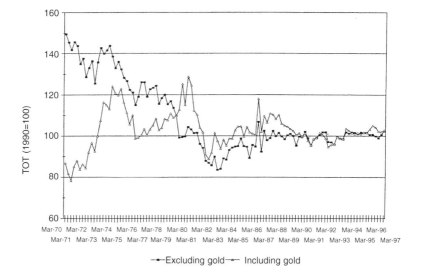

Figure 8.5   Terms of trade

South Africa's overall terms of trade excluding gold, show a deterioration during the 1970s with sharp declines associated with the oil price shocks. Apart from oil price shocks, the general downward trend in primary commodity prices during this period also contributed to this trend. During the 1980s, the relatively more stable oil prices and more favourable commodity prices reversed this trend. In addition, a greater proportion of South Africa's exports were manufactured and semi-manufactured goods, which to some extent reduced the impact of commodity price fluctuations on the terms of trade. Another factor contributing to the decline in the terms of trade during the 1970s was the fact that apart from oil, imports were dominated by capital goods where the rise in the price level of imported machinery was faster than the overall import price index (Gelb, 1991).

Capital flows

The third fundamental we consider is capital flows (see Figure 8.3). At the theoretical level it is assumed that long-term capital flows would be a long-run determinant of the real exchange rate, whereas short-term flows would be expected to influence the adjustment to equilibrium. Part of the rationale for this is that much of the short-term capital flow is speculative and responding to short-term factors. However, at least four factors complicate the interpretation of the South African capital flow figures and, in part, the long-term/short-term distinction. These are the existence of the financial rand mechanism; the disinvestment campaign against South Africa from the 1970s and the imposition of financial sanctions; the classification of sales of assets of an indefinite holding period; and, finally, the debt crisis of 1985. We deal with these issues in turn.

Under the dual exchange rate regime, non-residents selling assets would deposit the proceeds into a financial rand account (only transferable to other non-residents), which sale would be recorded as a long-term outflow, whereas the deposit into the financial rand balance would be recorded as a short-term capital inflow. Non-residents wishing to repatriate their funds had to sell these balances to another non-resident. Such a sale would have no net impact as it was simply a transfer of ownership. However, if the new holder of the financial rand balance then used it to buy assets, it would be recorded as a long-term inflow, but a short-term outflow from the financial rand account. Obviously, summing short- and long-run flows would net out such effects, while for the individual series these effects would be smoothed over time depending on the rate of transactions.

A related complicating factor is the disinvestment campaign to which South Africa was subject in the 1970s and 1980s. A number of companies began withdrawing from South Africa as a result of political pressure and in most instances these companies were sold to South African firms. This trend gained momentum in the early 1980s. From the time of the establishment of the dual exchange rate mechanism in 1979, direct foreign investment became subject to the financial rand mechanism and theoretically (abstracting from leakages) ceased to have an impact on the commercial rand and/or the balance of payments. However, when the financial rand was temporarily abolished in 1983–85, any disinvestment was recorded directly as a long-term capital outflow, which would have had a direct impact on the exchange rate and/or the balance of payments. This episode is apparent in Figure 8.3.

A factor potentially blurring the distinction between long-term and short-term flows is that the purchase of sale of assets of indefinite holding period is classified as a long-term flow, and includes the purchase or sale of shares or bonds of a maturity of more than one year. These assets could be held for speculative purposes and therefore could be viewed as short-term assets in terms of holding motive. Thus, the sale of a direct investment could be offset ultimately by the purchase of bonds by another non-resident. There would be no net impact on long-term flows, even though the nature of the investment is different. This general issue is not unique to South Africa, but is a generic problem.

The debt crisis of 1985 also had an impact on the structure of capital flows from South Africa. It became almost impossible for South Africa to raise long-term loans, while at the same time there was a commitment to repay previous loans on the basis of a series of rescheduling agreements. Although these outflows were partly a reflection of negative sentiment at the time, the timing of the outflows was dictated by the structure of the rescheduling agreements.

Long-term capital flows were generally positive during the period 1970–76 (except for the second quarter of 1973) and averaged 3.6% of GDP peaking in 1975 with an average of 6.5% (and over 9% in the fourth quarter alone). Much of this was due to long-term syndicated loans raised in the euro currency markets, particularly by the private sector and the parastatal corporations. The loss of access to the international markets following the Soweto riots of 1976 meant that inflows declined over the next few years and at the same time loans were repaid. The large outflows of capital in the fourth quarter of 1979 and the first quarter of 1980 (over 5% of GDP in each quarter) were attributable mainly to large repayments on foreign loans by the private sector and public corporations. These repayments were encouraged by the availability of funds in the domestic capital market and the high interest rate on foreign funds.

Net long-term capital inflows were generally positive from mid-1980 until the first quarter of 1985, partly in response to the higher gold prices, although the average level of net inflow was lower than that during the early part of the 1970s. This was in part due to the fact that long-term syndicated loans were more difficult to raise following the world debt crisis, as well the increasing tempo of disinvestment by foreign companies from South Africa. The debt crisis of 1985 resulted in a protracted period of net long-term capital outflows, although as mentioned, the timing and size of these outflows were dictated by the rescheduling agreements. Following the peaceful transition to democracy in April 1994, the capital account and net long-term capital flows became positive in the remainder of the period of analysis.

Not surprisingly, short-term capital movements displayed a higher degree of variability than long-term movements and also were greater in absolute value terms. Although a large proportion of the flows was related to trade credits during the early 1980s, the bulk of South African borrowing had become short-term because of the increased risk rating of South Africa (see Figure 8.3, where considerable hysteresis in investor confidence is apparent in the risk rating). In addition, apart from the period 1970 to mid-1972, net capital movements were predominantly negative, particularly between 1984 and 1990. The short-term outflows experienced in the latter half of the 1970s were mainly a result of the easy availability of domestic credit for trade financing purposes, and low interest rates. This situation was reversed in 1981 and 1983. Between 1984 and 1990 short-term capital flows were again generally negative, mainly as a result of the impact of the debt crisis, and since then they have displayed a greater degree of variability. It is important to note that the reserve bank has incurred significant losses on its forward book, that is, the manipulation of the forward rate in order to encourage importers and exporters to finance their trade offshore as a means of obtaining short-term capital inflows during the 1980s. By 1990 these losses totalled over R11 billion (see Van Der Merwe, 1996).[17]

Foreign exchange reserves

The stock of foreign exchange reserves is expected by the theoretical model to have a positive impact on the real exchange rate, consistent with its role as a relatively liquid indicator of the stock of national wealth. (The movements of net and gross reserves of the reserve bank can be seen in Figure 8.2.) Reserve movements have tended to reflect gold price changes as well as political events. Such movements are more pronounced for net reserves, given that the reserve bank borrows to bolster gross reserves at times when reserves come under pressure. Such actions tend to reduce the downward trend of the gross reserves. Conversely, when the balance of payments has improved, the reserve bank has used reserves to repay previous reserve-related borrowing, thus mitigating the rise in gross reserves, and at the same time reducing the difference between net and gross reserves.

Reserves in dollar terms reached an all-time high during the high gold price period around 1980. This reflects the substantial intervention of the reserve bank to prevent an excessive appreciation of the exchange rate at the time, and allowed for a repayment of reserve-related debt accumulated during the political shock period of 1976–78. Reserves, particularly net reserves, fell during 1984–86, again with the reserve bank intervening through reserve-related borrowing. The sharp down-turn in net and gross reserves during 1993 was related to the uncertainty associated with the pre-election period, and during this time net reserves were negative at times. Gross and net reserves recovered strongly after the 1994 elections for the remainder of the period under review.

Government expenditure

The next fundamental we consider is government expenditure, which showed pronounced cyclical movements during the 1970s. Moving averages (four-quarter) of government expenditure relative to GDP and government consumption relative to total government are shown in Figure 8.6. While the effect of higher government expenditure is theoretically ambiguous (Section 2), empirical regularity suggests that higher expenditure appreciates the real exchange rate. On the other hand, government expenditure on non-tradeables alone is theoretically expected to appreciate the real exchange rate.

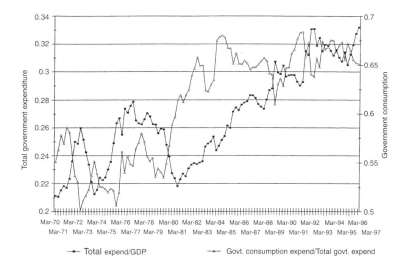

Figure 8.6   Government expenditure

The deficit before borrowing averaged over 4% of GDP in the 1970s with a peak of 6% in 1977. Part of the reason for the relatively high deficit was that government expenditure increased from 1973 on the assumption that there would be a sustained rise in the gold price. During the 1980s the deficit was more contained, averaging just under 3%, with a high of 5.1% in the 1988 fiscal year and a low of 0.6% in the 1990 fiscal year. However, there was a strong upward trend in expenditure. Government expenditure was boosted by increased expenditure on the military and police, particularly as internal opposition to the apartheid regime increased. In the late 1980s and early 1990s the increase reflected increased expenditure on social services, as the apartheid government attempted to redress some of the inequities of the past in anticipation of the democratic elections in 1994. Since 1991 the deficit has exceeded 4%, and in the 1993 and 1994 fiscal years, actually exceeded 9%. Despite the new government's commitment to fiscal restraint, government expenditure is likely to remain under increasing pressure for the foreseeable future.

Per capita real GDP growth relative to the OECD

Figure 8.7 shows the differential between South Africa's per capita real GDP growth relative to that of the OECD countries. This measure is a proxy for technical productivity growth differentials (see Section 4 and Table 8.2).

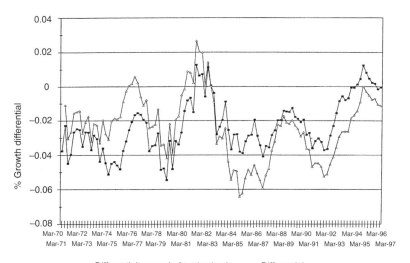

Figure 8.7 Real per capita GDP growth

The variable exhibits clear cyclical movements, which are strongly related to the South African and OECD business cycles. South Africa's economy has exhibited declining rates of economic growth since the mid-1960s, when real growth rates averaging 6% were recorded. There have been marked fluctuations around this declining trend, however, related in part to political crises and the variability of the gold price. The most severe and sustained recession was experienced between 1989 and 1993. Real growth averaged 1.6% in 1986–90, was negative in 1991 and 1992, due in part to the severe drought, and became positive again in 1993 and 1994 with growth rates of 1.3% and 2.7%, respectively, as the drought was relieved. In 1995 a real growth rate of 3.3% was recorded, which, given a population growth rate of around 2.6%, was the first time per capita GDP growth had been positive since 1982. Low rates of economic growth resulted in rising rates of unemployment, with less than 10% of new labour market entrants being absorbed into formal sector employment. There are differing estimates of total unemployment, although currently it is generally accepted to be above 30%.

Probably the dominant effect is political shocks. Figure 8.7 shows the productivity growth differential was positive only during 1981:3 to 1982:4 (apart from 1982:2). The downturn in 1976 reflects the political shock at that time, while the strong increase from 1979 follows the rising gold price. The downward trend from 1982 mirrors gold price and political developments, which at times were moving in opposite directions. The rise in economic growth is reflected in the upturn in 1988 as well as the subsequent decline in growth as the balance of payments constraint began to be felt. Political reforms in the country and more favourable growth prospects resulted in an increase after 1993.

4.   An econometric analysis of determinants of the real exchange rate in South Africa

In this section we estimate a version of the equilibrium correction model in Equation 9 of our theoretical model, with more generalised lags. The single equation equilibrium correction model is estimated using one-step non-linear least squares, which allows for direct estimation of the long-run cointegrating vector, as well as the short-run impact effects of the equilibrium correction specification.

Formulating regression variables

An important issue is regime shifts. We used two tests for parameter stability over different regimes. First, the chosen period of estimation, 1970:3 to 1995:1, is characterised by the almost continuous use of multiple exchange rates, with restrictions on both non-resident and domestic resident capital movements. Unification of the dual system and an effective end to non-resident capital controls occurred in the last quarter of this period, and we test the stability of the model when including the unified period for available data (to the end of 1995). Secondly, we also test the model for parameter stability over the 'regimes' of fixed and floating exchange rates (see Table 8.1). Otherwise, the only role this regime shift plays is perforce in the instrumenting equation for nominal devaluation (see below).

The variables used in the empirical regression as proxies for the theoretical variables in Equation 19 are defined in Table 8.2. It is important to note that the real exchange rate index we use is the measure deriving from the reserve bank, which given its policy relevance is the desirable index to model. Nevertheless, this definition of the real exchange rate is not exactly the same as the definition given in Equation 10 of the theoretical model.[18]

In the case of terms of trade, the theoretical variable has been disaggregated into the major mining commodity (gold) and non-gold terms of trade. Since the terms of trade give a theoretically ambiguous result depending on the relative importance of substitution and income effects, this allows us to capture the mining sector's expected income dominance more satisfactorily (there are few substitution possibilities).

Two measures of trade policy were used. Our preferred measure, *TARIFF*, uses trade taxes relative to GDP. However, this measure will not capture the presence of quotas, extensively used in the earlier part of the sample (see Section 2). Typically, a measure of openness (defined as exports plus imports relative to GDP) is used to proxy trade policy, including quotas. The version of *OPEN* used in one specification purges the variable of gold and non-gold terms of trade shocks (see Table 8.2), which otherwise dominate the evolution of *OPEN*. The two measures evolve fairly closely (Figure 8.4), although *TARIFF* reflects more immediately the periodic imposition of import surcharges.

While government expenditure is expected to influence the real exchange rate, the role of the composition of government expenditure is more controversial (Williamson, 1994). Due to unavailability of data, we test for the composition effect using government consumption as a proxy for government expenditure on non-tradables. Four-quarter moving averages of the government expenditure variables are used to remove short-run seasonal and cyclical noise.

To test for the long-run Balassa–Samuelson effect, a comparative measure of technical productivity levels between South Africa and her trading partners is required, though the equilibrium correction formulation suggests that both the levels and the rate of change are relevant. Due to data difficulties we use a comparative measure of real per capita GDP, which is averaged over three years to remove short-term seasonal and cyclical demand pressures. In order for this proxy to capture the Balassa–Samuelson effect, where productivity in non-traded versus traded goods is the critical comparison, we make two assumptions: first, that in this capital-intensive mineral exporting economy, growth in productivity in the traded sector far dominates that in the non-traded sector; and second, that trends in relative productivity in non-traded goods do not differ significantly between South Africa and her trading partners. Nevertheless, we were not confident that this measure would capture differential productivity trends cleanly, given the importance of commodity shocks in this economy and also pronounced political shocks via financial and other sanctions and foreign disinvestment. While the variable we use, *TECHPRO*, is purged of the effects of trade shocks (see Table 8.2), political effects remain that may have a strong impact, which can be interpreted both in terms of supply side productivity changes and changes in demand.[19] Thus there are likely to be systematic breaks in the relationship between our measure of relative productivity levels and the appropriate theoretical concept. First-differencing will typically turn structural breaks such as important political shifts into short-term noise, so that the differenced productivity measure could turn out to be significant while the level is not. (See Clements and Hendry [1995] on the effects of differencing on structural breaks; this is indeed what we find.)

Nominal depreciation is endogenous and was instrumented as described in Table 8.2, and the fitted value was used in the real exchange rate equation. No dummies were used in the real exchange rate equation, but the instrumenting equation uses two dummies to capture major discrete devaluations or revaluations in the fixed regime period and a dummy for the politically related debt crisis in the floating period. The other variable most likely to be endogenous of current-dated variables used in the real exchange rate equation is short-run capital flows. There are difficulties in instrumenting this variable given differing regimes for the control of non-residents' short-term capital flows in the period, the maintenance of capital controls on domestic residents, and the periodic effects of politics on the evolution of this variable. Thus, we simply examine the robustness of the parsimonious real exchange rate equation to the exclusion of this variable. We also examine total capital flows as well as the disaggregated short-term and long-term flows in a separate equation. A four-quarter moving average is used for long-term flows alone, to smooth short-run seasonal and reporting noise.

The empirical model

We have pointed out that it is important to deal adequately with the non-stationarity of the variables of interest. First-differencing does not offer a solution because it removes the long-run relationships that may be present in the data, and are the focus of this study. Thus, we follow a cointegration approach using quarterly data over 25 years. Ideally, one would use the full-information procedure of Johansen (1988) – generalised in Johansen and Juselius (1990) – which is asymptotically efficient. In our case, and given that we disaggregate the terms of trade into two components, and potentially also examine both the current and total expenditure of government, this could involve the estimation of up to a seventh-order vector autoregressive equilibrium correction model, with the components of vector **F** in Equation 16 and the real exchange rate as dependent variables.

Apart from degrees of freedom problems, the main difficulty is the interpretation of cointegrating vectors that include a large number of variables (see Juselius, 1994). While our theoretical model does give priors, in some cases the signs are ambiguous, while practically some proxies like *TECHPRO* are affected by significant regime changes. Dummies for regime changes would have to be included, and similarly, stationary variables such as *NOMDEV* (expected to have a very large short-run impact) should be included as well (Juselius, 1995). The empirical formulation from our theoretical model (Equation 19) allows for a range of short-run effects with stationary variables.

The practical problems with this approach are clear. One option is to examine a simplified model with very few fundamentals (e.g. Faruqee, 1995), though with the risk of an omitted variables bias. In this chapter, the preferred approach is to estimate a partial structural model for the real exchange rate, where given the large set of potential regressors, we use theoretical priors to achieve a parsimonious equation. We estimate a single-equation equilibrium correction model, using a non-linear estimation technique to obtain the long-run coefficients directly. In order to ascertain whether these estimates of the partial system are consonant with the full model (i.e. are efficient estimates), weak exogeneity tests need to be conducted (Johansen, 1992). Partial proof of exogeneity is offered by parameter constancy in the conditional model across different regimes, but strictly, weak exogeneity of the current dated regressors should be tested.[20]

Before estimating the single-equation equilibrium correction models, augmented Dickey-Fuller (ADF) test statistics were calculated for each of the variables in Table 8.2 to indicate the order of integration. The ADF statistics are shown in Table 8.3. Four variables were found to be stationary: short-term capital flows (*SRCAPFLO*), the rate of nominal depreciation (*NOMDEV*), the rate of monetary expansion (*DOMCRED*) and the comparative differential in productivity growth (*DTECHPRO*). For

Table 8.3   Augmented Dickey–Fuller tests for a unit root

Null order	I(1)	I(2)
log (*REER*)	–2.19*	–5.23
log TOTXG	–2.07	–14.35**
LOG (*PGOLD*)	–2.86	–3.79**
log (*TARIFF*)	–3.38	–4.82**
log (*OPEN*)	–2.35	–18.14**
LRCAPFLO	–3.32	–4.06**
TCAPFLO	–2.56	–5.39**
RESERVES	–2.77	–5.24**
log (*GOVEXP*)	–2.52	–5.41**
log (*GCUREXP*)	–2.40	–6.25**
NOMDEV	–4.73**	
DOMCRED	–3.70**	
SRCAPFLO	–3.89**	
DTECHPRO	–4.12**	

Notes
1. For a variable x, the augmented Dickey–Fuller (1981) statistic is the t ratio on π from the regression:

$$\Delta x_t = \Pi x_{t-1} + \sum_{i=1}^{k} \theta_i \Delta x_{t-i} + \psi_0 + \psi_1 t + \varepsilon_t$$

where k is the number of lags on the dependent variable, ψ_0 is a constant term and t is a trend. The kth-order augmented Dickey–Fuller statistic is reported, where k is the last significant lag of the 6 lags employed. The trend was included only if significant. For null order I(2), Δx replaces x in the equation above.
2. The sample is 1970:1–1995:1, except for log (*REER*) and *TECHPRO*, when it is 1970:3–1995:1.
3. Asterisks * and ** denote rejection at the 5% and 1% critical values. Critical values for around 100 observations with constant, and with and without trend, are obtained from MacKinnon (1991).

the remaining variables in Table 8.2, the ADF test fails to reject a unit root non-stationary process in levels but not in first differences. The unit root tests corroborate the consistency of our theoretical model. The four variables found to be *I*(0) are consistent with prior expectations: three are in differenced form, while short-term capital flows, by definition, should not influence the long-run equilibrium (consistent with evidence found for Chile by Elbadawi and Soto, 1994).

Three parsimonious equations from the general-to-specific estimation procedure for the entire period are presented in Table 8.4. The preferred parsimonious equation, which uses a fitted value for *NOMDEV*, is Equation 1. In Equation 2, short-run flows, which are potentially endogenous but as explained above are difficult to instrument, are simply removed from Equation 1 in order to show the robustness of the long-run estimates to short-run flow dynamics. In Equation 3, we replace the

Table 8.4 Single equation equilibrium correction models for the real exchange rate

Dependent variable Δlog (REER)$_t$	Equation 1[a] (1970:3–1995:1)	Equation 2[b] (1970:3–1995:1)	Equation 3[c] (1970:3–1995:1)
Long-run terms			
Equilibrium error	0.182	0.156	0.172
	(4.388)	(3.679)	(3.953)
Constant	0.876	–0.521	1.096
	(0.542)	(–0.249)	(0.614)
log (TOTXG)$_{t-1}$	0.639	0.896	0.608
	(2.113)	(2.271)	(1.819)
log (PGOLD) $_{t-1}$	0.398	0.426	0.339
	(3.927)	(3.342)	(3.536)
log (TARIFF)$_{t-1}$	0.263	0.290	0.204
	(2.479)	(2.194)	(2.116)
(LRCAPFLO)$_{t-1}$	4.040	3.451	2.156[d]
	(2.363)	(1.697)	(2.473)
(RESERVES)$_{t-1}$	1.491	1.523	1.268
	(2.919)	(2.431)	(2.515)
log (GOVEXP)$_{t-1}$	0.757	0.650	0.621
	(2.200)	(1.611)	(1.801)
Dynamic terms			
Δ log (TOTXG)$_t$	0.167	0.158	0.151
	(1.970)	(1.782)	(1.740)
Δ log (TARIFF)$_t$	0.056	0.045	0.050
	(2.612)	(2.024)	(2.310)
Δ log (GOVEXP)$_t$	0.525	0.533	0.527
	(3.629)	(3.514)	(3.576)
NOMDEV$_t$[e]	–0.916	–0.909	–0.938
	(–9.954)	(–9.436)	(–9.805)
DOMCRED$_t$	0.237	0.236	0.237
	(2.728)	(2.604)	(2.674)
SRCAPFLO$_t$	0.386	–	0.308[d]
	(2.998)		(2.712)
Δ log (PGOLD)$_{t-1}$	0.054	0.040	0.066
	(1.317)	(0.945)	(1.576)
NOMDEV$_{t-1}$	0.226	0.266	0.262
	(2.112)	(2.397)	(2.426)
DTECHPRO$_{t-1}$	0.527	0.815	0.586
	(1.815)	(2.842)	(1.932)

Notes

Diagnostics: (*t* statistics in parentheses)

Log of likelihood function	217.697	212.549	215.454
Number of observations	99	99	99
Std. error of regression	0.0295	0.0309	0.0302
R-squared	0.701	0.669	0.688
Adjusted *R*-squared	0.643	0.609	0.627
Durbin–Watson statistic	1.960	1.877	1.820
AR 1–5: F (5,77)	0.443 [0.817]		
Normality $\chi^2(2)$	0.583		
ADF test of equilibrium residual	–3.222*		
Chow: $F(17.65)$[f]	1.176 [0.309]		
$F(3,82)$[f]	0.772 [0.513]		

[a] Equation 1 is the preferred parsimonious dynamic ECM with short-run and long-run flows differentiated (see Equation 19 in Section 2). Variables are defined in Table 8.2.

[b] Equation 2 removes short-run capital flows (which are potentially endogenous) from Equation 1, to demonstrate the robustness of the long-run solution to short-term capital flow dynamics (see Section 4).

[c] Equation 3 demonstrates the robustness of the results using a measure of *total* capital flows.

[d] The measures of capital flows used here are *total* capital flows (short-run plus long-run flows), and the first difference of total flows.

[e] Note that nominal depreciation (NOMDEV) is a fitted value (see Table 8.3).

[f] For the Chow test the sample is divided into fixed and floating exchange rate regimes: 1970:1–1979:1 and 1979:2–1995:1. In the second parameter stability test, another three quarters are added to the sample (to 1995:4).

disaggregated long-run and short-run flows with a measure of total capital flows and its difference. In part, this is to answer objections that long-run and short-run flows in the South African data are not necessarily the theoretical versions of these variables (see Section 2 for discussion). However, despite some blurring of the definitions, in practice these variables do have distinctly different dynamics, where short-run flows influence the real exchange rate only in the very short-run, while the dynamics of the long-run flows suggest a long memory series. Furthermore, the long-run estimates of the fundamentals prove reasonably robust to the substitution of total flows for the disaggregated series.

It is important to distinguish long-run effects from short-run impact effects in interpreting the results of these equations, and this we do in the following two subsections.

The long-run equilibrium

The results in Table 8.4 show that the estimated parameters strongly corroborate the theoretical model outlined in Section 3. Starting with the long-run cointegrated estimates, a description and analysis of the main results from Equation 1 follows.

One of the most interesting findings in Table 8.4 is the importance of trade policy (*TARIFF*) in determining the level of the real exchange rate in this period. The positive and significant sign supports the notion that reforms aimed at reducing tariffs and eliminating trade restrictions are consistent with a more depreciated real exchange rate. Similar results were found for the volume of trade or degree of openness using the (negative of the) variable *OPEN*, purged of terms of trade shocks.[21]

The effects of shocks to the terms of trade, as remarked in Section 2, are theoretically ambiguous. The estimated elasticity for the real price of gold is positive and highly significant, which reveals the dominance of income over substitution effects that is normally corroborated in the empirical literature of real exchange rate estimation. This result is consistent with the strong income effect reflecting the important role of the gold sector in the South African economy, as well as its relative enclave status *vis-à-vis* the rest of the economy. Furthermore, a positive and significant effect on the long-term equilibrium real exchange rate was also found for non-gold terms of trade.

The ratio of total government expenditure, *GOVEXP*, is a conventional fundamental that was also found to have positive and significant effects on the equilibrium real exchange rate. Unsustainable levels of government expenditure lead to real exchange rate appreciation and over-valuation. The composition of expenditure variable, *GCUREXP*, performed very poorly even in moving average form in various alternative specifications of the model. This, however, may be a reflection of the inadequacy of the proxy (government consumption). To the extent that this variable is not strongly dominated by expenditure on non-tradeables, it may fail to provide any further information that contained in government expenditure.

Both long-run capital flows and the total flows variable in Equation 3 were found to be positive and significant, suggesting that a declining level of sustainable capital inflows requires a more depreciated equilibrium exchange rate. The data suggested an acceptable restriction in Equation 1 was to use a four-quarter moving average for the long-term flows indicating a long-memory series, by contrast with the short-run flows variable discussed below.

The stock of official reserves also had positive and significant effects, consistent with its theoretical role as a measure of relatively liquid foreign assets, and as an indicator of the capacity of the Central Bank to defend the currency. As expected, the levels measure of comparative technical productivity was insignificant, though positive.

The equilibrium-correction impact effects

The results reveal a wealth of dynamic effects otherwise missing and help sharpen the theoretical predictions. First, capital inflows are important in the immediate short run via the influence of the short-run flows, which leads to real appreciation. The same is true of the composite variable, *CAPFLO*, in differenced form. Secondly, the fundamentals that have both significant long-run and short-run effects are trade openness, government expenditure, non-gold terms of trade and the real price of gold. All of the four fundamentals have influences in the short run that are consistent with their long-run effects, indicating that in both the long and the short runs, more openness, worsening terms of trade and reduced capital flows lead to real depreciation. On the other hand, unsustainable government expenditure leads to over-valuation.

The most interesting result concerns the effect of (fitted) nominal devaluation, *NOMDEV*, on the real exchange rate. The estimated parameter for the contemporaneous effect of nominal devaluation is significantly negative, consistent with previous empirical literature, while that for *NOMDEV* lagged one period is positive and significant. In the current period, the very large estimated elasticity at -0.916 indicates that should the South African real exchange rate be over-valued in the current period, the impact effect of a nominal devaluation should be an effective instrument for an accelerated convergence towards the equilibrium real exchange rate, possibly minimising the transitional adjustment costs of real depreciation. It is possible to accept the hypothesis of a coefficient of −1 on *NOMDEV*, which would imply no reaction of domestic prices to devaluation within one quarter. However, the combined dynamics over two periods produce a combined coefficient for *NOMDEV* that is somewhat lower at around −0.7, which, coupled with adjustment delays through the lagged level of the real exchange rate, means that the effectiveness of nominal devaluation in achieving a real depreciation declines over time.

The effect of the excess supply of domestic credit, *DOMCRED*, has the expected positive sign and is significant, suggesting that with more expansive policies and associated domestic inflation, the real exchange rate will appreciate. Inconsistent policies therefore would lead to mounting disequilibrium and consequent over-valuation.

While a levels effect for technical productivity differentials was absent, as expected, given significant political regime changes, the lagged growth differential in comparative productivity, *DTECHPRO*, had a significant and positive effect. This is consistent with the theoretical predictions of models that assume differentiated productivities between the tradeable and non-tradeable sectors, with productivity growth being higher in the former. Under this structure, productivity growth in the tradeable sector leading to a rise in overall productivity will cause the non-traded goods supply schedule (Equation 6) to shift upwards, thus causing a deisequilibrium in the non-traded goods market (a shortfall in supply). To restore equilibrium this will require a real exchange rate appreciation (the Ricardo–Balassa effect). The variable is defined as an annual rate of change averaged over three years, and the *impact* coefficient of 0.527 suggests that a *sustained* 1% increase in the real per capita growth differential per annum over five years would induce a 3% appreciation.

A crucial parameter in the estimation of ECM is, naturally, that associated with the equilibrium-correction term. As mentioned, it measures the degree of adjustment of the actual real exchange rate with regard to its equilibrium level. When annualised, the estimate of the speed of adjustment is comparable to those estimated by Elbadawi (1994) using annual equilibrium correction models for Chile, India and Ghana, and by Edwards (1989) using quarterly partial adjustment models for a cross-section of countries. The equilibrium-correction coefficients can be manipulated in the context of the equilibrium-correction specification, to derive the corresponding adjustment speed in terms of the number of years required to eliminate a given exogenous shock. According to our calculations it would take 3.45 quarters (0.86 years) to eliminate 50% of the shock and 34.38 quarters (8.6 years) to clear 99.9% of it.[22] These calculations indicate that automatic adjustment in South Africa is comparable to estimates using annual data (1967–88) for the controlled economy, India. For the case of India, Elbadawi (1994) estimates that it would take 0.6 (6.2) years to clear 50% (99.9%) of initial misalignment.

5. Conclusions

The chapter has defined the equilibrium real exchange rate in accordance with the macroeconomic balance approach, focusing on the simultaneous attainment of *internal* and *external* balance for given sustainable values of variables such as taxes, terms of trade, trade policy, capital flows and technology. A theoretical model was outlined that specifies the equilibrium real exchange rate as a forward-looking function of the fundamentals, allows for a flexible dynamic adjustment of the real exchange rate towards the equilibrium real exchange rate, and the effect of short- to medium-run macroeconomic and exchange rate policy on the real exchange rate. The non-linear estimation of the quarterly dynamic equilibrium correction model for South Africa during 1970–95 strongly corroborates the theoretical model.

The main policy implications to flow from our results concern adjustments to equilibrium from disequilibrium positions due to short-run changes, and the likely real appreciation or depreciation required from a change in the fundamentals (e.g. liberalisation of trade controls and the potential for increased long-term capital flows in the democratic South Africa).

First, we deal with the question of trade liberalisation. Figure 8.4 shows there was a major decline in the volume of trade relative to GDP (purged openness) from the early 1980s, as a result of sanctions on trade and finance; that position began to improve around 1992. The series for trade taxes shows considerable volatility, mostly through the periodic use of import surcharges to protect the balance of payments, with a sharp increase in trade taxes from the mid-1980s and gradual liberalisation during the 1990s. Based on the coefficient in the long run, other things being equal, the implications for the real exchange rate are a 2.5% real depreciation in the medium term to compensate for liberalisation of the order of 10%, such has occurred during the 1990s. The impact or short-run effect of trade policy (via the differenced log(*TARIFF*)), is far smaller than the long-run effect.

Of course this is a partial effect. There is potentially a major offsetting factor via the increased availability of international trade finance and other loans, and the potential for increased foreign direct and portfolio investment. For example, the variable *DTECHPRO*, which represents the three-year average difference between real GDP per capita growth in South Africa and that of the OECD, shows that real per capita GDP growth has been well below the OECD average for many years (Figure 8.7). Poor growth performance, as discussed in Section 2, is related to the reduction of international trade and the virtual cessation of financial flows (other than trade finance) during the latter apartheid years. Figure 8.5 shows that long-term flows relative to GDP were negligible from the mid-1980s, while short-run flows were on average negative. Since late 1994 these flows have increased, though with considerable volatility (in large part related to uncertainty on the part of foreign investors about the timing of exchange control reform). If *sustainable* long-run flows increased from zero to about 3% of GDP, as in much of the 1970s, the long-run coefficient suggests a real appreciation of the order of 12% in the medium term to compensate. On the other hand, a 5% upswing in short-run flows relative to GDP would imply nearly 2% appreciation of the real exchange rate in the current quarter.

In the medium run, with foreign capital potentially available, one would certainly expect *DTECHPRO* to rise. If real per capita GDP growth in South Africa were to exceed the projected OECD average by 1%, and if the improved growth were sustained for some years (*DTECHPRO* is defined as a three-year annual average), the coefficient on *DTECHPRO* suggests that the real exchange rate would eventually (after some years) rise by 3%.[23] However, adjustment of the real exchange rate is slow, partly because *DTECHPRO* is a three-year moving average so that it takes three years of sustained growth for the improvement to be fully reflected in *DTECHPRO*, and partly because of the adjustment lags on the real exchange rate. It remains possible that increased growth and sustainable capital inflows could more than dominate the long-run and short-run effects of trade liberalisation.

Perceived growth possibilities in South Africa (including via an improvement in productivity) have a bearing on the question of the lifting of capital controls, since medium-term growth would be enhanced by inflows of capital. The importance of *short-run* flows under maintained capital controls in this model is not great. The historical 'crisis numbers' on the graph (Figure 8.3) are around –6% or –7% of GDP, subsequent to the estimated period, up to mid 1996, the largest short-run quarterly outflow to GDP just exceeded 3%. The estimated model of this chapter was intended to cover a period characterised by the almost continuous use of multiple exchange rates, with restrictions on both non-resident and domestic resident capital movements. However, despite the regime shift with the unification of the dual rate system in March 1995 (the last quarter of our empirical model) and an effective end to controls on non-residents, the empirical model continues to fit very satisfactorily when including for available data from the unified period (see Table 8.4). It is likely that a far more important regime shift would result from the lifting or significant relaxation of controls on domestic residents, inducing a transitional period of short-run outflows, as well as potentially large shifts in *long-run* capital to satisfy the pent-up demand for foreign assets in South Africa, particularly enabling the business and financial sectors to diversify portfolios abroad, thereby raising their creditworthiness.

Too much caution in removing exchange controls could be damaging. There is an urgent political need for growth, to substitute for high inflation: demands for high wages are less inflationary under growth, where they translate into real wage rises, while tax revenue rises with growth. That growth with low inflation may be a possibility is suggested by large potential gains in productivity, large returns on marginal investments given past distortions, a number of sectors with excess capacity and few labour shortages, at least in the unskilled labour market. On the other hand, too rapid a liberalisation remains a risky strategy. The high significance of (fitted) nominal depreciation (*NOMDEV*) is indicative of a high level of price rigidity in the short run (i.e. nominal devaluation for a time succeeds in achieving real depreciation). However, if wage demand pressures increase, and given that the reserve bank's current reserves could potentially be dwarfed by outflows of capital, the unpleasant possibility of a spiral of depreciation and inflation in the short run exists. A further risk for a government committing itself to a gradual liberalisation is vulnerability to costly speculative flows related to expectations of the timing of liberalisation, as events in 1996 showed.

Potentially there are 'vicious' and 'virtuous' circles, and it is critical to get onto the 'virtuous' circle, where the momentum of domestic growth attracts foreign capital inflows that more than compensate for outflows. It is important that growth should not lead to inflation, and this reinforces the need for a maintenance of conservative monetary and fiscal policy for the medium term, as well as the building-up of reserves by the reserve bank to prevent instability of the nominal exchange rate in the short run. It is particularly important that there be confidence that exchange controls once lifted will not be reimposed.

Government expenditure as a percentage of GDP showed a very strong upward trend in the 1980s (Figure 8.6), and is currently over 30% of GDP. One expects that the growth in this variable would be zero or negative in the future, given the large switching possibilities from defence to civilian expenditure, and the significant potential proceeds from privatised state industries. However, *DOMCRED*, the measure of excess money supply, is potentially more difficult to control. With the opening of the economy, investment opportunities will increase the demand for loans and the inflows of capital. If domestic credit grows 5% faster than GDP, this will generate 1% of inflation in the short run (an impact effect), reflected in an appreciation of the real exchange rate in the current quarter (holding the nominal rate fixed). This is slightly worrying since quarterly *DOMCRED* has on occasion been as high as 10%, although, on average during the 1990s, it has been less than 1%. This variable does not distinguish between investment and consumption uses of credit, the latter of which is more inflationary since it does not expand the economy's production possibilities. As a mineral exporter, the economy remains vulnerable to terms of trade shocks. While the importance of gold to the economy has decreased in the past decade, a sustained 20% fall in the real gold price would require a real depreciation of around 8% in the medium run.

Finally, we come to the question of management of the exchange rate. Adhering to nominal and real exchange rules is simply too rigid. Our model shows that the real exchange rate is *not* constant over time, but responds to changes in a range of fundamentals and shocks to the economy. With the current differential between South Africa's inflation rate of around 7% and the OECD average of around 2%, this suggests a fall in competitiveness of 5% per annum is currently taking place if the nominal exchange rate is assumed held fixed. It is crucial to bring down inflation, otherwise a large depreciation will be called for in several years' time (if the rate is not currently under-valued). It is obviously important that the reserve bank have sufficient reserves to be able to defend the nominal rate against large changes due to speculative attacks (though its ability to do so at present is limited).

Notes

1. The authors are very grateful for comments from John Muellbauer, John Williamson, Raimundo Soto, Terence Moll and many members of the CSAE, Oxford. Janine Aron is grateful for support from a Research Fellowship, Economic and Social Research Council, UK. (Award number H52427003594). The views expressed here are not necessarily those of the World Bank or affiliated organisations. Any remaining errors or omissions are the sole responsibility of the authors.
2. This chapter uses the real effective exchange measure of the South African Reserve Bank, which is a multilateral trade-weighted index for the real exchange rates of four trading partners, where an increase in the index denotes appreciation.

3. The authors are engaged in a long-term research programme on the foreign exchange market in South Africa, e.g., see Aron *et al.* (1998)

4. In recent years, Hendry (1995) has adopted the term equilibrium correction model for such models.

5. It was only after December 1988, and for a limited period between September 1983 and January 1985, that the reserve bank paid the gold mines in dollars and reduced its role in the foreign exchange market. From 1983 to 1985, 50% of gold production was paid in dollars by the reserve bank. Since 1988, 90% of the average of the previous two fixings on the London market has been paid in dollars. Nevertheless, gold mines are limited by the exchange control regulations that require them to sell these dollars to local authorised foreign exchange dealers within seven days.

6. The final 1994 Debt Arrangements provide for the full amortisation of outstanding affected debt (approximately US$5 billion at the end of 1993) in 15 half-yearly instalments, ending in August 2001.

7. Ironically, the debt crisis resulted in the new government inheriting a relatively healthy foreign debt situation. Since 1985, the foreign debt to GDP ratio declined from a high of 42% to 14% by the end of 1994. This figure excludes rand-denominated debt.

8. Equation 12 appears in similar guises in the empirical literature: see Edwards (1989, 1986), Elbadawi (1992), Mundlak *et al.* (1989), and Valdés (l985).

9. In a world of free capital mobility and market-determined interest rates, expected real depreciation could enter as a component of the uncovered interest parity condition, which would include the foreign interest rate. This approach is not appropriate for South Africa, where extensive exchange controls operated throughout the period examined.

10. Notice that the equilibrium solution in Equation 16 is not unique, since it is a function of policy fundamentals as well as external fundamentals.

11. F is stationary of order $k[I(k)]$ if $\Delta^{j}F$ is stationary for $j \geq k$, but not for $j < k$, where Δ is the difference operator.

12. A practical approach to introducing the concept of sustainability on the part of the fundamentals is found by obtaining the permanent (or sustainable) components of the fundamentals using the time series technique introduced by Beveridge and Nelson (1981). See Elbadawi (1994).

13. Note that the model is presented in a restricted form with current differences only, but in the estimation more general lag structures were considered.

14. South Africa has 35 *ad valorem* tariff rates, four levels of import surcharge rates, and 2,865 items with either specific or formula or other types of rates.

15. The average duty rate is twice as high as New Zealand's, the country with the next highest average tariff.

16. The most significant export promotion policy was the general export incentive scheme (GEIS), introduced in 1990 to help overcome the anti-export bias and to promote fully manufactured exports. GEIS provides cash subsidies for exporters of non-primary products, skewed towards higher value-added goods (GEIS is currently being phased out as it contravenes the GATT and WTO regulations).

17. As these losses are for the account of the treasury, they effectively form part of government debt. Before the 1994 elections these losses were made good by the issue of government stock to the reserve bank.

18. The main difference between the actual and theoretical measures is that the WPI for South Africa rather than the CPI is used in constructing the index. Since from Equation 10, the weighted average of foreign exportable and importable prices can be rewritten as the terms of trade (to the power α) multiplied by the price of importables (P_M^*, and given that the terms of trade already appear in the empirical equation, the link between the two definitions depends on how well P_N is proxied by the South African WPI. One might argue that given the predominance of gold in South Africa's exports until the early 1980s, and sanctions directed against manufactured exports in subsequent years, big divergencies between non-traded and manufacturing exportables sectors may be less likely. However, strictly, to correct for the discrepancy, the equation should include an additional variable, the domestic CPI/WPI ratio, as well as dynamic terms in the variable. These variables proved insignificant in the equation, suggesting that the measure we have used is a reasonable approximation (see Aron *et al.*, 1998).

19. For instance, a recovery in growth in South Africa in the 1990s relative to the OECD in part represents a politically motivated increase in demand for South African products. On the other, the resumption of investment and new availability of international capital is manifested in technical productivity improvements via catch-up.

20. In this chapter we report Chow tests for stability across different exchange rate regimes. A more detailed econometric investigation can be found in Aron *et al.*, 1998.

21. The influence of the trade regime has been even more dramatic in countries that effected considerable liberalisation. In the case of the Chilean reforms, tariffs were reduced from an average of 80% in the 1960–74 period to an average 20% in 1975–92. Subsequently the volume of trade increased from 29% to 55% of the GDP. Estimating an elasticity of the real exchange rate to openness of about 1, Elbadawi and Soto (1994) calculate that three-quarters of the 45% depreciation of the real exchange rate achieved during the period can be linked to the increase in trade volume.

22. The time required to dissipate $x\%$ of a shock is determined according to: $(1 - b_0)^T = (1 - x)$, where b_0 is the coefficient of the equilibrium-correction term and T is the required number of quarters.

23. This is bigger than might be expected for a pure Balassa–Samuelson effect. One reason is that our measure as explained earlier is an overly aggregated and therefore attenuated measure of the theoretical effect. The second reason is that our measure may also be reflecting relative demand growth in South Africa and abroad, which acts as predictor of relative interest rates to which the exchange rate responds.

References

Aron, J., I. Elbadawi and B. Kahn. 1998. 'Estimating equilibrium real exchange rates for South Africa'. Prepared for a World Bank-funded project: Exchange Rate Policy and Medium-Term Adjustment and Growth in South Africa. Mimeo. Centre for the Study of African Economies, University of Oxford.

Balassa, B. 1964. 'The purchasing-power parity doctrine: a reappraisal'. *Journal of Political Economy*, 72: 584–96.

Bell, T. 1992. 'Should South Africa further liberalise its foreign trade?'. ET Working Paper No. 16, Economic Trends Research Group, Development Policy Unit, University of Cape Town.

Beveridge, S. and C. Nelson. 1981. 'A new approach to decompositions of economic time series into permanent and transitory components with particular attention to measurement of the business cycle'. *Journal of Monetary Economies*, 7: 151–74.

Caballero, R. and V. Corbo. 1981. 'How does uncertainty about the real exchange rate affect exports?'. Policy Research Working Paper Series 221, Washington, DC: The World Bank.

Clements, M. and D. Hendry. 1995. 'Macroeconomic forecasting and modelling'. *Economic Journal*, 105: 1001–13.

De Kock Commission. 1984. *The Monetary System and Monetary Policy in South Africa*. Final Report of the Commission of Inquiry into the Monetary System and Monetary Policy in South Africa, Government Printer.

Dornbusch, R. 1973. 'Tariffs and non-traded Goods'. *Journal of international Economics*, 4: 177–85.

Edwards, S. 1985. 'The behavior of interest rates and the real exchange rates during a liberalisation episode: the case of Chile, 1973–83'. *NBER Working Paper No 1702*. Sept.

Edwards, S. 1986. 'Commodity export prices and the real exchange rate in developing countries: coffee in Colombia'. In S. Edwards and L. Ahmaed, eds, *Economic Adjustment and Exchange Rate in Developing Countries*. Chicago and London: University of Chicago Press, pp. 235–60.

Edwards, S. 1989. *Real Exchange Rates, Devaluation and Adjustment: Exchange Rate Policy in Developing Countries*. Cambridge, Massachusetts: MIT Press.

Elbadawi, I. 1992. 'Terms of trade, commercial policy and the black market for foreign exchange: an empirical model of real exchange rate determination'. *Journal of African Finance and Economic Development*, vol. 1, no. 2: 1–26.

Elbadawi, I. 1994. 'Estimating long-run equilibrium exchange rates'. In J. Williamson, ed., *Estimating Equilibrium Exchange Rates*. Washington, DC: Institute for International Economics.

Elbadawi, I. and R. Soto. 1994. 'Capital flows and long term equilibrium real exchange rates in Chile'. Policy Research Working Paper No. 1306. Washington, DC: The World Bank.

Engle, R. and C. Granger. 1987. 'Co-integration and error-correction: representation, estimation, and testing'. *Econometrica*, 35: 251–76.

Fallon P. and L. Pereira de Silva. 1994. 'South Africa: economic performance and policies'. World Bank Informal discussion papers on aspects of the economy of South Africa. Discussion Paper No. 7.

Faruqee, H. 1995. 'Long-run determinants of the real exchange rate: a stock-flow perspective'. *IMF Staff Papers*, vol. 42, no. 1: 80–107.

Garner, J. 1994. 'An analysis of the financial rand mechanism'. Centre for Research into Economics and Finance in South Africa. Research Paper No. 9.

Gelb, S. 1991. 'South Africa's economic crisis: an overview'. In S. Gelb, ed., *South Africa's Economic Crisis*. David Philip and Zed Press.

Hendry, D. 1995. *Dynamic Econometrics*. Oxford: Oxford University Press.

Johansen, S. 1988. 'Statistical analysis of cointegration vectors'. *Journal of Economic Dynamics and Control*, 12: 231–54.

Johansen, S. 1992. 'Cointegration in partial systems and the efficiency of single-equation analysis'. *Journal of Econometrics*, 52: 389–402.

Johansen, S. and K. Juselius. 1990. 'The full information maximum likelihood procedure for inference on cointegration – with applications to the demand for money'. *Oxford Bulletin of Economics and Statistics*, 52: 169–210.

Juselius, K. 1994. 'Domestic and foreign effects on prices in an open economy: the case of Denmark'. In N. Ericsson and J. Irons, eds, *Testing Exogeneity*. Advanced Texts in Econometrics. Oxford and New York: Oxford University Press, 161–90.

Juselius, K. 1995. 'Do purchasing power parity and uncovered interest rate parity hold in the long run?: an example of likelihood inference in a multivariate time-series model'. *Journal of Econometrics*, vol. 69 no. 1: 211–40.

Kahn, B. 1992. 'South African exchange rate policy, 1979–1991'. Research Paper No. 7, Centre for the Study of the South African Economy and International Finance, London School of Economics.

Kaminsky, G. 1988. 'The real exchange rate since floating: market fundamentals or bubbles?'. Mimeo. University of California, San Diego.

Kiguel, M., J. Saul Lizondo and Stephen O'Connell. 1997. *Parallel Exchange Rates in Developing Countries*. London: Macmillan and New York: St. Martin's.

Leape, J. 1991. 'South Africa's foreign debt and the standstill, 1985–90'. Centre for the Study of the South African Economy and International Finance, London School of Economics, Research Paper No. 1.

MacKinnon, J. 1991. 'Critical values for cointegration tests'. In R. Engle and C. Granger, eds, *Long-run Economic Relationships: Readings in Cointegration*. Oxford: Oxford University Press.

Mundlak, Y., D. Cavallo and R. Domenech. 1989. 'Agriculture and economic growth in Argentina, 1913–1984'. *Research Report No 76*, IFPRI, Washington, DC.

Polak, J. 1995. 'Fifty years of exchange rate research and policy at the International Monetary Fund'. *IMF Staff Papers*, 42: 734–61

Samuelson, P. 1964. 'Theoretical notes on trade problems'. *Review of Economics and Statistics*, 46: 145–54.

SARB. *Quarterly Bulletin*. Various issues. South African Reserve Bank.

Serven, L. and A. Solimano. 1991. 'An empirical macroeconomic model for policy design: the case of Chile'. Policy Research Working Paper Series 709, Washington, DC: The World Bank.

Valdés, A., H. Hurtado and E. Muchnik. 1985. 'Trade, exchange rate, and agricultural pricing policies in Chile', vol. 1 (*Country Studies*). The World Bank.

Van Der Merwe, E. 1996. 'Exchange rate management policies in South Africa'. SARB Occasional Paper No. 9, South African Reserve Bank.

Williamson, J. 1985. *The Exchange Rate System*. Washington, DC: Institute for International Economics.

Williamson, J., ed. 1994. *Estimating Equilibrium Exchange Rates*. Washington, DC: Institute for International Economics.

9

The Macroeconomic Effects of Restructuring Public Expenditure by Function in South Africa

Bill Gibson and Dirk Ernst van Seventer

1. Introduction

The extreme levels of inequality produced by the apartheid system seem to have overwhelmed South African policy-makers committed to the public sector as the mechanism by which the welfare of the majority of the people could be improved. In the face of staggering obstacles, the Government of National Unity (GNU) has adopted the rhetoric of 'fiscal discipline' as the organising principle for public policy. Still there appears to be some scope for setting new budget priorities along functional lines to improve the distribution of income and provide job growth. This chapter examines the macroeconomic impact of restructuring public spending using a multi-sectoral, dynamic computable general equilibrium (CGE) model calibrated to South African social accounting matrix (SAM). The principal conclusion is that functional shifts in government spending can make a significant difference to growth, employment, inflation and income distribution. Above all, it is necessary that public policies to stimulate demand be coordinated with more supply-oriented policies in order to stabilise major macroeconomic variables. A strategy that emphasises economic services and infrastructure investment performs best according the results of the CGE simulations.

The next section of this chapter locates the model in the context of the South African debate on macroeconomic frameworks structured in terms of 'demand driven' versus 'savings constrained models'. The section presents a stylised version of a macro-model that marries the concerns of both schools. The hybrid model is then subjected to a fixed public sector borrowing requirement (PSBR) to GDP constraint and it is shown that this will blind optimal fiscal intervention. This is followed by a brief empirical explanation of why fiscal policy is constrained in South Africa, based on a calculation of tax rates required to broaden the coverage of public sector benefits to the majority of the population. Since this option is effectively judged unworkable, the second best policy involved restructuring public sector intervention to improve the distribution of income. CGE model results are then presented, showing that a strategy that concentrates on economic services and infrastructure investment will work best in an economy in which private sector investment is crowded in to some degree.

2. Theoretical perspectives

Since the days of the Keynesian multiplier, it has been widely accepted that in a fixed price model with underutilised capacity and unemployed labour, a rise in government spending increases output. If wages and prices are flexible, however, this outcome is less certain and depends on how agents form expectations about the likely effects of government expenditure. Supply-side models question the proposition that the multiplier is even positive, noting that if taxes are not raised to pay for increased public sector spending, gross domestic savings will fall. As less is saved, less will be invested and thus the growth rate of the economy will slow down rather than speed up.

If taxes increase to match the rise in spending, the difference between the two models comes into even sharper focus. Growth in the supply-side model is unaffected by the rise in spending since no additional deduction from private savings need be made. Of course, if private savings decline with the higher tax burden, investment will follow and growth will be retarded. Since taxes usually do cause a reduction in savings, government spending slows down growth whether it is paid for by higher taxes or not.

On the other hand, a demand-side model will show that an increase in output accompanies a rise in public sector spending, whether taxes increase or the deficit is financed through the capital market. If government borrows to cover the deficit, output will rise. But even if taxes are increased, any decline in disposable income would have to be restored if total savings were to again equal investment.

The essence of the difference in the two perspectives lies in the determinants of investment. The Keynesian view holds that investment will increase when entrepreneurs foresee opportunities to profitably produce and sell their output. The source and cost of funds is not irrelevant, but the most important determinant of investment is markets. Orthodox models, by contrast, see investors as limited by the amount of available savings, chained to the past as it were, rather than forward looking. From the Keynesian perspective, savings adjusts to the vision of the future while in the supply-side model savings determines the future.[1]

The framework used in this chapter is based on the view that there exists a short run in which unbinding resource constraints are truly irrelevant, but this case is not the most typical. More generally, the effect of the constraint is inversely proportional to some measure of the distance between the constraint and the current period value of the affected variables. Past savings does indeed determine the available capacity to produce, but this constraint only becomes binding when that capacity is used. Whether the capacity is in fact used may have little to do with past savings; if anything, higher savings may well correlate with lower utilisation ratios.

It follows that models that focus exclusively on demand or supply are inadequate as a foundation for understanding the dynamics of the market system. Policy based on a one-sided view will be either impulsive or laconic, without motivation and cynical in its self-assessment. Confusing and conflating the two approaches, policy-makers often arrive at incoherent conclusions and resort to prescribed ratios or other rules of thumb. An example is setting the ratio of the public sector borrowing requirement (PSBR) to GDP as an economic (rather than political) objective of government policy.

A successful growth strategy must therefore take care to balance policies that stimulate demand with those that increase supply. If the demand side is over emphasised, the result is inflation, which may lead to a contraction of productive capacity. On the other hand, policies centred exclusively on supply run the risk of increasing capacity to an extent that growth in capacity itself becomes a drain on further investment.

The dynamics of a coordinated model

Consider a simple framework in which current output depends on consumption, C, plus autonomous expenditure, A (government and exports). Consumption is a function of disposable income, Y^d, but investment, I, depends on capacity utilisation. The latter is defined as the ratio of current income to capacity output. We have:

$$Y_t = C_t(Y_t^d) + I_t + A_t \tag{1}$$

$$I_t = I(u_t) \quad I_t' > 0 \tag{2}$$

$$u_t = Y_t/Q_{t-1} \tag{3}$$

Equations 1–3 constitute the usual demand-side or Keynesian model referred to above. For any given period t, Q_{t-1} is known. Investment is thus determined in Equation 2 and output is given by Equation 1.

The supply side says that capacity depends on the availability of the factors of production, capital, K, and labour, L:

$$Q'_t = Q(K_t, L_t) \tag{4}$$

Given factor prices, the firm calculates the optimal capital–labour ratio from the production function of Equation 4. Substituting Y_t and Q_t into Equation 4 and solving for the derived factor demand curves determines the rate of unemployment of capital and labour corresponding to the rate of capacity utilisation in Equation 3.

With I fixed, the demand-side model can be used to calculate multipliers in the usual way. The traditional long-run supply-side model allows the factor prices of labour and capital to adjust until the demand fully absorbs supply. The consumption function in Equation 1 then determines investment as a residual. Growth in the capital stock thus depends on savings and together with the growth in the labour force it determines the growth of income. In the traditional model, there is evidently no role for the independent investment function in Equation 2, and capacity in Equation 3 is always fully utilised.

But if the assumption that capacity is fully utilised, is relaxed, the full model then consists of Equations 1–4. A far more interesting set of dynamics unfolds when one assumes that both the demand (in Equations 1–3) and supply side forces (in Equation 4) are at work simultaneously. Capacity growth in Equation 4 is determined by the growth in the available factors of production, capital and labour. The last can be taken as exogenous, but the growth in capital depends on investment, which is itself determined in Equation 3. A rise in autonomous expenditure, for example, will increase capacity utilisation for the same supplies of capital and labour. But the higher level of capacity utilisation stimulates investment as suppliers increase capacity to meet the rise in spending.

The model's dynamics thus depend on the composition of the changes: a given percentage increase in output must be accompanied by the same percentage increase in capacity, or capacity utilisation will change. If output is growing in industries already characterised by significant excess capacity growth will be limited and capacity utilisation will rise; but if demand is slanted toward industries already operating close to full capacity, the only option is to increase capacity at close to the same rate.

As demand approaches full capacity in all industries, inflation begins to rise. In a homogeneous model, inflation makes no difference to the real side, but in a model in which some magnitudes are fixed nominally, inflation must reduce real expenditure. Inflation may also increase general uncertainty, which might well cause a decline in the rate of investment.

Once under way, the dynamics can be characterised as follows: The system may converge to some long-run equilibrium or it may diverge with some variables increasing without bound. If the long-run equilibrium exists, it may be at full capacity utilisation, or less. Clearly, a model that diverges is necessarily a 'medium-term' model, since eventually the environment to which the model is calibrated must change. But note that with a change in regime, the question of whether a long-run equilibrium existed for the initial set of parameters is clearly irrelevant. A sequential medium-term model is probably the most realistic approach to modelling economies as they actually work. A third possibility is that cycles develop in capacity utilisation. The cycles themselves may be convergent or divergent or on the boundary between.

Cyclical behaviour develops if the effect of investment on capacity growth is strong and there is significant depreciation. Imagine then an autonomous increase in investment that drives up income through the multiplier but increases capacity by a greater percentage. Capacity utilisation falls and this puts downward pressure on investment in the next period. Assume that this occurs and that investment is constant thereafter. If depreciation is rapid, the relatively low level of income will correspond to low capacity utilisation only initially. Soon, capacity utilisation will rise, even though income remains constant. The cycle then turns up again as investment increases in response to higher levels of capacity utilisation.

A model that allows for such a wide range of possibilities is clearly much richer than one for which the initial set of assumptions entirely prefigures the dynamic path. The issue, for example, of whether higher savings rates would accelerate growth is entirely open in the model presented here. Similarly, the timing of exogenous shocks, relative to the position in the cycle, is crucial. A rise in government expenditure could promote growth or slow the economy down, depending on the degree to which private sector investment was crowded in or out, by the intervention. In other words, policies that work at a low level of capacity utilisation might be ineffective at high utilisation rates and vice-versa. Since the impact of crowding in and crowding out is linked to the level of capacity utilisation, it is not possible to characterise one or the other as always dominant as is the case in more one-sided models.

The public sector in the model

Public expenditure is broadly classified into current, G, capital, I^g, the wage bill at wage rate w and employment, L^g, interest payments at interest rate i on debt D, and transfers, T^r. With Y as GDP and t as the tax rate, the PSBR ratio, p, can be expressed:

$$p_t = PSBR_t/Y_t = (G_t + I_t^g + w_t L_t^g + i_t D_t + T_t^r)/Y_t - t_t \tag{5}$$

From this formulation, it is clear that all major institutions in the economy play a role in the determination of the *PSBR* ratio. Government policy sets current and capital expenditure, employment, transfers and the statutory tax rate. But trade unions influence the total government wage bill, while the South African Reserve Bank (SARB) interest rate policy affects total interest payments. Transfers depend in part on demographic variables outside the control of government while the tax rate of Equation 5 is clearly an effective rate that is less than or equal to the statutory tax rate. Rate-payers across the economy evidently exercise some control over the PSBR ratio.

Government policy that seeks to control the PSBR ratio must first accurately predict income as well as the response of the remaining agents to government policy. Practice is more slipshod and policy often devolves into a search for a quiet residual in Equation 5. As noted by the World Bank (1994: 19), studies of fiscal adjustment typically find that capital expenditures are cut more than current expenditure with infrastructure investment, operations and maintenance suffering the most. South Africa appears to be no exception to this. Public investment then adjusts endogenously to conform to a given PSBR ratio.

To model this adjustment process, the level of the PSBR to GDP is set as an exogenous or policy-determined parameter. Note that the savings-investment balance from Equation 1 can be written as:

$$(s_t^p + s_t^x - p_t)\, u_t/k_t = g_t \tag{6}$$

where: s^i is the ratio of savings to output for the private and foreign sectors, respectively. u is defined as in Equation 3, the capital-capacity output ratio is k and g is the rate of growth of the private sector capital stock. The private sector investment function is taken in the model to be:

$$g_t = \alpha u_t + \beta_i^g\, t - \gamma r_t \tag{7}$$

where α is the accelerator coefficient, β is the crowding-in term, i^g government investment divided by income and γ is the crowding-out coefficient that measures the intensity of the (negative) impact of an increase in the interest rate, r, on private sector accumulation. Substituting the last equation into Equation 6, the solution for capacity utilisation is:

$$u_t = \frac{K_t(\beta_i^g\, t - \gamma r_t)}{S_t^p + S_t^x - p_t - \alpha k_t} \tag{8}$$

The short-run mechanics of the model are immediately evident from Equation 8. The first term in the numerator is crowding in. A rise in public sector investment, i^g, will increase capacity utilisation in the short run and an increase in the interest rate will cause capacity utilisation to fall. Consistent with the Keynesian short-run behaviour of the model, a rise in private (or foreign) savings will cause the utilisation rate to fall. An increase in the accelerator coefficient, α, or the capital output ratio, k, will increase capacity utilisation.

But observe from Equation 5 that an increase in any other component of government expenditure will have a dampening effect on capacity utilisation since it will crowd out public investment and therefore private investment. Thus, a non-zero crowding in coefficient, b, ensures that a rise in current government expenditure will cause capacity utilisation to fall. On the other hand, a rise in the tax rate will cause the current level of capacity utilisation to rise, since for the same PSBR ratio, more government investment will be forthcoming and thus with a positive, β, more private investment.

The dynamics of the model are also affected by the way in which the PSBR constraint is modelled. An autonomous increase in private investment, for example, will cause the current level of output to increase and hence the second-order effects of higher income on the PSBR ratio will cause government investment to rise. The multiplier is strengthened because of this effect, but there is also a rise in capacity due to the higher level of investment, public and private. Any increase in output will have the same effect of raising government investment, thereby toning down the possible mismatch between changes in capacity and changes in the current level of income. Holding the PSBR ratio constant provides an automatic stabiliser, which reduces the oscillatory character of the model.

Finally, inflation affects the public sector balance in subtle ways. Current government expenditure and employment are set by policy in real terms, and transfers are set as a share of GDP. Interest on debt and the wage bill depend on how closely the interest rate and the wage rate track the rate of inflation. Depending on the location of the economy in the cycle, the interest rate and wage rate may lag behind changes in the price level. When the economy is closer to full capacity, the adjustments are more rapid. This causes the public sector to have a slightly destabilising effect on the dynamics of the economy. The resulting slowdown in capacity growth, due to less public sector investment, increases the upward pressure on inflation. On the other hand, an unanticipated increase in inflation would produce higher levels of government investment, causing capacity to grow, thereby reducing the inflationary tendency in the economy.

Holding constant the PSBR as a fraction of GDP has a number of significant disadvantages when considered from the perspective of optimal policy. On the one hand, it robs the public sector of a major policy lever in that it causes the current government spending multiplier to become negative when crowding in is a factor, and zero if not. It also contributes to higher inflation due to slower rates of capital formation. On balance, then, one can conclude that this policy rule is destabilising and unlikely to produce the best macroeconomic performance for the South African economy. The next section addresses the question of why this approach to macro-policy-making was adopted when it is evidently defective.

3.   The policy environment

The second best macroeconomic policy of a fixed PSBR ratio can be seen as the legacy of the apartheid period. Lacking the political wherewithal to adopt obviously superior fiscal policies, the GNU has settled for a second best rule of thumb. A formal explanation is presented here for why optimal intervention has been effectively ruled out as a strategy. The magnitude of the disparities in public sector expenditures are so large relative to the available tax base, that the only workable option was to set arbitrary limits to the size of the public sector and to adopt the rhetoric of 'fiscal discipline'.

The spending dilemma

One measure of the depth of the apartheid period was the degree to which social benefits were skewed toward the white minority. While it is true that whites were also responsible for the majority of public sector revenues, they captured some 56% of social benefits in 1975 and 35% in 1987 (IMF, 1992: 28). In 1975 whites were 16% of the population and by 1987 they constituted 14%. Thus, spending on a per capita basis was becoming more egalitarian but with a considerable distance to go.

The official end of the apartheid period in 1991 also brought an end to the justification for large disparities in the distribution of social benefits. But it was far from clear how to redress the inequality inherited from the past. To appreciate the magnitude of the problem, let s be the ratio of spending per capita of blacks (including Asians and coloureds) to whites. If the tax rate on the white population were raised to pay for the equalisation of benefits at the level of the whites, the change in the tax rate would be:

$$\Delta t = \left[(1 - s)\frac{(1 - n)}{n}\right]g_w \tag{9}$$

where n is the share of the whites in the total population and g_w is government spending on whites as a share of white income.[2] The IMF estimates $g_w = 0.1$ (IMF, 1992: 28). Data for s are less certain. An often-quoted statistic is that the government spent four times more to educate a white than a black child, but other categories of expenditure, such as health, could be more equally distributed. As the graph in Figure 9.1 amply demonstrates, the increase in the white tax rates that would allow the equalisation of benefits ranges from 0.33 for health[3] to more than 0.5 for education. Thus, if all benefits were skewed in the same ratio as health benefits, the tax rate would have to rise from the present 31% to 64% of white income.[4]

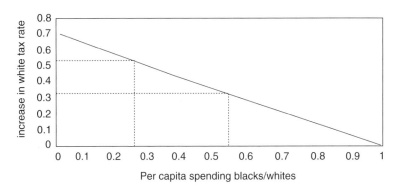

Figure 9.1   Equalising government spending

Reassessing spending goals

Since tax rates in such a high range are practically unenforceable, the Government of National Unity has opted to revise its goals of extending white benefits to other races. Instead, the composition of government spending is to be altered. The medium-term expenditure framework for public sector expenditure will be overhauled to reallocate spending within functional categories to achieve a more egalitarian distribution of benefits and between functional categories to raise employment within an 'envelope' or PSBR constraint.

In practice, fiscal discipline implies that most departments are unlikely to be able to meet the policy targets they have set out for the next five years. In particular, the goal of free and compulsory education for 10 years with acceptable pupil–teacher ratios, accelerated construction of new classrooms and equalisation of per pupil government expenditure after five years is all but unreachable. Neither will there be sufficient government funding for an acceptable number of average annual per capita visits to health care facilities.

Improvement in water supplies and housing subsidies to households, as well as land restitution and resettlement activities, will only be a fraction of the initial targets. Welfare maintenance grants could be phased out and social work services funded at current or declining levels. Expansion of economic infrastructure is limited and economic services such as the general export incentive scheme and the regional industrial development programme are to be phased out along with transport subsidies for commuters. The current approach to budget prioritisation replaces the goal of equalised spending with fiscal discipline.

In the next sections these priorities are re-examined by way of the computable general equilibrium model discussed above. Given that major changes in policy direction are unlikely to materialise, we examine some relatively minor shifts in the direction of public expenditure. Each of the three simulations involve a range of parameter changes and they are summarised in spirit under three headings: the welfare state model, the neoliberal model and a strategy that emphasises a state–private sector partnership, characterised here as 'Japan Inc.', with the understanding that these labels are used more as identifiers of a specific package of rather mild parametric changes rather than a basic change in course. It is to be stressed that these simulations are entirely macroeconomic in nature and we do not bring forward any of the underlying microeconomic issues of implementation and feasibility. Neither are the simulations intended to assess the overall welfare effects of the three directions in policy-making. The objective is more limited – to assess the impact of the changes on growth, employment, inflation and income distribution.

4.   CGE simulations

The debate around establishing new priorities in the budget has been confused by conflicting assumptions about the proper role of government in the economy. It is well known that neoclassical economics does not provide a complete theory of social choice (Hahnel and Albert, 1990: 28) The Coase theorem holds that efficient allocation of resources is independent of the distribution of income (Coase, 1960). An obvious derivative of this approach is the conclusion that the state should not meddle in the affairs of the private market but should limit its activities to lump-sum income transfers. Since such transfers affect no marginal calculations, the two tasks of promoting efficiency and a just distribution of income are, in principle, separable.

The theory of the modern welfare state grants that an equitable distribution of income is not required for efficiency, but holds that it is desirable for reasons of societal coherence. If the market does not provide a minimum level of welfare for the citizens of the state, it becomes the responsibility of the state to supply a safety net. In its most extreme interpretation, the state becomes the employer of last resort.

By contrast, the neoliberal model argues that income distribution is itself endogenous and the role of the state should be circumscribed. Incomes, in this view, are the product of intertemporal rational choice and the state has no logical or moral role in the allocation of resources in markets, neither should it play a role in determining the distribution of income. Like the price of any other resource, good or service, the distribution of income is the outcome of a market driven process. The neoliberal state does exist, but it is only for the purpose of repairing market failures. Were there no externalities in production or consumption, or no public goods, the state would optimally shrink to enforcing contracts and providing protection for private property. Health, education, security, justice and environmental protection are the traditional business of the neoliberal state since all involve some sort of market failure or externality. For positive externalities the state's participation is strictly complementary to the functioning of the market. Only when externalities are negative is the neoliberal state justified in limiting the right of the private sector to supply goods and services.

A third view of the relationship between states and markets is that the former should engineer the success of the latter. It is not adequate for the state to simply repair market imperfections; rather, the state has a fundamental role in developing markets and promoting domestic firms. In exchange for the guidance of the state, the firms agree to take over much of the provision of social welfare that in other regimes would be the responsibility of the state. Noting that a sequence of Pareto optimal states is not necessarily optimal when viewed as a sequence, the efficiency of static resource allocation is less of a concern than growth with full employment. So long as the state ensures that the markets will operate at maximum capacity, the question of income distribution can be left to private intertemporal choice. It is the role of the state to ensure that the incomes of its citizens are determined by their abilities rather than market opportunities.

These three models have been adopted with various degrees of success in Europe, the Americas, Africa and Asia. It comes as no surprise that the implications for welfare, growth and the size of the public sector depend in large measure on the model in place. Broadly speaking, the Western European democracies have opted for the welfare state approach, with the result that both real wages and benefits (public and private) have been higher than in the United States. But unemployment has hovered at about 10–11% in Europe while it has fallen to half that in the United States due to lower real wages there. Unit labour costs have risen most dramatically in Europe, and have been flatter in the United States, Canada and Japan. Real wages have risen in Europe but only in Japan and Canada have real wage increases been associated with declining unit labour costs (*New York Times*, 14 March 1994). In the developing world, productivity growth has been negative since 1980 in Latin America and the Caribbean, the Middle East and the entire continent of Africa (World Bank, 1995: 13). Budget deficits in the three models follow no prescribed tendency; taxes are higher in Europe but deficits lower, while the United States has attempted to reduce the size of its public sector by cutting taxes first and running high deficits as a result. Bloated public sectors in Africa have been associated with stagnant and declining GDP growth, while some (not all) of the fastest growing economies of Asia have large but efficient public sectors. Similar observations have been made for South Africa. Whereas the pre-election state in South Africa has been characterised as overstaffed and inefficient, leading to a financial crisis of the central state, calls have been made for a strong and slim state, giving a strong lead to economic transformation (MERG, 1993: 265–7). Clearly, the empirical record is mixed, offering at least some qualified support to each of the three schools of thought.

In the next subsections these stylised visions of public sector strategies are compared with reference to the debate on budget priorities in South Africa. Clearly, no pure strategy can or will be followed, inasmuch as a good deal of the budget is established by previous commitments. Historical policy also links future spending to more or less well identified cost drivers – population growth, labour force, inflation rates, etc. – and is therefore outside the scope of any but fundamental reform. Given that low level reform is unlikely in South Africa (as anywhere else) it follows that the relevant simulations must be cast in terms of changes in the direction of spending of fairly major aggregates and in fairly minor ways. The next subsection spells out the assumptions required to model these three approaches.

The assumptions

The parameter levels for the three simulations are summarised in Table 9.1 and are assumed to hold for the 1995–99 forecast period. The changes are classified into five groups: current government consumption, other spending related to current consumption, consumer subsidies, capital transfers for land reform, and assumptions about the macroeconomic environment. The latter include the ratio of the PSBR to GDP, the assumed inflow for direct foreign investment and public sector induced productivity change.[5]

The welfare state

The first column for the welfare state (WS) simulation emphasises health and education as well as social services and housing. The real current expenditure of goods and services for these government functions is assumed to increase for the next five years by 10% per annum relative to the 1994 levels. There is no increase for economic services in real terms and expenditure on security declines by 5% per year. Government employment (shown in row 2a of Table 9.1) is assumed to grow at the same rate as total government consumption; thus, its growth relative to the average of total current government expenditure is shown as zero in the table. In other words, there is no change in labour productivity in the public sector for this simulation. For all simulations, transfers are assumed to grow in proportion to spending on goods and services in the functional category of social welfare and housing. But in the WS simulation, transfers grow 2% per annum faster. Moreover, there is an RDP housing subsidy introduced as a fraction of GDP.[6] A direct electricity subsidy is granted equal to 10% of 1994 real consumption of low-income households for the forecast period. Row 4 shows that additional funds for land reform are made available in the first simulation.[7] We also assume that land reform stimulates small scale farming activities. This translates in the model economy into lower labour productivity in the farm sector.

Row 5 of Table 9.1 indicates key changes in the general macroeconomic environment in which the public sector spending programme is assumed to be taking place. Consistent with the concept of a welfare state, the PSBR as a fraction of GDP does not decline. On the other hand, spending designed to enhance the social wage does not lead to significant productivity gains, at least in the short to medium run as modelled here.

Table 9.1   Assumptions of the simulations[a]

	Welfare state	Neoliberal	Japan Inc.
1. Growth in real current government consumption			
a. Health	10	avg[b]	avg[b]
b. Education	10	avg[b]	avg[b]
c. Security	–5	10	0
d. Economic services	0	0	15
e. Social and housing	10	0	0
2. Growth relative to government consumption			
a. Employment	0	–5	–2
b. Transfers	2	–5	–2
3. Subsidies			
a. RDP-housing	yes[c]	no	no
b. Electricity	yes[d]	no	no
4. Land reform	10	no	no
5. Major macroeconomic variables			
a. PSBR/GDP(%)	6	3.4[e]	6
b. Capital productivity	0	1	0.5
c. Labour productivity	0	0.5	–0.25
d. Direct foreign investment	0	1	0

Notes
[a] % Changes unless indicated otherwise.
[b] Moves with the average of current government expenditure.
[c] RDP housing subsidy included at full amount (see note 2 to main text).
[d] Subsidy equal to 10% of real electricity consumption for low income households.
[e] PSBR declines linearly from 6% to 3.4% between 1995 and 1999.

Foreign capital is assumed to be neutral to the policy package, with no increase in direct foreign investment.

The neoliberal approach

Rectifying market failures and downsizing the government are the main objectives of the neoliberal approach. This is simulated by way of above average real spending increases on security (at 10% per year over the 1994 levels), an average increase in spending on health and education (3%–4% per year over the 1994 level), and no real increase in spending on economic services and social welfare/housing. In addition, the RDP housing and electricity subsidies, as well as the land reform programme, are scrapped. Government employment and transfers to households are growing at 5% and 2.5% less per year than the current expenditures to which they are linked. This implies that government labour productivity increases substantially and the effort to extend the welfare safety net to the majority of the black population is reduced, for example scrapping the child maintenance grants.

Downsizing the government is further emphasised by a declining PSBR ratio to GDP. The PSBR is assumed to fall from 6% in 1995 to 3.4% in 1999, more or less consistent with the stated objectives of the GNU. As a result of the fiscal prudence, capital as well as labour productivity increase (as shown).[8] Labour productivity increases across the board by 0.25%. Finally, assume that foreign investors react favourably to the adoption of the 'Washington Consensus'. The expectation is that the exchange rate is less vulnerable to rapid depreciation. This is reflected in the model by shifting the investment function up by an additional 1% compared with the previous simulation.

The Japan Inc. simulation

The spending programme in this last simulation is based on a pact between the private sector and the government. It emphasises the economic services function of current expenditures and public sector investment. The strategy is to generate sufficient employment and income to allow a larger fraction of the population to meet their own medical and education needs through normal market channels. Spending in the health and educational categories does not exceed the average (3%–4% per year over the 1994 level). Neither is there any real increase in current expenditure on social welfare/housing. The assumption is that firms receiving the support of the state will provide for their workers adequately . Employment and transfers decline relative to their respective functional lines by about 2%. Similar to the neoliberal strategy, will be no spending on subsidies and land reform. The state judges spending in these categories to be less effective, ultimately, than direct economic services. Neither is security a priority, as seen in Table 9.1.

The relatively slow growth in current expenditure will translate in the model into higher levels of government investment, given that the PSBR to GDP ratio is fixed. The government makes resources available not only by means of the economic services budget in order to directly accelerate capital productivity-enhancing activities, but also through the provision of infrastructure. The rationalisation of state services is assumed to promote higher capital productivity in the private sector, although not with the same boost as was assumed for the NL stimulation. An important part of the strategy is to target small and medium-sized enterprises (SMEs), characterised by higher labour absorption; this is modelled here by a small decrease in labour productivity. Finally, no additional foreign investment is expected to be forthcoming in this simulation.

Results of the simulations

Table 9.2 provides a picture of the macroeconomic performance of the three stylised experiments described above. The first column of Table 9.2 shows the capacity utilisation and should be interpreted as measuring the balance of the model. If capacity utilisation is rising, then supply is continually falling short of demand and thus supply-side stimulus would be called for; demand-side policies are warranted in the opposite situation.

Growth and capacity utilisation

Not surprisingly, the results shown in Table 9.2 suggest that the WS policies are more oriented toward demand expansion than the NL policies. Consequently, the capacity utilisation for the WS simulation rises over the forecast period, while the capacity utilisation in the NL scenario falls. What is perhaps a surprise is that in the JI simulation capacity utilisation rises to its highest level, a period average of 88.5%, despite the apparent supply-side focus of this set of policies. In none of the three cases, however, is the policy package so unbalanced that it produces capacity utilisation rates above 90% and as a result, inflation remains under control in all.

Growth is unquestionably the fastest in the third simulation. The JI simulation stimulates demand with a relatively large injection from the fiscus. But it is balanced with some growth in capital productivity to prevent a rise in capacity utilisation from igniting inflation and thereby choking off further expansion. This effect can be seen clearly in the first simulation: the rise in the inflation rate from 1996 to 1997 causes an increase in the rate of interest (shown in the 4th column), which stunts growth. Output falls momentarily in 1998, but then regains its momentum when the interest rate is stabilised.

In the NL scenario growth also dips in 1998, but it is now a reaction to the sharp drop in capacity utilisation due to insufficient effective demand. As noted, this is the product of the assumption of a declining PSBR/GDP ratio, which limits demand growth. When the interest rate falls, demand recovers somewhat and growth picks up in 1999. The same interest rate effect can be seen in muted form in the JI simulation. There, growth reaches a flat spot but then experiences another demand-led burst in 1998/99, as is evident from the increase in the rate of capacity utilisation in that year.

Individual Business Association (or Self-Employed Labourers' Association: *Geti laodongzhe xiehui)*. It was established by the government in 1986, is strictly controlled by the Bureau for Industry and Commerce, and has compulsory membership for all individual petty entrepreneurs who obtain business permits. Upon getting the permit, they are automatically enrolled in the Self-Employed Labourers' Association. Further, their leadership is picked by the government, and their operations are heavily subsidized by the government (Unger and Chan, 1995:39–40). Members include those who operate stalls or carts, as well as those who have small family craft or service businesses such as repair shops and small restaurants. By the end of 1992, the national Self-Employed Labourers' Association had close to 25 million members, all of whom were officially licensed (Pearson, 1994:44–5; Unger, 1996:796–8). However, in spite of membership being compulsory, the fact is that many small entrepreneurs operate without a permit and thus do not join the association. This no doubt reflects the questionable legality of their enterprises as much as it does a desire not to be under the thumb of the government.

Since 'civil society' is made up of that part of society which is both non-governmental and non-familial, its development in China is impaired by the continued emphasis within society on the family. Indeed, most of the self-employed are running family businesses. As in places such as southern Italy (Putnam, 1993), and as in so many developing countries, the Chinese have always shown a preference for businesses based on family ties, especially in the countryside. In the cities, businesses may be extended beyond the family on the basis of *guanxi*, personal relationships which are themselves often based on family ties. Rarely, however, have the Chinese been able to move beyond such personal ties to allow for the employment of outsiders, which has kept the size of Chinese businesses small by comparison with those in the West. As Francis Fukuyama has put it, they are not able to develop ties of 'trust' beyond the family and personalistic connections. By contrast, in the West, 'trust' (which is more reliant on contracts and the law) makes the building of large non-family corporations possible (Fukuyama, 1996).

For the many petty entrepreneurs and workers in the cities who have come recently from the countryside and lack *guanxi* in the cities, the Self-Employed Labourers' Association offers a sort of organizational *guanxi* (Nevitt, 1996:35). But at this point in history, unofficial associations, based on the province and even the town from which migrants hale, are well-established in the cities. While migrant entrepreneurs are often exploited by these mafia-like organizations, they also provide the essential *guanxi* to get them started in a new city.

Somewhat ironically, then, entrepreneurs in China, because they lack the state support offered by a *danwei* and need to pay taxes and apply for licenses and permits, as well as generally rely on the services (security, sanitation, transportation, and so on) provided by the state sector, must deal with local government officials much more frequently than those living in the cocoon of the state-owned *danwei*. This need to interact with the government is making entrepreneurs far more politically active and causes them to band together to press their concerns collectively. Indeed, although it was the government itself which insisted that all entrepreneurs and independent businessmen join a state-run association, those associations have turned out to be powerful lobbying organizations which represent the interests of China's new business class. Meanwhile, entrepreneurs, much like the employees of a *danwei,* continue to find developing ties with local officials through banqueting, the provision of goods and services, and gift-giving essential to their success in business (Shi, 1997).

In short, neither Communist ideology nor an authoritarian state can explain why China does not fully embrace a 'civil society'. What is missing in the explanation is China's culture, with its strongly authoritarian strains. Culture is deeply embedded in China's institutions, and in the family, which tends to be distrustful of all those outside the family and favours the promotion of family members above all others, regardless of competence, fairness or even legality:

> Chinese Confucianism ... does not legitimate deference to the authority of an all-powerful state that leaves no scope for the development of an independent civil society. If civil society is weak in China, that weakness is due not to a statist ideology, but rather to the strong familism that is basic to Chinese culture, and the consequent reluctance of the Chinese to trust people outside of their kinship groups. (Fukuyama, 1995:28; emphasis added)

Thus, those who think political reform alone will bring democracy to China are overlooking the critical role of the family and culture in maintaining an authoritarian and patriarchal system in China.

Thus, while interference by the state through corporatism may cut into civil society from the top down, perhaps even more important is the family closing in on civil society from the bottom up; for families, in order to protect their businesses against the intervention of the state, use bribery to cultivate *guanxi* with local officials. Through the cultivation of corrupt relationships between entrepreneurs and the state, the state becomes a rent-seeker, and in exchange, allows the family-run enterprises to make a profit. It may appear that a civil society is developing, but actually the corruption of officials by individual entrepreneurs impedes the development of a true public space that could be called 'civil society'. Alternatively, families and clans may even resort to forming underground ('black') societies (*heishe*) and use illegal methods, including violence, to protect and advance their businesses (Xiao, 1998; Xiong, 1999).

Therefore, Chinese culture, because of the distorted manner in which the emphasis on the family gets played out in China, and because of the culture's emphasis on the authority and dominant role of the state, bears some responsibility for the difficulties civil society has had in developing in China. Until associations can prove they are effective in protecting the interests of individual members, it will not be surprising if the family-run enterprises continue to count on the culturally reliable technique of corrupting officials to get what they want.

For such reasons, some Chinese argue that rounding up all the businesspersons into associations that represent their interests but also control them is essential if society is to be even partially protected against China's more rapacious entrepreneurs. All too many simply do not obey the law. Whether it is those who acquire marble for sale by using dynamite that decimates the side of a mountain into thousands of useless fragments, entrepreneurs who whip up cosmetics in the kitchen sink that cause serious rashes to those who use them, fishermen who use dynamite to fish, in the process killing tens of thousands of fish that are too small to eat, or entrepreneurs who sell defective or illegal products, Chinese society seems to need the state to exercise control.

In short, associations are not just useful for aggregating and articulating public (and private) interests. They are also useful for the society to be protected against the worst abuses of the unharnessed individual, for associations do not merely help expand the 'public space' of civil society; they also help control those who really need to be controlled (Nevitt, 1996:30; Professor XX, 1998). Looked at from a different perspective, then, associations bring an order which society both needs and wants. By providing both order and articulating their interests to higher authorities, then, the Self-Employed Labourers' Association serves the interests of both civil society and the state. The Association's officials really do want the petty entrepreneurs to do well, as the growth of the private sector under their supervision enhances their official status (Unger, 1996:801), while at the same time increasing financial support for the local government (Oi, 1992; Nevitt, 1996:37–38).

Whether in work units or associations, we see the patriarchal elements of traditional Chinese cultural perspectives emerging. For example, Jonathan Unger's study of the Self-Employed Labourers' Association in Chaoyang District, Beijing, notes that the Association's officials treat the stall vendors and petty entrepreneurs as 'children in need of protection from others' and, even more frequently, 'as juveniles needing a firm guiding hand'. They are viewed 'as dangerously unanchored in society,' and the role of the Association is to control them (Unger, 1996: 801).

In addition to setting up the Self-Employed Labourers' Association, the state also encourages them to organize themselves (Unger, 1996:801). The state's purpose in doing this is not, of course, to set up an organization that will give it trouble, but rather one which will link up with the state. The assumption is that both state and society benefit from this link. The association will represent its members' interests, but at the same time the association will help enforce the state's policy and regulations as they relate to the association. While at times the state *control* element may seem to outweigh the autonomy of the association,[5] the general trend in China seems to be in the other direction, at least in those periods when the state is less anxious about the control issue. Thus local association branches tend to support their members' objectives, such as to demand some of the benefits available to workers in state-owned *danwei*, or a better wholesaling network, or broader access to municipal services, or protecting them from unregistered entrepreneurs, and even defending their members against the interests of the state at higher levels. For example, the Self-Employed Labourers' Association is responsible for assisting the Tax Bureau to determine the taxes to be paid by each private enterprise; but according to Unger's study, the Association officials are unlikely to do anything that would negatively affect their relationship with the entrepreneurs in their association, such as helping the Tax Bureau collect taxes. The balance between the state's control and an interest group's autonomy is likely to be even more in favour of the latter in smaller cities and towns, where there are fewer powerful state officials in charge of associations than in Beijing. The balance also favours the autonomy of an association whose members are powerful in their own right, such as is the case with the All-China Federation of Industry and Commerce. Its members are large, wealthy and powerful businesspeople and businesses who *voluntarily* join the Federation, and the Federation's board is comprised of businesspeople, not officials (Unger, 1996:802–11).[6]

The ambivalent relationship between associations and the state exists in part, then, because local associations *do* have local government officials on their boards. Local government officials often see it as in their interest to promote local entrepreneurs in order to enhance economic development, *regardless* of whether they pollute the environment, produce dangerous or defective products, destroy scarce resources, or do little to fulfil the state's objectives.

In short, there is collusion between the state and civil society, with both sides hoping to gain something from it. As Wank (1995) concludes from his study of Xiamen City, efforts by some organizations to influence state officials may not necessarily come at the expense of state power. In some crucial respects, various associations, particularly those of private businesspeople, may actually enhance the power of local officials. This is because, as a result of economic decentralization, local officials control the allocation of resources and have the power to use regulations to benefit business enterprises. The end result is that private actors, such as businesses, work *in an alliance with the state at the local level* in order to enhance their autonomy *vis-à-vis* the central state (Wank, 1995:70): that is, the growing autonomy of 'civil society' is not that of autonomous private citizens or enterprises, but private citizens or enterprises *in collusion with* the lower levels of the state bureaucracy to promote their interests *vis-à-vis* the upper levels of the state.

If civil society is defined as that part of society which is not governmental or familial or individual (that is, private), then government-sponsored, organized and financed associations are not necessarily the sort of organizations that constitute elements of 'civil society'. Nevertheless, some of them are rapidly evolving into organizations that operate autonomously from the government and are responsive to constituent interests. This seems to be what the Chinese government leadership wants. For example, the Chinese government established certain national associations, such as the two federations of associations that replaced China's industrial ministries when they were abolished in 1993, and the 14 corporatist industrial associations that replaced Shanghai's 14 industrial bureaus when they were abolished in 1992. The state's purpose was to *replace* entire governmental sections which were based on ministries and bureaus that reflected the state's ownership of the industries, with corporatist associations that will reflect the concerns of a privatized sphere within each industrial sector. These associations are intended to take on the responsibilities for their own sector's welfare, thereby undermining top-down state corporatist control (Unger and Chan, 1995:42–3). The state went even further with the National Association of Light Industries, which it then broke down into some 50 corporate associations to represent the specialized interests of the many industries under each. These sub-associations are one step futher from the reach of the state.

The picture presented here, then, is a steadily larger and more complex chessboard of associations which press for the collective interest of their constituents. As in any 'civil society', China's associations are pursuing public interests through the aggregation and articulation of their needs, ideas and concerns, but they are simultaneously satisfying private interests. This is conspiciously true for businesspeople and workers, but it is equally true for, say, environmentalists (*Wenhui bao*, 1999) or consumers' rights groups.[7]

Some of the sectoral interests pursued by associations and interest groups springing up in China may, moreover, be in serious conflict with the overall good of the society. Thus, although a 'civil society' is supposed to be publicly, not privately oriented, there is inevitably some fallout for the private sphere.

In short, the corporatist associations that are proliferating in China are becoming increasingly like institutions of civil society as traditionally envisioned in liberal democratic societies. Residual state control over China's associations leaves something to be desired. But, even associations and interest groups in Western society are not perfect in their contributions to a civil society. As Benjamin Barber notes:

> by definition all private associations necessarily had private ends. Schools became interest groups for people with children (parents) rather than the forgers of a free society; churches became ... special interest groups pursuing separate agendas rather than sources of moral fiber for the larger society ... voluntary associations became a variation on private lobbies ... 'Even environmental groups were necessarily just another 'special interest group' pursuing their own special interests 'in competition with the special interests of polluters'. (Barber, 1995:28)

Still, China's broad collection of official and unofficial associations at national, regional and local levels are providing an increasingly strong institutional framework for representation of constituencies and specialized interests that are different from those of the state. They are seeking 'concessions, benefits, policy changes, relief, redress, or accountability' from the state. In doing so, they are steadily eroding the heavy hand of a centralized state. As in other civil societies, moreover, at the same time that they are cutting away at the state's authority, they are not standing in opposition to it. Thus, China's asssociations provide the Chinese people with opportunities to influence the state, especially at the local level. And, in so doing, associations provide them with an alternative to political parties for disseminating new ideas and for articulating, aggregating and advancing their interests. Finally, they also provide a training ground for new political leaders (Diamond, 1994:6–8, 10–11).

Peasant associations

Peasant associations were first created by the CCP in 1921, and they became a major organizational basis for revolution in China. After the founding of the PRC, and particularly with the formation of the people's communes as the structure for integrating the state with the society in rural China in 1958, the government decided that the peasants no longer needed to organize into associations as their interests were identical with the state's interests, so the peasant association was abandoned (Zhu, 1997:118–19).

Rural reforms and the introduction of the market economy since 1979 have, however, generated considerable discussion about reinstituting the peasant association. One argument is that, because peasants are now 'independent producers', their interests can no longer be assumed to be identical with those of the government. They therefore need an intermediary to regulate their relations with the government, and with the market. For its part, the government would itself benefit from an intermediary association (whether national, regional or professional) between it and the peasants to which it can delegate many of its functions, and which would help aggregate and articulate peasant interests. This peak association would form an umbrella over the nearly one and a half million specialized peasant associations which have developed to address the sectoral interests of the peasantry. But the government has not really paid enough attention to the peasantry, and has by default allowed the peasantry to organize as they please (Zhu, 1997:118–19). One result has been the re-emergence of 'black societies', unofficial (and illegal) organizations which engage in activities such as smuggling or take the law into their own hands to advance the 'interests' of their members. They are usually rooted in clans or religious cults. It would, however, be wrong to conclude that they form a part of 'civil society' as their activities are largely for private gain.

Trade unions

Like so many of China's associations, the government's willingness to negotiate with more autonomous workers' associations arose from changes in the labour market occurring as a result of economic decentralization. The proposition that the dismantling of the institutions of a command economy may help create a favourable environment for the growth of civil society (Rose, 1994:23) is aptly illustrated in China's labour sector. There the state has created associations to represent independent, self-employed entrepreneurs coping with the conditions of a developing, non-state-owned, market economy, but it has also encouraged trade unions to harness *unorganized*, and potentially dangerous, workers. The greater autonomy accorded to trade unions, however, illustrates the need for the state both to negotiate with and to control *organized*, and potentially dangerous, workers in the state-owned sector.

Like peasant associations, trade unions in China provide an example of the complex evolving relationship between the state and a developing associational society. They also reflect the shift during the reform period away from the view that the interests of the party-state and the workers were identical, and therefore that workers did not need autonomous organizations to represent their interests *vis-à-vis* state-appointed management in SOEs. By the 1990s, this view had changed, and state control and dominance over labour unions gradually relaxed to the point that unions could successfully negotiate for improved working conditions and welfare benefits for workers *vis-à-vis* the state.[8] In fact, workers felt they really had to fight for their rights with management because, as a result of economic reform, the state-party management of enterprises was replaced by a management-responsibility system. The new managers were under contracts with the state that pressured them to increase productivity and profits even at the expense of the workers' interests. Faced with the end of the 'iron rice-bowl,' and with it the possibility of unemployment and the elimination of pensions, workers began to demand greater organizational autonomy *vis-à-vis* their new managers (see Chapters 2, 3 and 6). The state was caught in a bind: it wanted management to move enterprises into profitability, but it could not risk millions of workers taking to the streets to protest about working conditions. The result was that the state turned to the trade unions to resolve the conflicts workers had with management (Zhang, 1997:128, 133–4).

The government also realized, as a result of the workers' efforts to create autonomous workers' unions during and after the Tiananmen Square demonstrations of 1989, that it needed to accede to some of the demands of an increasingly anxious and unhappy workforce to avoid continuing labour unrest. In short, the Party needed the support of the unions at the same time as it wanted to control them.[9] After 1989, the CCP and the unions developed a symbiotic relationship, wherein the trade unions would continue to support the Party in exchange for their having greater input into policy-making and greater negotiating power in the enterprise (Ng and Warner, 1997:57–8).

From the perspective of the ACFTU, the economic reforms that have threatened the workers' well-being brought it into conflict with the state. Under pressure from the workers, and for its own survival as a major bargaining unit in the state's structure, ACFTU sought to represent workers' interests and to attain organizational autonomy by confronting the state. Thus ACFTU's bargaining on behalf of the workers should be viewed as a 'pragmatic' policy to maintain its power as a major national 'peak' association. It was created by the state yet bargains on the workers' behalf 'against' the state (Jiang 1996).

Workers who bring grievances against state enterprises to labour arbitration have a better than 50:50 chance of winning their cases (Ng and Warner, 1997: Table 4.1).[10] Further, factory trade unions may now acquire independent corporate legal status, and have a far better chance of winning a case against the state, a state-owned factory, or even a privately-owned factory, if they have applied for such status. This status makes unions legally equivalent to factories: a factory may not, for example, treat the trade union's fund as part of the factory's own property. China's trade unions now use trade union laws passed by the National People's Congress for arguing their legal cases ('Progress ...', 1997; Qin, 1997:30–1).[11] This is another indication of the growing power of workers *vis-à-vis* the state, and of the willingness of the state to negotiate with workers who have been treated unfairly within a legal framework. In short, the state has recognized the power that workers have to challenge the Party-state, and it is trying to work with the associations which represent workers to avoid conflict and maintain stability.

Two of the major results of the shifting relationship between the state and this corporate association were the Regulations of the Minimum Wage in Enterprises and improvement of miners' safety, and the 1994 Labour Law, which it took ten years for ACFTU to negotiate with the government. The Labour Law led to the initiation of the five-day working week in January 1995, a 'quid pro quo' for ACFTU agreement to lay-offs of redundant workers necessitated by economic reforms (State Council, 1997:33–4). The Labour Law gave trade unions in enterprises the right to oversee the labour contracts within their respective enterprises, and to intervene to protect the workers' interests if employers cancelled or broke contracts without justification. Additionally, trade unions represent workers in negotiations and dispute mediation with management concerning wages, vacations and labour safety, as well as in such matters as workmen's compensation and insurance (Zhang, 1997:140). The Labour Law also gave workers the right not to work (essentially, to go on strike) if the workers' safety was at risk, and required that foreign-invested enterprises allow trade unions to be established (Howell, 1998:161–2).

Thus, in the 1990s, ACFTU changed from a 'top-down' transmission-belt to a two-way transmission-belt, from the old Maoist style of a 'mass organization' created by the state for the purpose of controlling all individuals and organizations in particular sectors (see Chapter 3), to an organization that, although it still functions to carry out state-assigned objectives, also pushes for its own independently-determined objectives. Like so many organizations in China, ACFTU has been forced to find much of its own financing. As a result, ACFTU, which had been dependent on state revenues and (inadequate) dues from its membership, has become involved in raising money to pay for the increased welfare benefits for workers that it had promised. ACFTU (that is, trade unions at lower levels within the ACFTU) now runs its own enterprises to increase its finances. By the end of 1995, ACFTU's 138 000 enterprises generated an income of 45 million yuan. Of the total, 67 000 were economic enterprises, and most of the rest were in the service sector. Employing more than one million workers, they are considered 'collectively-owned enterprises' (Ng and Warner, 1997:57–8). This has produced the paradoxical situation in which workers have become managers of workers; and in which a reputedly state-run organization, ACFTU, which was originally created in order that the Party-state could control China's workers, now runs its own enterprises, which are neither state-owned nor state-controlled. Overall, ACFTU has greater autonomy from the state as a result of its greater financial independence.

Equally important is the increased control the memberships of some local trade union associations now exercise over their own officials. For example, in many of the trade unions at the enterprise level in the city of Qingdao, enterprise trade union presidents are no longer appointed. Instead they are directly elected by workers in the enterprise. Further, because the Party was, under the management-responsibility system, removed from administrative affairs, and because workers are almost solely interested in material benefits, not ideology, Party committee leaders are essentially ignored (Zhang, 1997:138–9).

As the government has steadily decentralized and rationalized administration, bureau-level trade unions have been eliminated in some cities. Trade union federations of local level trade unions in enterprises that fall within the same industrial sector have emerged in their place in such broad sectors as chemicals, light industry, textiles and heavy machinery. These federations are far more autonomous from state control than were their smaller isolated predecessors. And, of course, their larger size makes them far more powerful *vis-à-vis* both enterprise management and the state (Zhang, 1997:139).[12]

Trade unions in foreign-funded enterprises

Economic liberalization has also led to dramatic changes in ownership forms, as well as in the categories of workers in China: migrant labourers, workers in foreign enterprises, and TVE workers were added to the categories of peasants and workers in SOEs. No organization, however, was representing these new categories of labourers (Howell, 1998:152). For example, some 20 million new workers in TVEs were recently peasants tilling the soil; and some 15 million workers are now employed by foreign-funded (FFEs) and private enterprises, not by SOEs. They have become a source of discontent and industrial action since, not being workers in a state-run enterprise, and without an official union to negotiate for them, they face problems of late payments of their wages, job insecurity (most being hired on short-term contracts), appalling working conditions and inadequate housing (see Chapters 3 and 6) (Ng and Warner, 1997:53).

At the level of local governments in particular, the desire to attract foreign investment has tended to outweigh any concerns government officials might have for protecting and advancing workers' interests, for local officials do not want workers to make demands which drive foreign investment out of their locality. However, while foreign business people (most of whom are Hong Kong or Taiwanese entrepreneurs) do introduce efficient capitalist-style management in China, their enterprises (often in the form of sweat-shops) are not known for progressive labor practices. Workers in the more than 120 000 FFEs[13] are, in fact, far more likely to suffer from exploitative labour practices than the workers in China's SOEs. A study of Qingdao's FFEs, for example, noted that they did not pay overtime for working extra shifts, did not provide safety equipment to workers, did not sign contracts with workers that specified their terms of employment, and even revived once-common practices of corporal punishment and personal humiliation (including strip searches) as methods by which to control workers. Of course, these kinds of practice tend to anger workers and, because FFEs have no Party committees to discipline workers, labour militancy against management was far more likely to occur in them. Thus, it was in the state's interest to set up trade unions to act as mediators in the foreign-funded companies (Zhang, 1997:143–5).

Since trade unions have been established in the foreign-funded sector, most labour disputes with management have occurred in those enterprises not having trade unions. In part, the success of trade unions in the foreign-funded sector may be attributed to the fact that, although they were originally established by cadres from local Party committees or high-level trade unions, their leadership soon came to be elected on an annual basis by their own union memberships. Because these unions no longer have Party committees, and can sometimes enlist the support of the local government in its disputes with management, their union leadership has gained significant autonomy from the Party and the state to negotiate with management. Generally this pleases the state, as it helps stabilize labour–management relations in the potentially explosive foreign-funded sector (Zhang, 1997:143–5).[14]

In short, the development of more associations in the labour sector, many of which are almost completely autonomous from the state, has not necessarily been confrontational with the state. Indeed, the state sees their development as essential to cope with the problems introduced with economic liberalization. Thus, even the Chinese state has viewed this advance of civil society as a non-zero-sum game, in which both the state and the society win (see Warner, 1999).

Associations for enterprises with foreign investment

In addition to establishing trade unions in some FFEs, in 1987 the Chinese government established the China Association for Enterprises with Foreign Investment (CAEFI) as a national or peak association, with 40 sub-associations at levels below the national level. Members are usually groups (that is, the enterprises themselves), not individuals, and most individual members are Chinese, not foreign. At the national level, CAEFI has deep ties with the Chinese state, especially with MOFTEC. At lower levels, however, it is often local officials who have founded the associations. At both the national and local levels, the association is 'primarily self-funding', although some of the start-up costs for CAEFI were paid for by MOFTEC. The high level of self-funding does not, however, necessarily translate into greater autonomy. Further, at both the national and branch levels, CAEFI has an 'interlocking directorate' of officials from MOFTEC (or retired from MOFTEC), and CAEFI managers. Many Chinese managers in the foreign enterprise sector, however, do not regard CAEFI as 'a serious channel through which to make suggestions or have complaints redressed'. But, without these personnel links with the government, it might be considerably more difficult for CAEFI to achieve such objectives as attracting more foreign investment and functioning generally in the way a chamber of commerce might do in a capitalist state (Pearson, 1994:37–8).

Further, CAEFI associations do challenge the state's authority over FFEs, especially at the local level where local government officials interfere with their operations, and they frequently win. Finally, although these business associations have a foot in both the state and private sector, they are successfully pushing for greater autonomy, especially at the local levels where the foreign enterprises are actually located. Nevertheless, because the CAEFI associations are made up of businessmen who benefit from many of the state's policies to promote a strong business environment today, they are in general not 'anti-statist' in their orientation (Pearson, 1994:39–42). In short, the efforts of CAEFI associations to become more autonomous need not be viewed as fundamentally conflictual or adversarial by the state.

Altogether, then, China has gradually introduced conditions under which workers have gained the right to negotiate with their employers, regardless of whether they are private, collective, foreign or state employers (see Chapter 6). Still, labour disputes and demonstrations go on. By 1993, China had reported 12 358 labour disputes, an increase of 50 per cent over 1992 (Pei, 1997:20). In turn, the new forms of employers – private, collective, TVEs, and FFEs – have also gained more autonomy from the state. Like the workers, their relationship with the state is often one of mutual advantage.

Unofficial, underground workers' organizations

Some of China's workers in non-SOEs where no trade unions exist are joining unofficial or underground workers' organizations. This is particularly true in the Free Enterprise Zones in the coastal areas, where workers feel they are being exploited by foreign-run companies; but it is also true for workers hired by Chinese entrepreneurs. In addition, unofficial and underground unions are organizing workers to protest against economic reforms that adversely affect workers' benefits in state enterprises. Workers have even hired gangsters to take care of their grievances with exploitative managers. Unemployed workers, laid off due to economic reforms, are joining underground workers' organizations (see Chapter 13). These unofficial organizations use far cruder tactics than do branches of ACFTU, including violence against employers and destruction of employers' property (White, 1995:29–32).

4   Problems for democracy created by a multiplicity of associations

As Diamond has persuasively argued, the proliferation of interest groups is not necessarily a sign of a 'civil society' or a more democratic society (Diamond, 1994:5, 15). Focusing exclusively on the development of civil society may, in fact, distort our understanding of democratic change in China. 'Societal autonomy' (that is, the proliferation of genuinely autonomous associations) 'can go too far ... even for the purposes of democracy'. Associations in civil society must have limits on their autonomy:

> A hyperactive, confrontational, and relentlessly rent-seeking civil society can overwhelm a weak, penetrated state with the diversity and magnitude of its demands, leaving little in the way of a truly 'public' sector concerned with the overall welfare of society. [Civil society] must be autonomous from the state, *but not alienated from it*. It must be watchful but respectful of state authority. (Diamond, 1994:14–15, emphasis added)

The view that a weak state is not the best breeding ground for a true civil society is exemplified by Russia, where the weakening of state institutions has significantly thwarted the creation of a civil society. If state institutions wither too quickly, it

> may actually hinder the growth of a strong civil society. The presence of a decrepit state structure – one whose offices can be bought or coopted by private interests – engenders patterns of interest organization that deviate sharply from those associated with a normal civil society ... The organizations of civil society must enjoy independence from the state in order to function normally, but state institutions also must possess a degree of autonomy if they are to respond to demands in a manner that encourages pluralist competition. (Fish, 1994:32)

In Russia, the 70-year-old legacy of socialism, and the replacement of a fairly strong state with a web of interpersonal networks dedicated to their own interests and not to those of the greater society, have truly been detrimental to the development of a civil society beneficial to democratization (Fish, 1994:41). In short, a multiplication of interest groups, especially if they are of the 'rent-seeking' sort, do not add up to a true civil society. Instead, the state may be weakened by them, but in a way that benefits the rent-seekers rather than the associations on which a civil society is built.

Similar conclusions concerning this seeming paradox, that a strong civil society needs a strong national government, have been reached by those who have studied European history. In early modern England, 'the evolution toward a strong, coherent central state was as critical for the emergence of the institutions of a civil society as the growth of an ideology of individual rights or the increase of nonstate associations' (Davis, 1995:17, note 27). By contrast, the ability of Shanghai's bourgeoisie in the early twentieth century to turn increased associational autonomy 'into a viable civil society' suffered as much from 'the weakness of the central state' as it did from its own weakness as a class. Thus, neither a totalitarian *nor an anarchic system* provides a satisfactory environment for social forces to mobilize. Both are hostile to the development of the institutions that comprise a civil society, and the public sphere cannot take root (Davis, 1995:17, note 28, emphasis added).

The competition among interest groups to affect policy may not necessarily benefit the whole society, or it may benefit only the most powerful constituencies represented by interest groups. And, because the most powerful interest groups are likely to be funded by the wealthier segment of society (or large numbers of not so wealthy people, such as retired persons, or trade unions), the interests of individuals unable to organize into a powerful association will tend to be neglected. Thus, the already dominant class (or interests) will tend to become even more powerful. Moreover, for individuals and groups still burdened by many of the practices and institutions of an authoritarian society, which require negotiating complex bureaucracies in order to obtain licences, permissions, resources and access, it may be difficult to participate effectively in an emerging pluralistic society. It may turn out that 'informal collusion or clientelistic connections' work better than organizing interest groups and associations (Schmitter, 1992:169, 172).[15]

If state institutions in today's China become so weak that they are corrupted by the particularistic interests of powerful associations, are overwhelmed by them, or alternatively, are unable even to offer protection to nascent associations, the proliferation of associations will not necessarily lead to a more democratic system. Thus, the development of too many associations fighting for their own interests without strong state institutions still in place to protect collective societal interests may hinder China's democratic development. Only a strong state can avoid the corrosive impact of the uncontrolled expression of narrowly-based constitutent self-interests through competing associations, associations which have no loyalty to the state as a collective whole. By contrast, a strong state (which is willing to relinquish strong centralized control over the society) has a potentially protective role in helping build a civil society. A strong state can act to protect weaker associations against more powerful associations, thereby maintaining some degree of social equilibrium and order. In China's case, its state institutions may be disintegrating faster than new ones are being constructed to replace them, and society is becoming increasingly ungovernable (Pei, 1997:48). Indeed, the less able the government is to control China, the less likely it is that it will tolerate the growth of a pluralism that further undermines its control. Nevertheless, the state may have enough residual control to give China a better long-term chance of developing democracy than Russia and the former Soviet republics.

China's associations which have large memberships are becoming increasingly effective politically, while those Chinese with narrower concerns are still inclined to work more on the basis of family ties and 'relationships', (*guanxi* established through patterns of favours, gift-giving and banqueting) than they are through interest groups (unless, that is, the interest at stake is so broad that one individual's efforts at *guanxi* would be ineffective). Further, interest groups and associations, like virtually all organizations in China, are being forced to turn increasingly to private financing; and this is necessarily leading to the wealthier organizations having more clout. Thus, in the stand-offs between environmentalists and private entrepreneurs in business associations, the power of the purse held by the business associations is often dispositive. The problem is aggravated by the fact that local leaders responsible for both business development and for implementation of environmental controls tend to favour business because of the tax revenues generated by business for the locality. In some cases, however, the pressures from environmentalists on the government have led to serious action, such as the shutting down since 1996 of hundreds of small paper-producing factories that had proliferated once free enterprise was allowed ('Analysis of Sustainable Development', 1997).

To summarize, the Chinese government may officially reject 'peaceful evolution' towards civil society or, perhaps better stated, towards 'associational pluralism', yet this appears to be what is happening, and with the support of the state. To the degree that the whole political and social system can tolerate this dramatic challenge to its control structure, the development of these many associations and the creation of a civil society will benefit the Chinese people and advance democracy. So far, the institutions and associations that are being created as part of China's civil society are not fully autonomous. But autonomy may turn out to be far less important to China's democratic development than whether China's corporatist associations contribute to stability or instability (cf Perry and Selden, 2000).

The power of associations and interest groups and their effect on the development of civil society in China today

China today still maintains controls over associations and interest groups, and still has adequate state power to resist their demands if they push beyond their narrow sectoral interests to challenge overall state control. But, in general, as long as associations and interest groups do not publicly oppose the government in their activities or statements, the state seems unworried about the details. On the contrary, the state sponsors efforts by associations to address the problems created by economic reform. This is particularly noticeable in the modern enterprise sector, where entire ministries have been transformed into associations. Similarly, various economic sectors, such as the automobile sector, and the bank and financial sector, have been encouraged to move together into horizontal associations (Li, 1987:23–5).

The language still used by both the government and such associations and interest groups is, of course, that the associations are advancing the interests of their own clientele in order to serve the goals of the Party and state (cf. Chapter 2). Thus Shanghai's Brain Olympics Association was established to 'advance the four modernizations' by training students to go to the International Brain Olympics Contest. Shanghai's Cooking Association was established for 'supporting reform and the open door policy, and abiding by China's laws' to unify all the city's cooks in spreading the art of Chinese cooking abroad. It also publishes a bimonthly magazine, and sponsors exhibits and workshops. The Rural Enterprises Association promotes 'spiritual civilization' by supporting basketball, soccer, chess, films, singing and karaoke among its members. All academic and research societies, from Futurology, Family Planning,

Qigong, Fishing Economics, *The Dream of the Red Chamber (Hong Lou Meng,* a famous novel) and Food Therapy Research Associations to Playwrights', Musicians', Film Producers', and Calligraphers' Associations have in their mission statements the aim to 'support the four principles', 'the open door policy', and 'the two 100's'. ('Let a hundred flowers blossom, let a hundred schools of thought contend'.) The Leprosy Prevention Association 'upholds the four basic principles' by eliminating leprosy within this century. And the Association for Eliminating the Four Pests (mice, mosquitoes, flies and cockroaches) also exists 'to uphold the four basic principles' by uniting, organizing and co-ordinating all technical forces and contributing to the 'four modernizations' by safeguarding people's health. In 1982, this association established a company in Pudong District (the Shanghai Health and Pest Prevention Company) which provides consulting, processing and marketing services and sells pesticides (Ma and Liu, 1993:108–74). It is, in short, the money-making arm of the association.

The jargon notwithstanding, the importance of these changes for civil society are real. As Nevitt concluded from his study of associations for entrepreneurs and businesses in Tianjin:

> It seems that in the Chinese context a civil society may not develop separate from and in opposition to the state but rather in the niches and spaces that the state leaves open, and that it will grow in response to opportunities deliberately engineered or accidentally created by the state. And, in turn, such a civil society may make demands upon the state – not to undermine or weaken it but to constrain its behavior in some circumstances and to endorse and support it in others. (Nevitt, 1996:43)

Conclusion

Thus, any simplistic view of 'civil society', in which individuals and associations must be seen as fully independent of, and even in opposition to, the state ignores the subtle and complex intertwinings in China. Economic liberalization in the last 20 years has created a new role for associations, and a friendlier environment for the evolution of civil society (see Lane and Luo, 1999). Ultimately, it has turned out to be in the state's interests to create still more associations, and to give greater autonomy to certain associations, while at the same time maintaining tight control over others which it fears might go too far in undermining the state's power. In addition, the state's control is being eroded by other forces set in motion by economic liberalization, forces whose interests are not aggregated and articulated by official associations, and forces which are also not in the best interests of a developing civil society or associational pluralism.

It is not easy to know just how much state control is good for the development of China's public sphere. Like all societies, China continues to wrestle with the proper balance between autonomy and control. If associations become deeply institutionalized, the state may not be able to confer and retract power and responsibilities at will.

Notes

1　I am indebted to Fang Cheng for his comments on an earlier draft of this chapter.

2　Another perspective on why interest groups are being formed in China is that a large number of retired or idle cadres still remain energetic and want to retain their social status, as well as their influence over political and economic policies. So they are establishing all kinds of academic, economic and professional groups, or are appointed by the state to head them. The leaders in power today, being the former subordinates of these retired cadres, cannot prevent them from doing this. Instead, they cater to the requests of their former superiors! (Li, 1997). This view is confirmed by Margaret Pearson, who found retired officials on managing boards in her own 1994 study of socialist corporatism in foreign enterprises (Pearson, 1994:38). It is unlikely that a retired or idle worker would, however, have as much power or influence as someone who still possesses all the perquisites of office.

3　The Writers and Artists Federation is truly controlled by the Party, and it reports directly to the Department of Propaganda. If the writing, production or art of a member is unacceptable to the Party branch within the Association, the member might have his or her privileges removed, but rarely more (McDougall, 1999).

4　At the time the organization was banned, it had 215 artists (Jin, 1996:72–3).

5　Unger notes how the Industry and Commerce Bureau, under whose aegis the Self-Employed Labourers' Association falls, forced members of the association to do its bidding at such times as 1993, when Beijing was being visited by the head of the Olympics Committee to consider the city as the site for the year 2000 Olympics (Unger, 1996:801).

6　Nevitt's study of the Self-Employed Labourers' Association and the All China Federation of Industry and Commerce in Tianjin arrived at similar conclusions about the latter, but found that the Self-Employed Labourers' Association did little to advance the interests of the petty entrepreneurs (Nevitt, 1996:30–1).

7　The name of the magazine *Zhongguo zhiliang wan li xing (Quest for Product Quality in China)* is also the name of the consumer rights organization, which is very influential in China. It sends out teams to investigate consumer complaints concerning product and service quality, but also deals with broader issues of criminality, such as swindling (Xiong, 1999).

8 The term 'negotiate' is used not in the sense that China's trade unions come to the bargaining table with independent status and power in some sense equivalent with the government's. Rather, the government has had to make concessions to the trade unions because of its need to placate disgruntled workers who threaten to strike, demonstrate and cause major societal upheaval unless some of their demands are met. Because of the extraordinarily large numbers of workers angered by the negative effects of economic liberalization on them, the government cannot simply use force to maintain order; it must also make concessions. Hence 'negotiations'.

9 Ironically, the 1989 demonstrations illustrate the frequent overlap between the official and the unofficial, making it difficult to discern to what degree an association is truly autonomous from the state. For example, during the 1989 Tiananmen demonstrations, workers joining the Beijing Workers' Autonomous Union were required to be regular employees in one of the city's state-controlled work units, in spite of the fact that the whole purpose of developing an independent unit was to protest to, if not against, the state. The same was true for the more than 20 autonomous workers associations that sprouted in 19 of China's provinces at that time (Perry 1995:317).

10 Settlement of Labour Disputes Accepted and Handled by Labour Arbitration Committees in the PRC (State Statistical Bureau, 1995).

11 Other regulations, such as the Regulation of Minimum Wages in Enterprises, also now provide a basis for workers bringing legal action.

12 Based on Zhang's study of trade unions in two cities, Weifang and Chanzhou.

13 As of April 1995, more than 240 000 foreign-invested enterprises had been approved, of which at least half were already operational (Howell, 1998:150).

14 Zhang is drawing these conclusions from his study of the establishment of trade unions in the foreign-funded sector in Qingdao in 1993–94.

15 Illiya Harik notes that in Arab countries, their 'most "modern" associations – business groups, labor unions, professional and intellectual societies – show little or no interest in democratization' (Harik, 1994:48; emphasis added).

References

'Analysis of Sustainable Development' (1997) *Qiu shih (Seek Truth)*, 7.

Barber, B. R. (1995) 'Jihad vs. McWorld', from *Jihad vs. McWorld*, New York: Random House, pp.281–7, in S. Myers and P. Parsekian (eds) (1996) *Democracy is a Discussion: The Handbook*, New London: Connecticut College.

Brook, T. and Frolic, B. M. (eds) (1997) *Civil Society in China*, Armonk, NY: M. E. Sharpe.

Chan, S. (1995) 'Building a "Socialist Culture with Chinese Characteristics"? The Case of the Pearl River Delta', *Issues and Studies: A Journal of Chinese Studies and International Affairs*, 31, 5 (May), pp.1–24.

Chinese Law Society (1998) 'Overview of Work by Associations and Societies under the Ministry of Justice', Section 9, *Zhongguo Xinzheng Sifa Nianjian 1997*

(*China Judicial Administration Yearbook, 1997*), Beijing: China Legal Publishing House, pp.621–9.

Davis, D. S. (1995) 'Introduction' in D. S. Davis, R. Kraus, B. Naughton and E. J. Perry (eds), *Urban Spaces in Contemporary China: The Potential for Autonomy and Community in Post-Mao China*, Cambridge: University of Cambridge Press and Woodrow Wilson Center Press.

Diamond, L. (1994) 'Rethinking Civil Society: Toward Democratic Consolidation', *Journal of Democracy*, 5, 3 (July), pp.4–17.

Fish, M. S. (1994) 'Rethinking Civil Society: Russia's Fourth Transition', *Journal of Democracy*, 5, 3 (July), pp.31–42.

Forney, M. (1998) 'China: Voice of the People', *Far Eastern Economic Review*, 7 May, pp.10–11.

Fukuyama, F. (1995) 'Confucianism and Democracy', *Journal of Democracy*, 6, 2 (April), pp.20–33.

Fukuyama, F. (1996) *Trust: The Social Virtues and the Creation of Prosperity*, Harmondsworth: Penguin.

Harik, I. (1994) 'Rethinking Civil Society: Pluralism in the Arab World', *Journal of Democracy*, 5, 3 (July), pp.43–56.

Howell, J. (1998) 'Trade Unions in China: The Challenge of Foreign Capital', in G. O'Leary (ed.), *Adjusting to Capitalism: Chinese Workers and the State*, Armonk, NY: M. E. Sharpe, pp.150–71.

Hui, W. (1998) 'Contemporary Chinese Thought and the Question of Modernity', *Social Text 55*, 16, 2 (Summer), pp.9–44.

Jiang, K. (1996) 'The Conflicts between Trade Unions and the Party State: The Reform of Chinese Trade Unions in the Eighties', *Xianggong Shehui Kexue Xuebao (Hong Kong Journal of Social Science)*, 8.

Jin, Y. N. (1996) 'Perspectives on the Failure of the Fine Arts Village in 1995', *Ershi yi shiji xuan yuekan (The 21st Century Bimonthly)*, 33 (February), pp.72–80.

Jin, Z. R. (1999) 'More than 200 Scientific and Technological Journals Signed the Moral Covenant', *Guangming Ribao*, 2 February (http://www.gmdaily.com.cn).

Lane, K. and Luo, Y. (1999) [eds.] *China 2000: Emerging Business Issues*, Thousands Oaks, CA; London and New Delhi: Sage publications.

Li, G. (1997) 'Prospects for Post-Deng China', *Contemporary China Studies*, 1.

Li, Y. Z. (1987) 'Rise of Horizontal Associations', *Beijing Review*, 30, 15 (13 April), pp.23–5.

Ma, Y. L and Liu, H. B. (1993) *Shanghai Shehui Tuanti Gailai (Overview of Shanghai's Societal Organizations)*, Shanghai: Shanghai Publishing House.

McDougall, B. S. (1999) Conversation.

Nevitt, C. E. (1996) 'Private Business Associations in China: Evidence of Civil Society or Local State Power?', *The China Journal*, 36 (July), pp. 25–43.

Ng, S. H. and Warner, M. (1997) *China's Trade Unions and Management*, London: Macmillan and New York: St Martin's Press.

Ogden, S. (1974) 'Chinese Concepts of the State, Nation, and Sovereignty', PhD Thesis, Brown University. Available from University Microfilms. Ann Arbor, Michigan.

Ogden, S. (1996–1997) Notes and interviews, China.

Oi, J. C. (1992) 'Fiscal Reform and the Economic Foundations of Local State Corporatism in China', *World Politics*, 45, 1 (October), pp.99–126.

O'Leary, G. (ed.), (1998) *Adjusting to Capitalism: Chinese Workers and the State*, Armonk, NY: M. E. Sharpe.

Pearson, M. M. (1997) *China's New Business Elite: The Political Consequences of Economic Reform*, Berkeley: University of California Press.

Pearson, M. M. (1994) 'The Janus Face of Business Associations in China: Socialist Corporatism in Foreign Enterprises', *The Australian Journal of Chinese Affairs*, 31 (January), pp.25–46.

Pei, M. X. (1998) 'Chinese Civic Associations: An Empirical Analysis', *Modern China*, 24, 3 (July), pp.285–318.

Pei, M. X. (1997) 'Racing Against Time: Institutional Decay and Renewal in China', in W. A. Joseph (ed.), *China Briefing: The Contradictions of Change*, Armonk, NY: M. E. Sharpe, pp.11–49.

Perry, E. J. and Selden, M. (2000) [eds] *Chinese Society: Change, Conflict and Resistance*, London: Routledge.

Perry, E. J. (1995) 'Labour's Battle for Political Space: The Role of Workers' Associations in Contemporary China', in D. S. Davis, R. Kraus, B. Naughton and E. J. Perry (eds), *Urban Spaces in Contemporary China*, University of Cambridge Press, pp. 302–25.

Professor XX (July 1998) Fudan University, Shanghai, conversation.

'Progress in the Cause of Human Rights in 1996', (1997) *Xinhau yuekan (New China Monthly)*, May.

Putnam, R. (1993) *Making Democracy Work: Civic Traditions in Modern Italy*, Princeton: Princeton University Press.

Qi, H. C. (1997) 'From Concept to Social Action: The Green Movement in China', *China Strategic Review*, II, 3 (May/June), pp.39–49.

Qin, X. C. (1997) 'How Can the Funds of a Trade Union Be Forcibly Transferred?', *Legal Herald (Fazhi daokan)*, 5, pp.30–1.

'Regulate Various Social Relationships in Accordance with the Law: China Launches Legal Service Telephone Line', (1999) *Shidai chao (The Tides of Time)*, Beijing, 27 (January).

Rose, R. (1994) 'Rethinking Civil Society: Postcommunism and the Problem of Trust', *Journal of Democracy*, 5, 3 (July), pp.18–30.

Schmitter, P. C. (1992) 'Interest Systems and the Consolidation of Democracies', in G. Marks and L. Diamond, (eds), *Reexamining Democracy: Essays in Honor of Seymour Martin Lipset*, London: Sage Publications, pp.156–81.

Shi, T. J. (1997) *Political Participation in Beijing: A Survey Study*, Cambridge, MA: Harvard University Press.

Shue, V. (1994) 'State Power and Social Organization in China', in J. Migdal, A. Kohli, and V. Shue (eds), *State Power and Social Forces: Domination and Transformation in the Third World*, New York: Cambridge University Press, pp.65–88.

Solinger, D. J. (1992) 'Urban Enterpreneurs and the State: The Merger of State and Society', in A. L. Rosenbaum (ed.), *State and Society in China: The Consequences of Reform*, Boulder, CO: Westview Press.

State Council Information Office (1997) 'The Progress in China's Human Rights' Cause in 1996', *Xinhua yuebao (New China Monthly)*, 5, pp.33–4.

State Statistical Bureau, *et al.* (compilers), *Zhongguo Shehui Fajan Zhiliao: Zhiguan, Keguan He Guoji Bijiao (Data on the Development of Chinese Society: Subjective, Objective and International Comparisons)* (Beijing: China Statistical Publishing House), December 1992.

Structural Transition Project Team (1998) 'Medium and Short-Term Trends and Problems in the Structural Transition of Chinese Society', *Strategy and Management (Zhuanlue yu Guanli)*, Beijing, 30 (May), pp.1–17.

Unger, J. (1996) '"Bridges": Private Business, the Chinese Government and the Rise of New Associations', *The China Quarterly*, pp.795–819.

Unger, J. and Chan, A. (1995) 'China, Corporatism, and The East Asian Model', *Australian Journal of Chinese Affairs*, 33 (January), pp.29–53.

Wang, S. G. (1995) 'The Politics of Private Time: Changing Leisure Patterns in Urban China', in D. S. Davis, R. Kraus, B. Naughton and E. J. Perry, (eds), *Urban Spaces in Contemporary China: The Potential for Autonomy and Community in Post-Mao China*, Cambridge: University of Cambridge Press and Woodrow Wilson Center Press, pp.149–72.

Wank, D. L. (1995) 'Private Business, Bureaucracy, and Political Alliance in a Chinese City', *Australian Journal of Chinese Affairs*, 33 (January), pp.55–71.

Warner, M. (1999) [ed.] *China's Managerial Revolution*, London: Frank Cass.

Wasserstrom, J. N., and Liu, X. Y. (1995) 'Student Associations and Mass Movements', in D. S. Davis, R. Kraus, B. Naughton and E. J. Perry (eds), *Urban Spaces in Contemporary China: The Potential for Autonomy and Community in Post-Mao China*, Cambridge: University of Cambridge Press and Woodrow Wilson Center Press, pp.362–93.

Wenhui Bao, Shanghai, 26 January, 1999.

White, G. (1995) 'Chinese Trade Unions in the Transition from Socialism: The Emergence of Civil Society or the Road to Corporatism?', Working Paper No. 18, Institute of Development Studies, University of Sussex.

White, G., Howell, J. and Shang, X. Y. (1996) *In Search of Civil Society: Market Reform and Social Change in Contemporary China*, Oxford: Clarendon Press.

Xiao, S. (1998) 'Reconstructing China's Civil Society', unpublished paper, Zhongnan University of Finance and Economics, Wuhan.

Xiong, F. (1999) 'Analysis of Consumer Complaints in 1998 Received by This Periodical', *Zhongguo Zhiliang Wan Li Xing (Quest for Product Quality in China)*, 73 (January).

Zhang, J. (1998) *Fatuan Zhuyi: Jiqi yu Duoyuan Zhuyi de Zhuyao Fenqi (Corporatism and its Major Differences with Pluralism)*, Beijing: China's Social Science Publishing House.

Zhang, Y. Q. (1997) 'From State Corporatism to Social Representation: Local Trade Unions in the Reform Years" in T. Brook and B. M. Frolic, *Civil Society in China*, Armonk, NY: M. E. Sharpe, pp.124–48.

Zhu, G. L. (1997), *Dangdai Zhongguo Zhenfu Guocheng (Government Process in Contemporary China)*, Tianjin: Tianjin People's Publishing House, pp.191–4.

Index